A Landscape Manifesto

A Landscape Manifesto
Diana Balmori

Introduction by Michel Conan

Yale University Press
New Haven and London

This book was supported by a grant from the Graham Foundation for Advanced Studies in the Fine Arts.

Copyright © 2010 by Diana Balmori.
All rights reserved.
This book may not be reproduced, in whole or in part, including illustrations,
in any form (beyond that copying permitted by Sections 107 and 108 of the
U.S. Copyright Law and except by reviewers for the public press), without
written permission from the publishers.

Designed by Alan Dye/Brian Scott
Set in Greta (Typotheque), Akkurat (Lineto), and Replica (Lineto) by Tina Henderson
Printed in China by Kwong Fat

Cover illustration and endpapers: *Robert Smithson's Floating Island to Travel Around Manhattan Island*,
rendering (detail of fig. 143)

Library of Congress Cataloging-in-Publication Data

Balmori, Diana.
 A landscape manifesto / Diana Balmori ; introduction by Michel Conan.
    p. cm.
 Includes bibliographical references and index.
 ISBN 978-0-300-15658-4 (cloth : alk. paper)
 1. Landscape architecture. 2. Balmori, Diana. I. Title.
 SB472.B35 2010
 712—dc22   2009011966

A catalogue record for this book is available from the British Library.

This paper meets the requirements of ANSI/NISO z39.48-1992 (Permanence of Paper).

9 8 7 6 5 4 3 2 1

An original idea is never new.
It is as old as humanity.
It reveals what is real, what
is true. It can only vary in
its form of representation.

Dorothy Ling
The Original Art of Music
(1989)

Contents

Introduction

viii   **Reinventing Landscape Form and the Experience of Beauty**
Michel Conan

Prelude

1   Prelude

1

5   **History and Nature/Nature and Art: A New Departure**

5   The Present

5   History

6   Nature and Art

12   Historical Achievements and Contemporary Failures: The American Lawn

18   Retrieving Past Achievements: Hedgerows, Espaliers, Sunken Gardens

2

27 Transformations: Overcoming the Past

27 The Ecological Transformation of Human-Made Forms

30 From Green Corridor to Thick Edge: The Linear Park

54 From Roof to Fifth Façade

68 From Ditches to Rain Gardens

79 From Drainage Pipes to Stormwater Parks

88 Inscribing Urban Forms in the Larger Geographical Context

104 Accommodating Natural Processes in Cities

117 Making Temporary Landscapes

136 Straddling Borders: Jordan River Peace Park

139 Conclusion: Searching for the Present

3

143 Interweaving Architecture, Landscape, and City

143 Interface

144 Aesthetics

145 From Thin to Thick Edge

219 Embedding the City in Nature

Coda

221 Coda
224 A Landscape Manifesto

226 Notes
230 Selected Project Credits
233 Acknowledgments and Collaborators
234 Index
236 Illustration Credits

Reinventing Landscape Form and the Experience of Beauty
Michel Conan

Diana Balmori's works aim at the production of new forms, turning away from commonly held views of nature.[1] Her project for the equestrian grounds in the New York City proposal for the 2012 Olympic Games provides an example of—and a metaphor for—her position. She grew up with horses. Her father, a linguist studying native languages, used to take her and her brother on long rides to the sites where he worked, in northern Argentina. She has come to know horses very well and to develop a friendship with them. Horsemanship is a perfect metaphor for her understanding of human stewardship of the earth. It bespeaks the mutual transformation of humans and nonhumans when they pursue the achievement of beauty together (fig. 1).

There is little doubt that many New Yorkers familiar with the earthworks of the 1970s and 1980s would have assumed a filiation between the large S-shaped berm that Balmori proposed for the site of the equestrian games and Robert Smithson's gestures in the Utah desert (fig. 2). That would not, however, have been the main reason for their visit there, in 2012. They would have come to watch extraordinary riders and their horses. Dressage may be the most telling of all the Olympic equestrian events because it displays only the marvelous agreement between a steed and a rider that testifies to the combination of trust, understanding, and will that they share, without any taint of the athletic sense of performance and goal-directed action present in jumping, steeplechase, or polo playing. This unique agreement is not easily achieved. Horses are not naturally submissive, and humans are not naturally endowed with an innate capacity to ride. On the contrary, young horses resist the presence of people on their backs as much as they can, and inexperienced riders are regularly misguided by their bodily reflexes and intuitive understanding. Horse riding demands a mutual transformation of rider and horse, through which both achieve a new natural state in which they share some deeply felt mutual acquaintanceship—a preverbal relationship—while at the same time remaining separate, subject to different biological processes and social rules.

This provides a fitting metaphor for the transformation of nature pursued by Balmori. Nature always comes from the past, already present and in flux, engaged in becoming. It is the whole world—comprising matter, forces, and life—to which humans belong. She understands landscape as a human tool for constructing this new, civilized form of nature, resulting from interactions between humans and nonhumans and radiating a sense of beauty (fig. 3).[2] This form should enable humans and nonhumans to

Fig. 1. Diana Balmori.

Introduction ix

Fig. 2. Earthworks: NYC 2012 Olympics, Equestrian Venue, Staten Island, New York, 2004. S-berm with fens in the background.

Fig. 3. Earthworks: NYC 2012 Olympics, Equestrian Venue. Poppy-covered berm.

Fig. 4. Earthworks: NYC 2012 Olympics, Equestrian Venue. Transformation of the site after 2012 Olympic Games.

thrive together peacefully, to engage in mutually beneficial developments at a remove from the present onslaught of human actions upon nonhuman living beings. Human art, or landscape invention, contributes to the creation of this form, and yet we should immediately recognize that no artist could claim to have created it; it can be the result only of interactions among human subjects and the forces of life, the elements, and matter—the expression of an artistic will that transcends individuals.[3] This is a form that should fulfill the requisites for the egoless art that the New York art world has stridently advocated since the abandonment of abstract expressionism, in the 1960s. In Balmori's art, this form implies the mutual transformation of humans and nonhumans in the most literal sense. It is the expression of a shared engagement in which nonhumans and humans equally see their existence in the world deeply transformed. It is not the form of a thing, but the form of a process to which a myriad of living subjects and material forces contribute, and yet it depends on the creation of a sustainable substratum, a landscape or—in her words—a topographical art work.[4]

The phrase "humans and nonhumans" does not, however, imply a sense of symmetry any more than horse riding does. Rider and steed never exchange positions, and any form of cooperation results from human initiative, even if that can succeed only when submitting to the demands and needs of the horse. Balmori understands landscaping as a process initiated by human endeavors. It implies transforming an initial state of nature—very often a derelict state—into a new one, while establishing sufficient conditions for the spiraling growth of new living processes. A landscape project is based not on the claim that it will achieve a particular result, but on the establishment of a sustainable process of mutual changes in an appropriate site.[5] It depends in particular on the changing ethics of human subjects who contribute to its existence, and on their desire to sustain a process of changing relationships with nonhumans. It does not imply the constant presence of the same plants or an unchanging use by humans. The site of the equestrian games would have been devoted to different activities after the Olympic season in New York and would have created opportunities for practices and nonhuman forms of life that can be only dimly anticipated (fig. 4). Any single object created at the very beginning by a landscaping team is open to change as a result of interactions between nonhuman forces and human desires—thus modifying the material form of the object and deflecting the initial course of its development—but the substratum, defining a mutual process of interaction between humans and nonhumans, must remain operational. In addition, the initial topographical art must be sufficiently pleasurable and aesthetically captivating to trigger and sustain a new engagement of humans with nature. The dramatic form of the S berm offered wide panoramic views over the competition grounds and beyond, extending over the fens to the horizon before leading into a walk in the woodland or the fens themselves (fig. 5). Moreover, the landscape must be a source of pleasurable activities, inviting a continuous flow of people to indulge in being there. It should promote a new sense of beauty that gives clear access to the central intention, the historical project of a renewed interweaving of human and nonhuman lives. Balmori insisted in her proposal that the project allow visitors to enjoy the formal events and the training sessions equally, to get a full view of the whole process and see the equestrian demonstrations as a moment in a thrilling process of civilization. Thus the sense of beauty is to be derived from contemplation of a fleeting moment in a process, and of the invitation to invent in the present that is addressed by the past to the future, not from a commemoration of ancient deeds.[6] It would have enabled people to discover the beauty of the fens and be attracted back after the games were over.

This is an aesthetic of engagement with the flow of nature, and yet material form is essential to this experience. The landform created for the games had to be significant enough to stimulate a strong response on the part of first-time visitors and ecological enough to abide with the local forces of nature. This was intended to remain over time as a testimony that human will had engaged in a quest for a new compact with nature there, as part of the Olympic equestrian games. We can see that the site

Fig. 5. Earthworks: NYC 2012 Olympics, Equestrian Venue. Walkway on canal along the fen.

Fig. 6. Earthworks: NYC 2012 Olympics, Equestrian Venue. Roof surfaces planted to prevent runoff.

Fig. 7. Earthworks: NYC 2012 Olympics, Equestrian Venue. Pattern of plants on ground and on buildings, with a detail of its composition.

5

6

would not have been conserved as a commemoration of the Olympic Games but would have developed as a living place subsequently devoted to complex interactions between humans and nonhumans. And yet the landform would have remained a visible symbol of the human will to contribute to a new course of nature; moreover, the careful management of water and waste circulation, put in place from the start of the project, would have ensured a more diverse biotope and more intense human activity than had existed before the games (fig. 6). The landscape project, as Balmori conceives it, should trigger the creation of a new nature without dictating its future form and content. Allow me to stress that this proposes an anthropic nature, not a representation of some prelapsarian wilderness. The choice of a strongly patterned planting of exotics under the cover of amelanchier trees, uniting the ground of the plaza in front of the walls and the roof of the canopy around the arena, gives a clear sense of a created nature. It would have changed dramatically over time; the arena would have been dismantled, but a large part of the planting would have remained in place and grown at its own pace, modifying the initial pattern as plants adapted to their particular location and its changing microclimate (fig. 7).

7

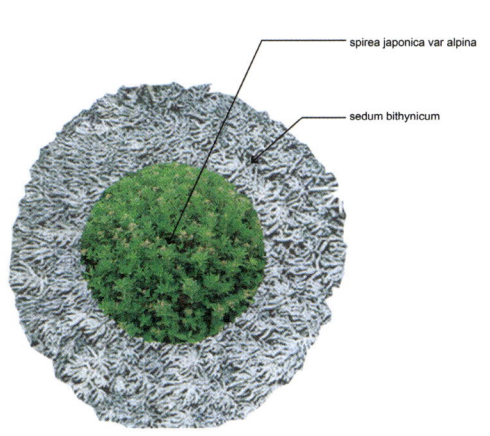

The Formation of a Radical Project

Landscape architecture moved away from garden art in the first half of the twentieth century, when it broadened its scope to include not only residential land but also any place that could be devoted to planting. Balmori may be moving away from landscape architecture by shifting the stress on the site as object to the site as process, transforming landscape creation from an art of space to an art of movement.[7] This is a radical project, and if it appears difficult to grasp, it was even more difficult to conceive.[8] It should be seen as the result of an exploration rather than a scholarly speculation—an experimentation in action, as presented by Donald Schön (1930–1997) in *The Reflective Practitioner*.[9] Whatever the name, it is the outcome of a long and complex process in which the practice of design has constantly borrowed from an understanding of landscape architecture achieved through scholarly or critical writing, and which allowed subtle developments in Balmori's thinking before it was voiced or expressed in writing. She wants to confront and move beyond the successive crises ushered in by architectural modernism, ignorance of the environmental destruction it precipitated, and the failure of environmentalism to merge the demands for large-scale architecture and sustainable public space in contemporary cities around the world. All her works aim at a renewal of the profession of landscape architecture, predicated on new ethical and aesthetic commitments.

In a book of poignant beauty dedicated to the ephemeral gardens of homeless people in New York, *Transitory Gardens, Uprooted Lives,* Balmori shows how garden making can be empowering in three different ways. It enables people to build a sense of self by giving a creative focus to their lives, and to engage bodily with a place that reflects their self-construction; it changes their relationships to others by enabling them to control some of these relationships (their self-presentation, in particular); and it enables them to monitor new forms of sociability. During her stay in Japan, where she worked in the 1990s, Balmori learned to appreciate the Buddhist perspective on the

8

transience of life and the importance of enjoying the ephemeral. However, we should not read the lives of the New York homeless as a metaphor for all urban dwellers' lives; this is not a doomsday allegory. And yet Balmori's book strongly suggests that urbanites could achieve a new sense of accomplishment if they made public spaces into city gardens and simply learned to engage with nature and appreciate the ephemeral quality of their own presence in the world, as the homeless do. This paradoxical attitude, bringing together the engagement in a construction process and a focus on the present, also merges the individualistic pursuit of aesthetic appreciation with an ethical engagement in an open process of reinvention of city life (figs. 8, 9).

The celebration of individual action and collective responsibility is also at the heart of Balmori's *Redesigning the American Lawn*.[10] This is a study devoted to a critical understanding of the modern landscape. The suburban lawn is a recent invention in America.

Fig. 8. Angelo's garden, from *Transitory Gardens, Uprooted Lives* by Diana Balmori and Margaret Morton (New Haven: Yale University Press, 1993).

Fig. 9. Guineo's garden, from *Transitory Gardens, Uprooted Lives*.

Introduction xiii

It provides a family pleasure ground and status symbol. It may even be a source of community pride. However, when observed as an aggregate phenomenon of today's America, it constitutes an environmental problem, with deleterious effects on nonhuman lives, and is a source of pollution detrimental to human lives as well. The interactions between industrialists, retailers, horticulturists, landscaping firms, community organizations, and millions of families have coproduced the American lawn, thus giving new forms to suburban cities, creating avenues for a new sense of self, and promoting new forms of collective desire. No criticism, however well grounded, can erase these realities (fig. 10). Modern America has produced a new form of nature, a new desire for this nature, and a self-sustaining process of land production. All of these should be reformed to achieve sustainability of the world we live in. This demands working at the invention of new forms of nature, at the corresponding development of new desires, and at new processes of landscape making, embedded in the development of economic activities. It also demands acknowledging the limited power of ideas and the powerful role of collective interactions. Balmori's art aims at transforming public space in such a radical way that it becomes a source of bodily pleasure and aesthetic delight for each individual urban dweller. Her reinvented public space should lead to, and provide a striking material symbol for, a new sociability and a mutual reinforcement of a commitment to the creation of a new balance between humans and nonhumans.[11]

Fig. 10. Ro Wilson garden, Cape May, New Jersey.

A New Doctrine of Imitation

Aesthetic appreciation of this new art should invite an ethical commitment to the pursuit of its deep agenda of reform of human engagement with nature, as suggested by Balmori's homage to Robert Smithson (see fig. 140). This agenda makes three important demands of the production of new public spaces. First, they should sustainably support future long-term development of mutual interactions between humans and nonhumans. Second, they should be highly pleasurable and stimulate ongoing interest. Third, they must be strikingly different from existing environments, signifying a new engagement with nature.

First and foremost, the process of transforming nature must itself be transformed. Balmori uses two resources to devise her strategies. First, along with a number of other contemporary landscape architects, such as Andropogon, Scott Murase, Michael Van Valkenbergh, and Nelson Byrd Woltz, she turns to natural processes as models to imitate.[12] She has devoted a book, *Guidelines for Sustainable Land Development*, to a simple presentation of a large number of such methods.[13] The imitation of the hydrologic cycle of a planted countryside, for instance, is clearly highlighted in her project for Memphis, as is the use of local stream flows to avoid silting in a harbor in the Canary Islands, or the construction of an open-air drainage system modeled on wetlands at Farmington, Minnesota (fig. 11). In the same way, heat absorption by the canopy in the countryside is imitated by developing a green cover on flat city roofs. The choice of plants for the roof cover is inspired by the imitation of Alpine rock lands with very poor soil, long periods of drought, and exposure to the sun, snow, wind, and very low temperatures in the winter—conditions that can also be experienced on the roofs of Long Island. This is obviously not a return to the classical art principle of the imitation of nature, since Balmori considers that processes—not forms—are to be imitated, and that nature is not a given, but a becoming.[14] Because she wants visitors to become aware of the public will to change urban dwellers' engagement with nature, she wants the topographical form to express intentional human intervention, as in the first project she had proposed for Farmington, where the retaining pools for the runoff were designed to imitate and recall the organization of cranberry bogs created for farming purposes (fig. 12).[15] Whereas the classical doctrine of imitation aimed at engaging spectators in a moral dialogue with the work of art in a quest for self-improvement, her own imitation of nature aims at fostering the construction of a new ethical attitude toward nature in a broadly altruistic direction.

Second, unlike most other landscape architects, she is also willing to turn to historical precedents to learn about the dynamics of relationships between humans and nonhumans, as we have just seen in the example of Farmington. This is a very difficult endeavor because historical circumstances change constantly over time and space.[16] When writing about the history of streets in Europe and the United States, she took great care to present their multiple functions from the Renaissance through the nineteenth century, and to analyze the demise of many of those functions and the resulting problems for contemporary society. The history of landscape forms enables her to articulate new problems, not solutions, for contemporary design. This is clearly illustrated by her history of hedges in America and in Great Britain.[17] However, some British hedges have survived for centuries, demonstrating that a simple man-made ecological construct can evolve into a very complex ecosystem, supporting a wide variety of nonhuman life while at the same time serving human interests. This invites us to look beyond the simple imitation of the spontaneous regulation of natural phenomena and to establish the basis for enduring forms of urban landscape open to colonization by wildlife. One of the great lessons Balmori derives, on multiple occasions, from studies of recent historical developments in America is the importance of individual initiatives and popular movements that bring these initiatives together (fig. 13).[18] This is borne out in her studies of the Freedom Lawn and the development of green roofs, and especially of the urban linear-park movement. Thus the dynamics of public opinion and

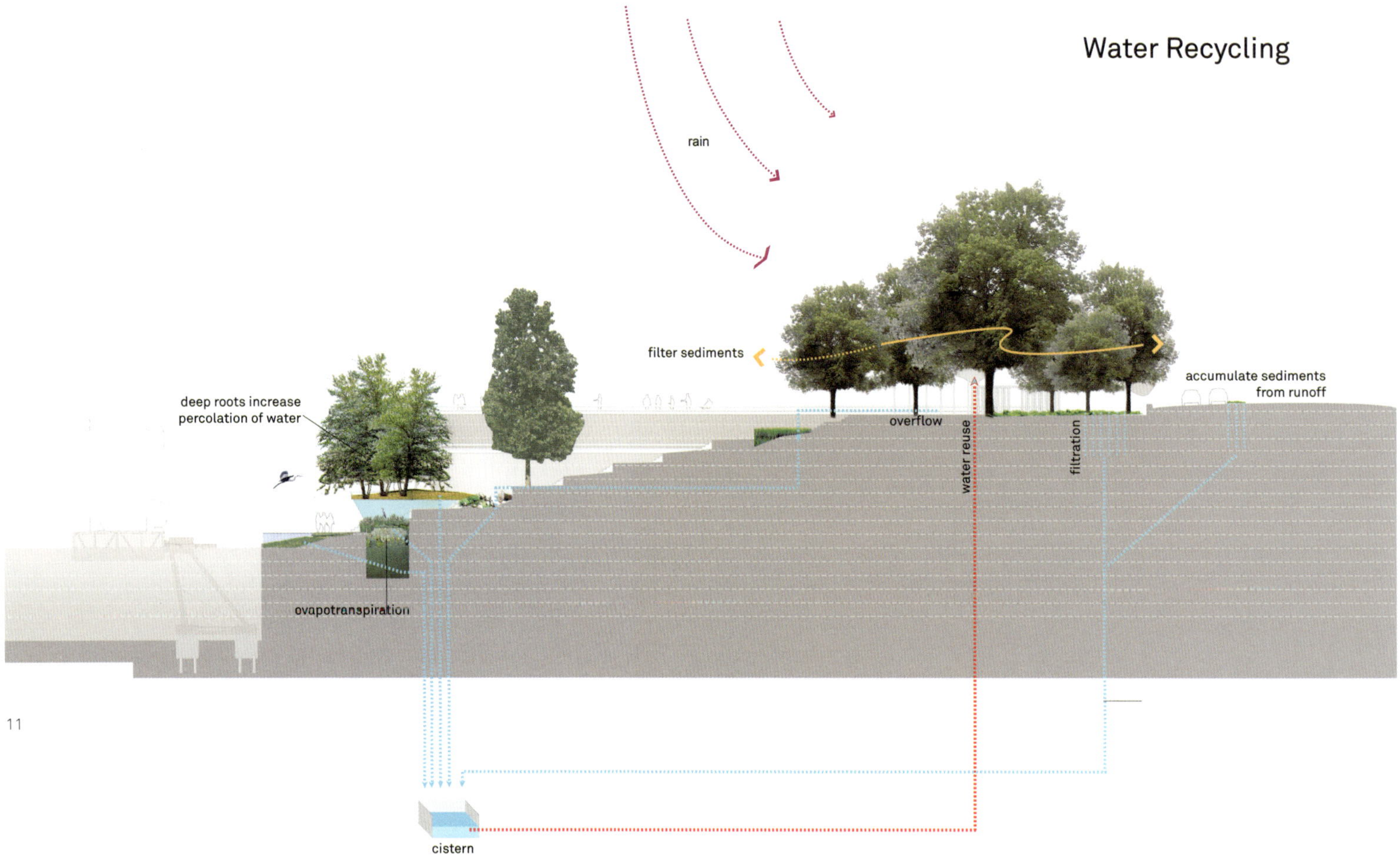

Water Recycling

Fig. 11. Beale Street Landing, Memphis, in progress. Schema of water circulation.

Fig. 12. Prairie Waterway/Park Place, Farmington, Minnesota, 1996. The project featured a runoff strategy imitative of cranberry bogs, in the red frame.

Fig. 13. Notice for a house designated a wildlife sanctuary.

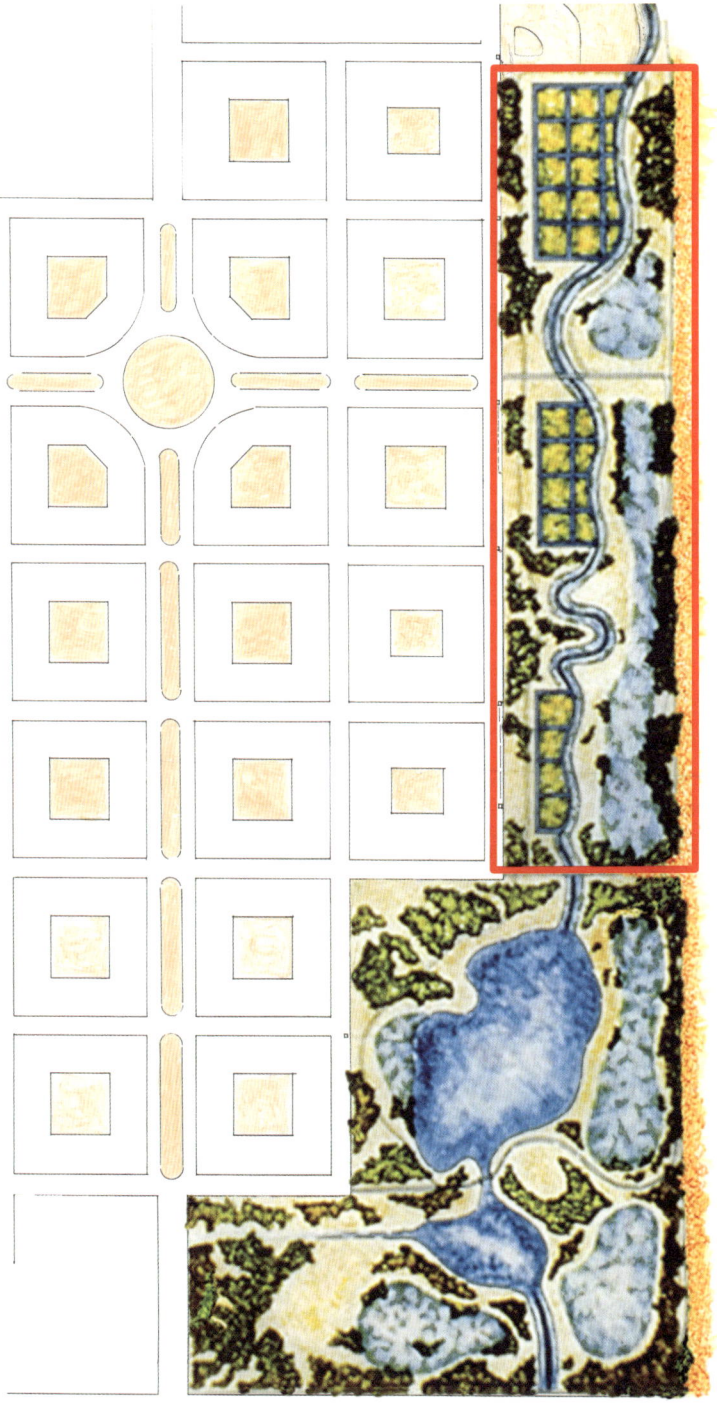

attitudes have to be reckoned with in devising long-term strategies of change in the urban landscape. This raises a central question of contemporary landscape architecture: how can a topographical art foster the desire among a growing number of urban dwellers to contribute to a balanced relationship between humans and nature?[19]

Diana Balmori's Topographical Art Form

The usual answer proposed by environmentalists and late twentieth-century landscape architects is to provide, on formerly derelict grounds, a rehabilitated natural environment, undefiled (apparently) by human intervention. However, this is a self-defeating approach. It hides the effort involved in ecological rehabilitation by presenting a form of nature that is taken for granted by everybody, and thus does not mobilize public opinion. Moreover, it does not apply in spaces of intense human use, thus segregating humans from nonhumans. Balmori's answer is quite different, and yet extremely simple in its general principle: create a pleasurable and attractive site endowed with topographical forms that are explicitly expressive of a new constructed nature and that achieve a sustainable balance between humans and nonhumans. The challenge is threefold. It demands the creation of a new biological process, a new topographical form compelling aesthetic appreciation, and a site for a desirable public life. We shall now turn to Balmori's projects, since they (even more than her writings) provide her answers to these challenges.

The new biological process is meant to enable the sustainability of the newly created form of nature. It depends to a large extent on the introduction of urban-based control of hydrological phenomena, modeled after spontaneous processes in nature and their successful imitation in other urban areas. It usually encompasses a carefully defined space where both nonhuman and human ways of dwelling in nature can thrive. It may call for the introduction of plants or other nonhuman life forms on the site. The coastal park for the city of Qing Huang Dao, China, provides a clear-cut example (see fig. 120). The city, located where the Great Wall meets the China Sea, has destroyed much of its preexisting landscapes. The park Balmori proposes aims at offering urban dwellers the possibility of coming into close contact with some of these former local landscapes; it is a mosaic of coastline, tidal marsh, dune prairies meadow, red pine forest, oak woodland, and a purely urban space. Each of these rests upon a regulation system inspired directly by local ecologies, but none of them is strictly speaking local, other than the coastal area itself (which remains untouched, though it can be used by visitors).

Each of these ecological landscapes supports a number of other interventions, architectural buildings, pathways, and belvederes, which are set in the specific ambiance of each ecological zone. Balmori uses setting, together with contrast, passage, merging, collage, weaving, connecting, and heterogeneity, to compose her topographical art. These are very important aspects of her contribution because they correspond to a new set of design issues that open the way to a renewal of topographical and aesthetic inventions. Let us examine them in turn.

Setting

Setting is a composition issue; just as words are set to music, so is architecture set into a landscape. Balmori noted in her early writings that the problem of the boundary between architecture and landscape was rarely addressed, even though it was always an acute one in contemporary corporate architecture, because the passage from architecture to landscape involved a dramatic change of scale along the vertical dimension (fig. 14).[20] That problem called her attention to the points where a transition is made from the rules and materials of one art form to those of another.[21] This issue should be addressed every time these two arts—architecture and landscape—contribute to the construction of a site.[22] Yet instead of looking for a visual frame that would ensure the independence of one from the other, she thought that they should merge into a unit of a more encompassing nature. Some historical precedents pointed to this possibility. Hamilton Hazelhurst, for instance, has shown with great clarity how Mansart and Le Nôtre engaged a dialogue between landscape and architecture at Dampierre.[23] This dialogue, however, constitutes only one form of setting. In a more general way, setting concerns the inscription of any two different works of art into a background, creating a higher sense of the unity to which they then belong. The project for the Public Administration Town (PAT) at Sejong, in South Korea, is an example of setting gardens, orchards, streets, and architecture into an encompassing ensemble that can be discovered through many distinct experiences (fig. 15). From the point of view of a pedestrian in the street, most of the architecture is set within the three-dimensional landscape into which it is woven. As soon as the same pedestrian walks on the city slopes leading to the green terraces which cover much of the city, she reaches a new point of view: architecture now appears within the setting of a larger landscape defined by the mountains, the sky, and the mosaic of fields and planted terraces.

The topographical features sustain the emergence of the specific mood, or *stimmung,* of a landscape when people interact with one another and with nonhumans there.[24] The setting can comprise hedges, fences, walls, and ground forms; these can be sunken, elevated, patterned, or folded. It sets the city apart as a place where distant mountains, nearby roof gardens, architecture, and trees create a specific embedding of human lives. The setting in the most recent project for Bilbao, achieved by a sophisticated folding of planted surfaces and passages, concerns the relationships of the park not only to the newly created architecture, but also to the elevated streets around it. Balmori envisages different points of view and so designs solutions to their corresponding problems. The elevated bridge and the traffic noise that it produces are masked from the attention of park visitors by a green wall that evokes other terrace walls in the park. Thus the setting also creates an imaginary expansion of the park. For visitors in the buildings, the rolling meadows of the park establish a common setting for the architectural structures, thus enabling each to be seen independently of the others; at the same time, the whole Campa de los Ingleses,

Introduction   xix

Fig. 14. NationsBank Corporate Center Plaza, Charlotte, North Carolina, 1991.

Fig. 15. Public Administrative Town Master Plan, Sejong, South Korea, 2007.

Fig. 16. Campa de los Ingleses, Bilbao, Spain, 2007.

Fig. 17. Frances Daly Fergusson Courtyard, Vassar College, Poughkeepsie, New York, 2003.

Fig. 18. Frances Daly Fergusson Courtyard.

16

covered by the park, will be perceived as an idiosyncratic urban space (fig. 16). In addition, we should note (in the aerial view of the convex lawns cut by concave pathways) the existence of small architectural constructions, which are literally hidden inside the hillocks and yet project a serviceable space in front of them, thus overlapping with the landscape. These examples show that setting is a design problem that arises from the coexistence of different artworks and various points of view.[25] They also demonstrate the complexity achieved by the mutual inclusion of landscape and architecture that Balmori introduces in her setting solutions.[26]

Contrast and Passage

In fact, she introduces contrasting elements of landscape and architecture in the very construction of the setting. Thus, in striking contrast to the reduction of green space to a homogenous expanse of lawn or groundcover typical of modernist architecture, she calls upon a multiplicity of internal contrasts to construct her setting in a way reminiscent of some developments in the early twentieth-century visual arts.[27] Throughout her career as a landscape designer, Balmori has been interested in exposing the ideological character of the distinction between artifice and nature. All human-produced, artificial objects are made out of natural materials. Yet it is true that there are many degrees in the transformation of natural elements into artificial objects. Appreciating this, Balmori undertook a systematic exploitation of the contrasts between different forms of nature, thus inviting an aesthetic experience of the diversity of nature that rejects the opposition between nature and artifice, between natural environment and architecture. She highlights the most dissimilar elements, usually large and towering buildings on the one hand, and the wildest aspect of nature on a site on the other. They usually contrast starkly along several dimensions, such as volume versus flatness, smooth versus rugged texture, dead versus live material, fixed versus changing appearance, and internal homogeneity versus heterogeneity. Then she weaves a passage between them by juxtaposing elements that present partial contrasts.[28] The treatment of the garden for NTT, in Japan, has often been presented as one example of this technique.[29] Another is a much more recent project: the courtyard linking the Avery Hall art center and a Boyar dormitory to the campus grounds, with an older faculty building facing them, at Vassar College, in Poughkeepsie (fig. 17). The project consists of a flat, rectangular sunken lawn framed by flat, white alleys, giving the campus green an architectural form. It plays on five contrasting qualities: modern versus picturesque style, volume versus surface, curved versus straight line, fixed versus evolving form, and live versus dead material. It makes them vary separately, rather than simultaneously. On the longer side of the quadrangle, a slanted surface with a regular grid of shrubs makes a transition to the vertical façade of the Boyar building, and on the opposite side an undulating hedge of topiary softens the contrast between the flat lawn and frame and the vertical trees. The succession of partial contrasts establishes an almost continuous passage between the trees and the buildings (fig. 18). The lawn is planted with a mix of grasses and clover, which mediates between the deciduous trees and the unchanging materials of the alley and the buildings. This apparently simple project thus proposes three forms of nature: the picturesque planting of the campus green, the lawn, and—on opposite sides—the buildings, two modern and one picturesque. The construction of such passages with contrasting elements is one of the sources of Balmori's design invention (fig. 19).

Merging

The braiding of internal contrasts is used to create an aesthetic appreciation of the underlying unity of a setting in contrast with the heterogeneity of architecture, civil engineering, and landscaping. This appreciation results in part from the experience of a succession of subtle changes introduced by partial contrasts as a visitor enters, lingers in, and passes across the site. In Balmori's projects, it plays very often between two extremes that seem difficult to reconcile—the modern city and the banks or the mudflats of an untamed waterway, for instance (fig. 20). One of her approaches consists in merging the edges on both sides. Balmori compares this technique to the blurring of the limits of rectangular patches of color in Rothko's painting to allow spectators to become immersed in the experience of color and to lose even the peripheral vision of the geometric form. This is a metaphorical relationship.[30] Merging is not a way of suppressing the edge, but of overcoming the existence of a sharp edge between adjacent elements, such as infrastructure and landscape. Thus it helps focus attention on the setting of her landscape, just as it helps focus attention on the material color in Rothko's painting. In Trenton, she has created a bridge that allows pedestrians to access the islands nearby and experience their natural environment, while on the city side she has planted cherry orchards that seem to run down from the elevated green terraces around the major buildings to form a long garden alley along the major street that separates the project from the dense city. In an even more dramatic confrontation between the river and the landscape, in St. Louis she has introduced a series of floating islands along the river; on some of them, people can walk, rest, and enjoy boating or dining (fig. 21). The same intention is at play in the proposal for Stapleton, New York, where the floating islands allow visitors to walk around a

19

21

22

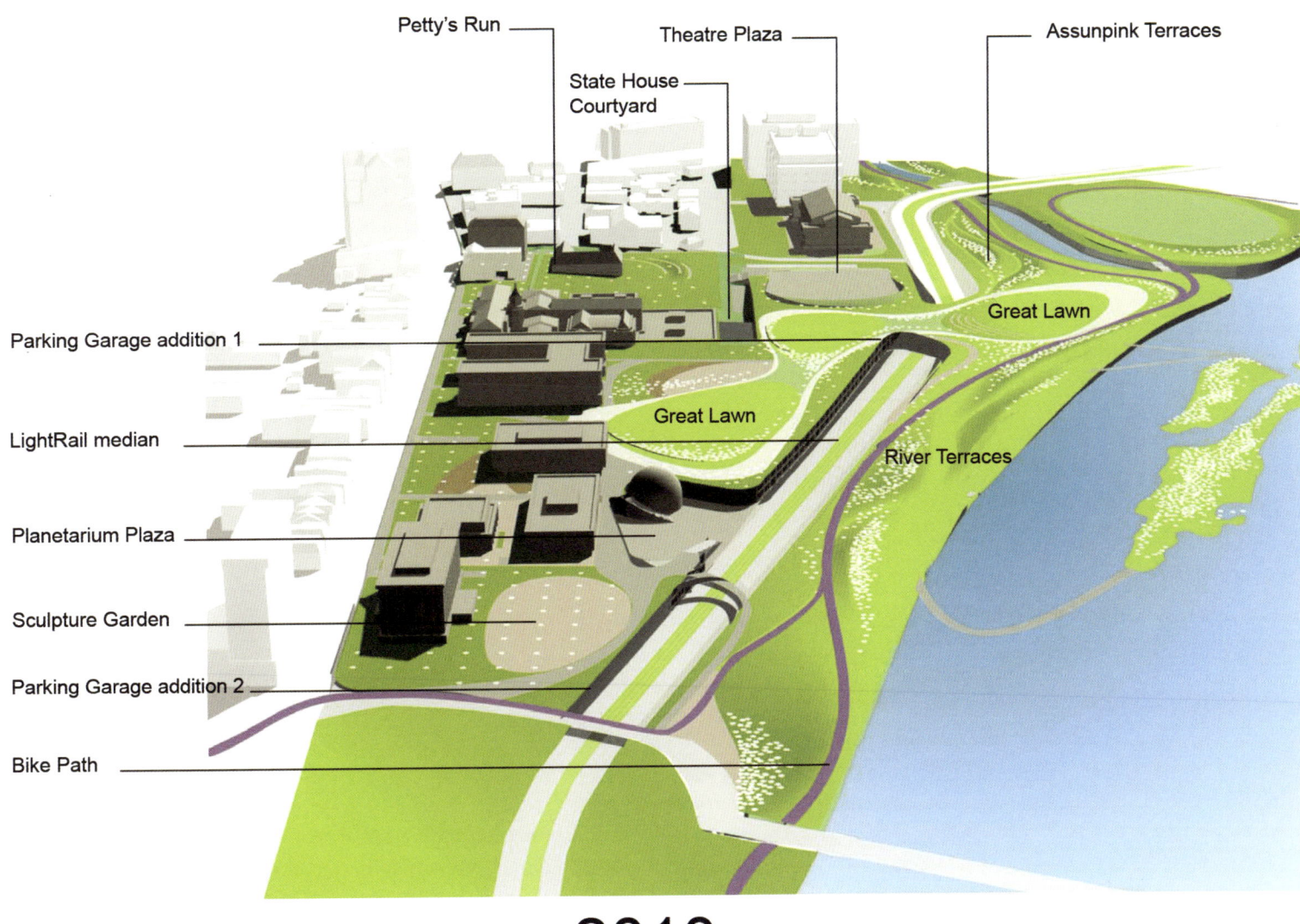

Fig. 19. Campa de los Ingleses, Bilbao, Spain, 2007. Passage between ground level and vertical wall.

Fig. 20. PARK(ING) Trenton, Trenton, New Jersey, 2006. Projected view in 2010.

Fig. 21. St. Louis Waterfront, in progress.

Fig. 22. Stapleton Waterfront, Staten Island, New York, 2004. Views before and after project.

23

marsh growing in the river bed and to see the river as an inland pond, thus confusing the limits of the city grounds and the wild river (fig. 22). People can even view gardens made according to an unmistakable geometric pattern that apparently float freely on the river. Merging in her work has more to do with the imaginary relationship between nature and artifice, of course, than with peripheral vision. It transforms edges into landscapes in their own right, where the forms of nature that are separated by the edge are merged into an ambiguous unit belonging to neither and to both at the same time.

Collage

In a project along a harbor in the Canary Islands, Balmori wanted to create a three-tiered park, evocative of different forms of nature on the island, with halophytic plants in the coastal zone, vegetated dunes along the coast, and thermophytic forest in the interior (fig. 23). None of these ecosystems remained intact, and similar ecosystems thus had to be re-created. Fernando Chacel, who has successfully re-created vegetation along the derelict coastline of the new extensions of Rio de Janeiro, calls this an ecogenesis. This is an anthropic nature, re-creating the conditions that have formed sustainable biotopes in similar circumstances. Yet it is only a "parvula natura," a small quotation from the great book of nature (fig. 24). In the Canary Islands project, the first of these biotopes grows in the intertidal zone, which is covered twice a day by the rising tide, the second in artificial dunes close to the seashore, and the last on higher, dry ground in the mountains. Collages of each of these man-made biotopes are patched on the corresponding areas of the topography designed by Balmori between the shore of the harbor and the ribbon of high-rise buildings that encloses the park and protects it from some of the dry, cold winds coming from the northeast (fig. 25). These man-made biotopes are framed by the specific topography on which they rest and the pedestrian footpaths that run between them. The same collage technique was used to allow people in Memphis to see the relationship between the level of flooding of the Mississippi

Fig. 23. Parque de la Luz, Las Palmas, Gran Canaria, Spain, 2005. Thermophytic forest.

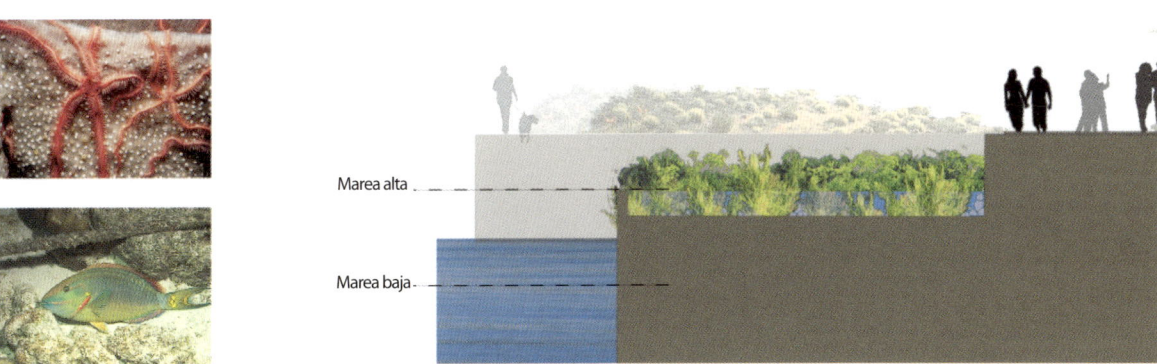

Marea alta

Marea baja

Fig. 24. Parque de la Luz. Halophytic plants in the coastal zone.

Fig. 25. Parque de la Luz. Aerial view of the park.

Fig. 26. Beale Street Landing, Memphis, in progress. Diagrams illustrating flood levels.

Fig. 27. Stapleton Waterfront, Staten Island, New York, 2004. Plan.

Fig. 28. Public Administrative Town Master Plan, Sejong, South Korea. Architecture under green roofs.

River and the development of specific forms of landscape (fig. 26). These collages are placed in huge terraces hanging over a sculpted stairway going from the top of the bluff overlooking the river down to its lowest water level at Beale Landing. Here the setting is achieved by the flow of the river, which makes each of these ecogeneses into a hanging garden, floating in the air when the river is low and appearing to be an island only when the river rises to its level. It should also be noted that the planting does not seek to imitate the density of the mangrove but only to evoke the dynamics of mangrove formation and to allow visitors to engage bodily with an imaginary landscape along the Mississippi. Collage is typically an artistic move that enables Balmori to evoke a specific form of local landscape and all the cultural memories it summons.[31]

Weaving

All the topographical devices discussed so far, from setting to collage, contribute to an aesthetic experience of the continuity between man-made and untamed nature (fig. 27). Weaving together strands of nature of different kinds constitutes a late achievement in the development of Balmori's topographical art. In these projects, instead of cutting a succession of parallel sashes of land beginning at the river, or between the sea and the city fabric, and attributing a unique function to each of them, she weaves them horizontally and vertically, allowing green sashes of land to braid together and rise from ground level along ramps. All of them support some human activities, as well as some nonhuman beings, each in completely different ways (fig. 28). Some buildings, such as the large parking lots in Trenton, New Jersey, or the housing and stores at Sejong PAT, in South Korea, thus become literally embosomed in the landscape; other buildings, such as the State Capitol and the museums at Trenton, or the ministries at PAT, stand out above the highest green terraces. The same aesthetic applies in the project for Toronto; the Stapleton redevelopment area, in Staten Island; and the St. Louis project, in front of Saarinen's arch and Dan Kiley's landscape. It gives a recognizable form to a few of Balmori's master plans for recent projects.

It produces more than a signature effect, however (fig. 29). We can see that the weaving topography always appears as an intentional anthropic landscape that mediates between some untamed waterway or the larger horizon of the distant mountains (as in the Korean project) and the dense human space of a city. The recycling of rain and stormwater is designed to ensure the sustainability of its vegetable cover and allow its development over the coming decades. Hence, these unusual topographical forms should appear to future generations as a testimony to the will to change relationships between untamed and urbanized nature.

Connecting

Balmori is deeply interested in transforming city life, and she sees the creation of public space as an opportunity for a change that concerns many more living beings than just the people working or visiting the buildings on or near the site.[32] This is expressed in many projects by her efforts to provide long-distance connections between the public place she designs and both the city and tamed—or even untamed—nature near the urban area. We have seen earlier how she availed herself of streams circulating around the Canary Islands to expose the whole harbor and its halophytic planting to the direct influence of oceanic life, but in that project we can also see how she proposed to link the city to this unique park (fig. 30). In other projects, she has proposed bicycle trails and light-rail connections to suburban areas. Connecting the inner city to the larger natural environment may be a more difficult task, and Balmori has explored different ways to achieve this. She worked for several years on the development of linear parks, since they offer the possibility of creating a nature corridor—as in the Farmington Linear Park in New Haven, Connecticut (fig. 31)—and they are supported by citizen groups in many U.S. cities. In recent years she has proposed weaving sashes of land to link internal city spaces and the broader environment, as in the project for the University College Dublin Gateway (fig. 32).

Connecting the different strands woven together on each site, however, is even more important since it makes it possible for users and visitors to experience the passage from one form of nature to another, and to experience bodily the unity of man-made and untamed nature. She thinks of connecting as an absolute necessity. This is clearly visible in her projects, since she creates numerous views of the bicycle trails, pedestrian bridges, floating pathways, and handicapped access routes that are meant to enable all people, whatever their physical needs and capacities, to roam the whole landscape comfortably (fig. 33). These are not only convenient paths linking independent land sashes, but also invitations to a variety of experiences—walking, jogging, cycling, running on skates, feeling the slope of the land, fancying a flight in the air or a stroll on the river. Connecting means not only creating links between places but also—more radically—connecting the body to the elements of nature in a way that is orchestrated by the design itself.[33] The project does not even include all the connections she wanted to establish, such as those to East St. Louis, across the river, where she proposed a linear park along the bank. In addition, she proposed connections between areas north and south of the project, but they were also postponed to a later phase. The importance of the experience of connecting is also clearly visible in the project for the Toronto Waterfront, where the skating rink allows a long race on a flat curving track that creates a sensation of compression when one passes through a tunnel and a sense of elation and freedom, as if one were reaching the sky, when one enters the dancing rink (fig. 34). Each connector, in fact, can be designed as a landscape with its own setting, contrasts, and weaving bands, as in the case of the Plaza de Euskadi, in Bilbao.[34]

Heterogeneity

All of Balmori's strategies for the creation of new forms of nature that merge human and nonhuman lives rest upon a deep refusal of zoning as a planning instrument. Zoning implies a functional specialization of different parts of the city and encourages the implementation of homogeneous land uses. While some of these zones may be devoted to nature conservation, at best that practice allows a segregation of human and nonhuman interests and encour-

Fig. 29. Public Administrative Town Master Plan, Sejong, South Korea. Detail of structural plan.

Fig. 30. Parque de la Luz, Las Palmas, Gran Canaria, Spain, 2005. Collage showing connections between city and park.

Fig. 31. Farmington Canal, Yale University, Malone Engineering Center, New Haven, Connecticut, 2006.

Introduction xxix

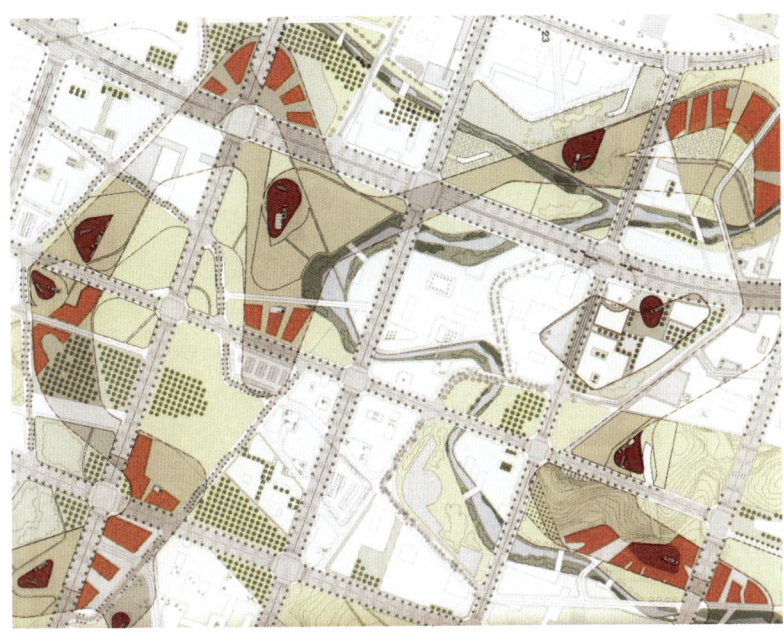

29

30

31

Introduction xxx

Introduction xxxi

Fig. 32. University College Dublin, 2007. Plans showing ecological corridor.

Fig. 33. St. Louis Waterfront, in progress.

Fig. 34. Toronto Central Waterfront, 2006. Skating rink.

ages the ideological opposition between man and nature that Balmori fights. Her strategy instead aims at proposing heterogeneous land units that allow different human and nonhuman functions to coexist without impinging upon one another. This applies on all scales in her projects, since it is a corollary of the engagement with natural life; whereas American lawns attempt to impose a homogeneity of plant material, the meadows planted by Balmori on any of the large landforms she creates are always heterogeneous and open to developing in unpredictable ways that include the incorporation of patches of new plants brought by visiting birds. They make her man-made landforms look as if they were cared for by nature herself.

Experiencing Diana Balmori's Topographical Art

There is, indeed, much more to Balmori's landforms than a reinvention of earthworks (fig. 35). These swaths of planted meadowland are also the sites of pleasurable activities attracting large crowds. People come from a long distance across the city, thanks to dedicated transportation systems, new connections to previously existing city thoroughfares, and the creation of light bridges and pathways enabling pedestrians to move in the air, on the ground, or on water across the whole landscape. This is a landscape of motion as much as a landscape to be contemplated from the buildings that rise from it.

Her landscapes always serve three functional levels: urban work life, internal and external connections, and a variety of pleasurable activities and attractions for everyone in the city. They bring typical urban activities at a high level of intensity into this newly invented form of nature (see fig. 204). The conjunction of these activities and the braided landscape, with its partial contrasts linking the natural and urban environments, makes these projects into symbols of a renewed compact between human and nonhuman activities in nature. The people in this landscape are not the decorative figures of a seventeenth-century Dutch landscape painting; they are the stuff of which the new nature is made. This is a public landscape because it offers urban dwellers the experience of community. But it does much more. It brings people into a place that is enjoyable because it allows free circulation between engaging with nature in many different ways and engaging with other inhabitants in highly social activities. Humans respond to the intensity of their engagement in the world with an appreciation of the uniqueness of the moment, a heightened sense of the passing of time. They cannot fail to notice the singularity of their experiences, whether they are fishing along the river a few hundred yards from the State Capitol, practicing extreme sports under a high bridge, biking down a bridge toward a floating bikeway, racing on their skates in Toronto, or simply gazing at the river flooding an island at Beale Landing (fig. 36). Moreover, these experiences are all framed by the driving force of this landscape: the will to see humans and nonhumans share in a new form of constructed nature that has been created as a background for all their activities by both large- and small-scale design elements, and that, as we have seen above, pervades the forms of the project. The aesthetic pleasure derived from the enjoyment of time in these public spaces enables people to share an appreciation of the will toward a new course of nature that is inscribed in Balmori's landforms. Beauty in her landscapes derives from public enjoyment and an aesthetic response to the clear ethical purpose of the landscape artists, a new *pulchritudo adhaerens*.[35] We must understand precisely how they propose to create these new kinds of experiences.

New Experiences of Nature and Time

The quest for more respectful attitudes toward nature has been a leitmotif of American landscape architecture during the last forty years. It has been driven by a shared sense that human actions during the previous century were destructive to nature on an unprecedented scale. The surge of concerns about human behavior has been predicated upon an opposition

Fig. 35. PARK(ING) Trenton, Trenton, New Jersey, 2006. The Great Lawn leaping over the highway.

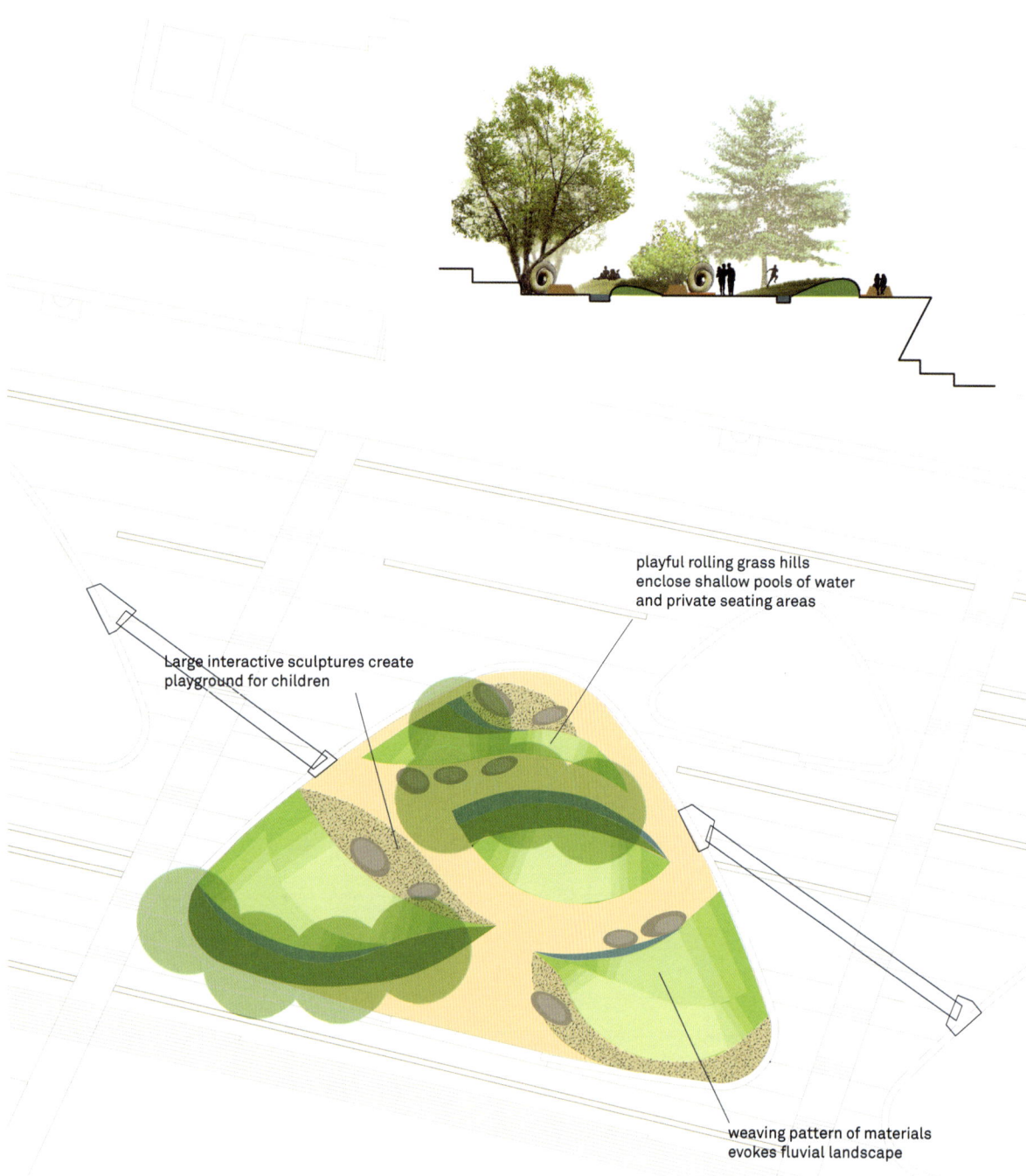

Fig. 36. Beale Street Landing, Memphis, in progress. Mesophytic island as playground.

between humans and nature. It has resulted in many positive changes, and yet it is a limited approach because it does not allow exploring the positive contributions that humans can bring to developments in nature.

Balmori does not see nature as a fixed entity for humans to plunder, but as a dynamic manifold of relationships between physical and living forces not subject to any teleology. Humans are part of the process, and contribute to it. Balmori wants a sense of being part of nature and being able to engage in the co-development of nonhuman life to be a central experience of urban living. She wants to turn places of intense urban activity into places of coexistence and co-development of humans and nonhumans. She wants those who use or visit the places she designs to sense that evolution is an open-ended process, and to share responsibility for its course. She expects them to feel the desire to contribute to the changing attitudes toward nonhuman nature that are presented on the site: the interweaving of human and nonhuman lives, the creation of new environments for nonhumans, and the encouragement of respect for nonhuman life. The aspects and the uses of the places that she creates will change over time. She does not design them to establish an ideal Arcadia that would enable people to find relief from the everyday urban world; on the contrary, she aims to create places where people will be active participants in the transformation of that world. And yet, even though this is an open process that will change many aspects of each site, she also wants future urban dwellers to be aware that each place is expressive of a new ethos initiated at the historical moment of its construction. Unlike the idealized forms of nature produced by garden and landscape architecture during past centuries, the places she designs are intended to expose the changing forms of nature that result from the conscious behavior of urban people over time. She also wants future generations to be able to see the traces of an initial period when a city moved intentionally from unreflective relationships with nonhumans to an open pursuit of a new ethic. Unlike monuments intended to freeze a moral example for eternity, these places invite a sense of moral engagement toward the pursuit of an ethical construction.

The Experience of Beauty

To achieve these goals, the places Balmori creates have to be multifunctional, highly pleasurable, and able to produce an aesthetic experience that distinguishes them from places that, in contrast, are merely pleasant and do not invite reflection upon their origins or the intentions of their creators. This seems to coincide with Immanuel Kant's description of the adherent beauty (*pulchritudo adhaerens*) shared by the practical arts, architecture, and landscape architecture. And yet Balmori's idea of landscape beauty is quite different from the idea proposed by Kant, because Kant's perspective rests upon a strict opposition of nature and art: "Nature is beautiful," Kant wrote, "because it looks like art, and art can only be called beautiful if we are conscious of it as art while yet it looks like nature."[36] There is an implicit stasis of nature in this perspective. Balmori wants art to contribute to the dynamics of nature, and to have the sense of beauty derive from the ethical will to change that is made manifest by the project in its urban context. Beauty is not a property impressed into physical forms by the genius of a landscape artist who would impose a rule as nature does, since there is in fact no absolute rule of nature. It results from a sense of radical change in the relationships between a city and its living environment, experienced through contrasts between the dynamics of nature in that new place and in the urban spaces that preceded it. According to Kant, the experience of beauty is achieved through the aesthetic appreciation of form, but the form at stake here is not fixed; it is a movement spanning decades of spatial changes. Space is important as an embodiment of a shift in urban ethics, a reflection of the collective attitude toward nonhuman nature and its developments, to be experienced physically. Moreover, Balmori assumes neither the universality of formal beauty nor the universality of a desire for the beauty of material objects. She knows, from her historical studies of the American lawn and of the gardens of homeless people in New York City, that not all inhabitants of a city share the same desire for nature, and that some may have tremendous difficulty accepting what other people desire. On the other hand, she expects the conjunction of the functionality of these sites, the pleasure of togetherness in them, and the sense of a new ethos that is attached to them, to stimulate the cultural construction of new shared desires. In that sense, she acts in the hope that the beauty of the place, as a marker of a historical moment, might eventually become universally acknowledged as the new desires become universally shared.

The Construction of a New Landscape of Desire

How can a desire come to be shared by a growing number of people in a city? Historical precedents show that this may result from new bodily experiences of place and debates about their interpretation.[37] There is already an ongoing debate about the relationships between humans and the rest of nature, so it remained for Balmori to create the sources of new bodily experiences for urban dwellers. This demanded, in turn, creating new forms of urban space that would be attractive to a large number of city inhabitants. To this end she has elected to work as often as possible on central city projects, in places of intense activity, or in sites closely linked to a major activity center that also offer a variety of leisure services. The places have to be functional and pleasurable in order to attract large numbers of people. Yet that alone is not enough to introduce the new bodily experiences that support a sense of continuity between human and nonhuman lives in nature.

Since Balmori wants each place to establish a passage between unfettered nature and densely urbanized natural environments, the forms she creates have to merge seamlessly with both. And because the newly formed desire should issue from a bodily experience of each particular landscape, the forms she creates also have to give a sense of visual continuity and introduce a distinctive experience. These topographical landscape forms challenge intuitive understanding and impose a sense of mystery. Their invention is therefore an artistic achievement.

37

38

Fig. 37. World Mammoth and Permafrost Museum, Yakutsk, Russian Federation, 2007.

Fig. 38. Campa de los Ingleses, Bilbao, Spain, 2007.

Rather than proceed from formalist principles to produce a sense of topographical distinction in her projects, Balmori has constantly called upon a set of creative gestures—setting, contrast, passage, merging, collage, weaving, connecting, and heterogeneity—to be reinterpreted in each particular context. They are abstract instruments—schemata—to be used for a creative purpose: the production of a horizon of interpretation of the place. Thus the form is a feature of the background of common experience, not an aspect of the world that has been foregrounded in the way a sculpture on a public square can be. These experiences are not to be confused with experiences of objects or signs disseminated through a site that invite personal interpretation, such as objects in an English landscape garden or a memorial landscape; instead, they result from being in the place, moving through it, and engaging with other people there, while sensing that it is part of the interweaving of human and nonhuman creatures. When confronted with mystery, we feel compelled to seek an explanation. In Balmori's spaces, city inhabitants will use their own words to invent a proud narrative of place that they interpret to others.

A Contribution to the Renewal of Landscape Architecture

How can we assess Balmori's claim that her work breaks away from the complacencies of contemporary landscape practice (figs. 37, 38)? Her ideas may be new, but not all new ideas result in meaningful change. On the contrary, many proposals for redirecting landscape practice during the past forty years are already long forgotten, and the majority of new art forms remain only in museum archives, following the same path toward oblivion. Neither classical, modernist, nor postmodernist architecture was born from the proposals of a single artist because the renewal of useful arts depends on the agreement of many creators and patrons on the value of innovative ideas. So we should examine the ways in which Balmori's topographical art fits within a larger context of innovative practice in landscape architecture throughout the world. On the other hand, before discussing her contribution to the forefront of landscape praxis, one would like to know whether her work exhibits strikingly new features on the American scene.

In the 1980s, Peter Walker had already forcefully criticized the lack of interest in landscape design, just as Balmori did later.[38] His works have been acclaimed ever since as proof that he succeeded in giving a new direction to landscape design in the United States. He inspired many talented landscape architects, such as Toru Mitani and Yoji Sasaki, in Japan; Thorbjörn Anderson, in Sweden; and Kathryn Gustafson, in France. It therefore seems pertinent to compare Balmori's and Walker's design perspectives.

The Parallel Lives of Two Artists

Balmori and Walker seem to have led almost parallel professional lives, separated by twenty years. Both are deeply committed to the creation of form and to the renewal of the idea of beauty in landscape architecture. They have achieved a recognizable mastery in the production of their work after many years of professional practice, involvement in academic education, and a constant engagement with the history of garden and landscape architecture and contemporary visual arts. Like many other landscape architects in the United States, they also both experienced the specific constraints of corporate patronage and collaboration with architects and numerous other professionals. However, these parallel experiences did not lead them to the same conclusions. Walker moved away from allotment planning and landscaping to discover how to accommodate the demands of corporate clients creatively, while Balmori has moved from the unequal partnership with architects imposed by corporate clients to a broader engagement with public-space creation for urban managers.[39] This may reflect a time difference in their careers: Balmori has entered, at the turn of the century, a world of landscape architecture made visible and attractive to city managers, to a certain extent, by the work Walker has done for corporate managers since the end of the seventies. Thus we should not be surprised to discover that their intense formative periods have led to strikingly different positionings of their craft and its aesthetics.

Walker, in Greenbergian fashion, has produced a normative discourse. He was undoubtedly deeply influenced by formalist principles that were predominant in the days of abstract expressionism and by the efforts of visual artists to create objects entirely devoid of references to other arts or narrative.[40] He asserted that landscape architects could achieve this kind of objectality by stressing flatness, repetition, seriality, and gesture to create designs exhibiting visual unity on their project sites. And yet, because—unlike Greenberg—he is a creator, he has constantly breached the purity of his doctrine by introducing pictorial representations of rivers, rocks, boulders, historical allusions to Olmsted or "Egyptian ziggourats" (as Jane Amidon astutely underlined in her dialogues with him about the Nasher Sculpture Center Garden, in Dallas), or even elements of surrealistic inspiration into some of his projects.[41] Thus many of his works are far more interesting than are those of some of his followers because they achieve a tension between an underlying formulaic adherence to his doctrine and the presence of exceptions to it that stimulate unending questioning. The forms he achieves both illustrate and break away from the formal principles he proclaims.

Balmori has not formulated a design doctrine. Instead, as we have just seen, she has developed a number of design issues—setting, contrast and passage, merging, collage, weaving, connecting, and heterogeneity—which are quite different from Walker's, and which enable her to analyze the context of a project and to define the grafting of new ecological processes onto it. However, the deliberate subordination of the project to the preexisting ecological context and the natural forces at large in its environment precludes any systematic doctrine of design. And yet, in recent years, her work has developed a definite signature, weaving landforms that support both nonhuman lives and human activities together with architecture (fig. 39). In spite of a real attention to site-specificity and the local issues she has encountered, her master plans exhibit a certain stylistic unity.

Balmori and Walker have thus both been led to create a distinctive design method and also to contradict it, to a certain extent, in their works. This observation bespeaks the importance of understanding the difference between landscape design and discourse, but it also invites a better understanding of the difference between Walker's and Balmori's design approaches themselves. The first major source of difference proceeds from their respective views of nature. Nature seems to be absent from Walker's critical thinking about landscape design. It is treated as the given world, a universal reference exterior to human life and intentions. Eventually, in sites like the Tanner fountain at Harvard or the IBM Solana campus, it can also be used, in humanist fashion, as a source of forms to be imitated to achieve beauty and create a sense of mystery. Balmori, on the other hand, sees nature as a process in flux, open to reflexive criticism because humans have some responsibility for its course. This flux itself is neither given nor predestined, but rather a historical development that is reflected in the presence and diversity of human and nonhuman lives. Human action can be detrimental—the unreflective use of nature is currently greater than it has ever been—or it can be constructive, as it has sometimes been in human history. Thus she thinks of nature as a historical construct to be reinvented.[42] She also sees the processes of interaction between nonhumans (rather than landscape forms or the grouping of plants) as the source of the models to be imitated by landscape artists in their attempts to create a new nature that supports all forms of life.

Walker and Balmori also differ in their understanding of the role of history in their art. Walker is interested, rather like Ian Hamilton Finlay, in the recurrence throughout history of the view of classical art as an expression of the universality of man. Finlay and he also both proposed a new form of universal art, different from all that preceded it, in the hope that it would last, like them, through the centuries. Neither sees history as process. From their point of view, each new development in classical art gives

Fig. 39. Governors Island, New York, in progress.

form to the human discovery of an essential aspect of nature, making it subsequently accessible forever to people as long as the art form endures. Balmori shuns this essentialism. She is interested in the processes of human interaction with nonhumans, and in the way they have resulted in rich biotopes—as in the hedges of English fields—or in dramatically impoverished ecologies—as in the American industrial lawn. She wants to understand these processes not in order to duplicate them, but so that she is better able to think about the current dynamics of nature and, importantly, about the dynamics of human action in relation to it as well. She does not think that her work can by itself create a new form of nature—a new form of the process of interactions between humans and nonhumans—but rather that it may trigger a cultural change, the ultimate result of which depends on other people's actions and desires. These differences in Walker's and Balmori's perspectives with respect to nature, history, and design methods have important consequences.

While they are both very much interested in twentieth-century American visual arts, they have pursued opposite directions in regard to the relationships between the arts and their own practice of landscape design. Walker has borrowed the formalist principles proposed by Greenberg and the sense of gesture characteristic of earthwork artists and minimalists like Richard Serra to create a flat landscape background set in contrast to the volume of architectural structures. The framing of his landscape is achieved by a grand gesture that imposes a large-scale patterning on the ground surface. In many of his projects he sets an object against this background. For example, Mile Long Drawing (1968), by Walter de Maria, was set against the Mojave Desert; Spiral Jetty (1970), by Robert Smithson, against the background of the Great Salt Lake landscape; Secant (1977), by Carl Andre, against a meadow background; Steam (1974), by Robert Morris, against the forest background of Washington University; and the Running Fence (1970), by Christo, against the rolling hills of California. In other projects, such as the Nasher Sculpture Center Garden, the entire collection of sculptures constitutes the object.

Balmori has been directly involved in many ways in the New York art world, and yet she has not written much about the relationship of her topographical art to the other arts. In a conversation we had when she was preparing this book, she expressed how important that relationship was: "I try to express in the drawings [representing the project] how my approach of landscape is inspired by art. It has much to do with the history of painting, with the dissolution of the object. Landscape has been burdened with the idea that it is about the placement of objects (flowers, plants, fountains, seats . . .). Clients may include a list of objects in their demands. And yet landscape is beyond the objects. The satisfaction it procures does not depend on the objects. [There are objects in a landscape, but] the appreciation of the landscape does not result from focusing attention on them. These objects contribute to a feeling of space. They contain or expand you, but you are not aware of them as things. So we erase them in our presentation [drawings] of a landscape [project]. We make each object less important (breaking its own frame), we insist on pattern and avoid [the duality of] foreground and background."[43]

Thus both landscape designers have drawn inspiration from American art in the same period (the 1970s) and have been led to opposite conclusions. Walker stresses the dialogic nature of landscapes—both real object and background—whereas Balmori seeks to create a specific art form—the topographical art—that embodies a sense of mood beyond the existence of objects and background. Walker, like the earthwork artists, strives for "thingness" in his art; Balmori, for the beauty of the flow of nature and the sense of ephemerality in the present. Whereas Walker takes a stand in favor of a purely aesthetic approach to landscape architecture, Balmori adopts an ethical position,[44] making aesthetic pursuit instrumental to the development of new forms of cultural desire.[45] It constitutes a definite renewal of the attention to design in landscape architecture, thus inviting it to become a topographical art, folding the earth surface in deliberately anthropic forms and anchoring them in a structural harmony with the elementary forces of nature.

Fig. 40. Stig L. Andersson, Anchor Park, Malmö, Sweden, 2001.

The International Front Line

Late twentieth-century landscape designers have learned—from Roberto Burle Marx, in Brazil, Martha Schwartz and Peter Walker, in the United States, and Ian Hamilton Finlay, Bernard Lassus, and Dieter Kienast, in Europe, among others—to relate their creative work to transformations of the contemporary visual arts. The historical encounter of a large movement of public engagement with environmental issues and ecology on the one hand, and a movement of attention to the contemporary visual arts among a few landscape architects on the other, has created a large front line of research, which is rapidly transforming the practices and debates among landscape designers. Where does Balmori's work stand in this context?

Her ideas about nature contrast with the positivist view adopted by a majority of Ian McHarg's followers, but it recalls the attitude of Fernando Chacel (a former collaborator of Burle Marx), who stresses that even though we cannot reestablish ecosystems that have been thoroughly destroyed by human activity, it is possible to understand scientifically how they worked, and then to implement that knowledge in the creation of new ecologies—for example, the ecogenesis of mangrove and restinha near Rio de Janeiro—that allow human and nonhuman beings to exist in close proximity.[46] Chacel agrees with Balmori's view about the indeterminacy of these processes, and with the importance of public-opinion movements in supporting the development of ecogenesis; he also hopes that aesthetic appreciation of these new urban ecologies will stimulate a desire for the protection of natural environments. Yet unlike Balmori, he does not actually undertake the creation of new ecologies, and instead falls back on an imitation of the forms of nature, and of Burle Marx's park design.

We have already mentioned that Balmori's attention to the creation of topography is unlike that of most earthwork sculptors, who either pursued formalist strategies (as Herbert Beyer did, at Mill Creek Canyon Park, near Seattle) or a metaphysical grounding of human existence in the aesthetic appreciation of celestial phenomena (as Jane Holt or Michael Heizer did). Balmori's topographical creations, as can be seen in the projects for Trenton or Sejong PAT, are neither earthworks nor architectural forms, like the Hundertwasser projects for housing and gas stations around Vienna, or Emilio Ambasz's ACROS conference center, in Fukuoka prefecture (1995). They propose a new kind of interweaving of architecture, horticulture, and living ground. Heterogeneity—of both urban ecology and landscape aesthetics—is the central notion that distinguishes her topographical inventions from recent parallel proposals.

True, the Beale landing project, with its floating islands, does bring to mind much of the work by the Danish landscape architect Stig Andersson. For example, collage is also systematically employed in his project in Holbaek, Denmark, giving rise to an abstract rendering of the plan, and at Ankarparken, in Malmö, Sweden, where large "suspended garden islands" are used to bring elements from some typical biotopes that form the Scania landscape into the center of a residential neighborhood (fig. 40).[47] There is even an underwater garden, quite comparable to Balmori's intertidal garden in the Canary Islands. Both artists use collage to evoke—rather than reproduce—an existing landscape, unlike Dominique Perrault's and Eric Jacobsen's unsuccessful attempt to create a "forest" in the center of the Mitterrand Library, in Paris.[48] However, Andersson tends to intensify the density of the ecological precedent he uses, in an effort to create a poetic distance, whereas Balmori seems to be more interested in making her created landscape accessible to visitors, open to leisure or cultural activities. This may seem a subtle difference, but I think that it reveals two very different directions that poetic creation has taken in contemporary landscape. Andersson attempts to engage visitors in a very personal and intimate experience of natural phenomena made more intense by his art: dense birch forest, or, as in Byhaven in Nørresundby, intense reflections of the sky in artistically designed water puddles (fig. 41). Balmori aims at allowing people to choose their public or private engagement with places, and she wants nature to appear as a coproduction of human culture and elemental forces.[49] She insists on designing spaces which are planted according to ecological principles and in making part of them available for cultural activities.

Among the small group of innovative designers whose art is engaged in the construction of a new ethic of relationships between humans and nonhumans, Balmori distinguishes herself by this aesthetic engagement in the creation of a new nature. She is not driven by the nostalgia for a lost nature that has marked the environmentalist movement since the 1960s; instead, she creates an art geared toward imagining new urban forms that allow a new course of nature to develop. The strength of her position derives from the conspicuous visibility of her formal inventions, which weave sheaths of urban nature between the wild environment and the dense urban center. Their appreciation depends on the creation of the desirable new experiences of urban and natural life that she proposes. Each of her sites offers an interweaving of anticipated individual and group experiences, of casual and formal events. Mostly, however, each proposes a distinctive experience of beauty: the experience of the tension between the mutability and fragility of connections between all living things, and the strong will to create new relationships between humans and nonhumans. This is an aesthetic of time that highlights the anonymous efforts of those who came before us and who cared for their descendants, as opposed to the aesthetics of memorials that command crowds of descendants to venerate a celebrated ancestor.

Fig. 41. Stig L. Andersson, Urban Garden, Nørresundby, Sweden, 2005.

Prelude

Landscape's role for our time must be redefined. Now. The need is urgent. This book sketches two major new tasks that come out of such redefinition, and shows how they can be accomplished. First, landscape can now create a new kind of livable city; second, through design it can broker the coexistence of human beings with the rest of nature. To design a livable city that coexists with nature as a whole will require establishing different relationships among the parts. The harmful relations created by nineteenth-century industrialization will have to be revised in some cases, reversed in others.

I have chosen a Manifesto as the format to express the critical shifts needed to carry out these tasks. You may be surprised by the use of the word Manifesto. Usually it means a rigid set of rules, pronounced in a stentorian voice, that you must follow rigorously (lest you fall off the right path). This Manifesto instead proposes the realignments required of our work and our lives in order for us to participate in the permanent re-creation of our world. I have used the word Manifesto because it transmits a certain urgency and telegraphs that its message is vital. These realignments offer a way to live in our world as it is today. Each Manifesto point is called out in the following pages with a bold numeral; the corresponding point is adjacent.

This book is not about my work, though some of it appears here because it provides concrete illustrations of the emerging landscapes described early in the text. But these particular projects represent only one set of possibilities; the general typologies described in Parts 1 and 2 can be taken in different directions by others.

These are my words, but many other practitioners, both in the United States and abroad, also voice an awareness of the issues raised in this book and wrestle with them in their work. Incorporating the hints and partial descriptions that it provides, this text aims to extract and put into words the critical points of our moment in time that can lead to a new coexistence with nature and a new kind of city. The medium is landscape. The tool is design. Design must broker the new relationship with nature and make new arrangements for coexistence visible through an aesthetic resolution. It can create the framework for a new kind of urban life that leaves behind nineteenth-century urban design and twentieth-century master plans.

New manifestos become necessary whenever our vestments no longer fit their time. Such is our situation.

1
History and Nature/ Nature and Art: A New Departure

The Present

Seeking refuge in the past or in the future is futile. "Before" and "after" are dimensions of time that are not in our hands. The present is. By the present, I mean the intersection of one's own life with that of one's society and culture; by the present, I mean the time in which we exist. To grab hold of this present and to describe it as well as possible is the intent here. This is not an easy task. We need absolute concentration to be granted fleeting and intermittent glances of our own present. An understanding of our own time, and the need for new words and new forms in the field of endeavor called landscape, gradually emerge out of this effort. Indeed, landscape design itself ultimately takes on a new meaning. In transmuting old forms and words into new ones, we are given new eyes with which to look at the world in all its width, height, depth, and temporality.

History

The weight of the eighteenth-century English Landscape School on landscape design in our time has been onerous. So onerous that one is tempted to avoid dealing with landscape history at all, for fear of remaining in its grip. Putting history first in writing on landscape seems to cave in to it. Instead, it is an act of confrontation. This is not a history of landscape. It is an attempt, in considering how we design landscape, to understand what our relation to the history of landscape design is, in order to free ourselves from it, and in particular from the English Landscape School. Though not from the extraordinary practitioners that brought it about: William Kent, Alexander Pope, Capability Brown, and Humphrey Repton, up to the great Frederick Law Olmsted—figures one can't hope to emulate. This is not a competition.

The English Landscape School developed in the eighteenth century and was started socially in a literary circle, the Kit-Kat Club. Visually, landscape painting—particularly the landscape paintings of Lorrain and Poussin—served as a point of departure for landscape design, which at this time therefore began to be described as Picturesque.

But the key word to describe the new style that replaced the Dutch and French formal layouts was "natural." Nature was the new ideal. In *The Moralists*, of 1709, Shaftesbury, a member of the Kit-Kat Club, declares his preference for "things of a natural kind; where neither Art, nor the Conceit or Caprice of man has spoiled their genuine Order."[1] Though many waves of fashion came and went from the eighteenth through the twentieth centuries, the English School's attachment to the natural was a constant in landscape design. Its call for the emulation of nature crossed the Atlantic, and, by Olmsted's time, the resulting designs were confused with nature itself in the mind of the general public.

The English Landscape School represented its creations as a close approximation to nature. At times, indeed, even of *being* nature. Paradoxically, these claims were made while its practitioners were busily at work artificially constructing landscapes. Kant excluded landscape from his list of the arts because of this aping of nature: "It seems strange that landscape gardening could be regarded as a kind of painting despite the fact that it exhibits its forms corporeally. It does, however, actually take its forms from nature . . . and to this extent it is not art."[2]

In the wake of the English Landscape School, fueled in part by the Romantic movement, a view of nature arose which, when paired with landscape, made landscape-as-nature into an indissoluble pact. Under the effect of the ideas of the Romantic movement, nature acquired traits of a deity in an age that was moving away from religion. This development is echoed in the popular desire for "being in nature." As we sat by a river with our feet in the water, at the foot of several chains of the Andes mountains, a friend said to me that "we seldom have the chance to be so close to nature without any human artifacts standing in between."

The asphyxiating legacy of the English movement continues to this day, aided by the lack of development of a new landscape aesthetic, the exile of landscape from the arts, and the emergence of the field of ecology. Any attempt to reinvent landscape design has to wrestle with its powerful ideas and its worn-out forms, as well as those three other forces. That wrestling sometimes seems to require a rejection of landscape history itself; it seems that only rejection can free one from the Picturesque's heavy hand and allow one to see things in the present, one's own present. The ambiguity that results from resisting landscape's history—in part by ignoring it—while the hold (only now being loosened) of its dead hand on the practice remains, is remarkable and tragic.

A concentrated effort, a painful tearing of ourselves from the past after many attempts and false starts, can bring us to a deeper understanding of the present and to the possibility of decoupling landscape design from nature and of releasing us from the bonds of its history. An understanding of landscape design's confused representation of itself as nature is the first step in this effort. The second is to depict clearly our current understanding of nature. **1**

Nature and Art

Nature has always been our name for observed phenomena. However, we are constantly shifting

1. Nostalgia for the past and utopian dreams for the future prevent us from looking at our present.

what we observe and how we observe it. And through this process, we reinvent it. What we understand to be nature now is not only forest, river, cloud, trout, daisy—but also us, and us interdependent with all the rest.

Examining the number and variety of definitions of nature given by the cultural historian Raymond Williams in his book *Key Words* (1976), we can begin to appreciate the historical shifts in how people have thought about nature. Williams presents "nature" as the most complex word of our present culture. He gives three meanings for it, of which *nature as the material world itself* is the one that concerns us here and the one that relates directly to landscape. To paraphrase Williams, the moment we have been looking at—the Picturesque in the eighteenth century—reveals a transition from nature as Reason, with discoverable laws, to a nature that has not been altered by human hands, a transition from the Enlightenment to the Romantic movement, with its view of society as an artificial construct with problems that must be cured by learning from nature.

This view of nature prevailed from the eighteenth century to the middle of the twentieth century. For all that time, nature meant the countryside, unspoiled places, plants, and creatures other than humankind; it meant everything that humans had not made. It was also seen as fixed and unchangeable.

So the Picturesque represented as important a transition in the concept of nature as the one we now are making in our own time. The present shift started in the late nineteenth century, with the concept of natural selection, which made nature both historically diverse and active. Darwin and the concept of evolution put nature in motion, took away its fixity. Then came the twentieth-century concept of ecology, which made humankind part of nature again, with all of nature's parts considered to be interdependent. (The word *ecology* was coined in 1868 by the German biologist Ernst Haeckel to designate the totality of relations between living species and their environments.) We emerge thus into the twenty-first century with shifts in our understanding that challenge the foundations of the Picturesque and its concept of nature. But to these formidable changes in the view of nature itself there is added the complicated relation of Nature and Art.**2**

The present shift in the concept of nature requires a renewal of our ideas about the relationship of nature to art. We see nature now as multifaceted, changing over the centuries along with our actions, thoughts, and arts. This invites a historical examination of the different forms of nature that result from human interventions. We could attempt a history of these forms (such as meadows, ponds, canals, harbors, forests, gardens, and parks) to learn how the arts contributed to ecological changes. It would show how common practices—ethics and aesthetics—variously affected historical environments.

Once you include the human species in nature, the issues of art and nature get very complicated. Many painters and sculptors in the twentieth century have denied that they have any relationship with nature or that it is a basis for anything in their work. Robert Irwin: "I began to recognize the difference between imagery and physicality, that everything had both an imagery and a physicality, and furthermore that for me, the moment a painting took on any kind of image, the minute I could recognize it as having any relationship to nature, of any kind, to me the painting went flat. Now, I don't know where I got that idea, but there it was. Imagery for me constituted representation, 're-presentation,' a second order of reality, whereas I was after a first order of presence."[3]

Robert Irwin's acute observations on landscape touch on some of its modern preoccupations, including, in particular, the issue of recognizable objects, and he has contributed important concepts to that discussion. He has made it clear that he wishes to distance himself from anything suspected of being nature in his art. Curiously, at the same time he has both moved his work into the field of landscape (Getty) and has declared landscape to be the most interesting area of artistic inquiry.

The strained efforts to refuse a dialogue with nature appear in the works and thinking of many other artists. Of all modern artists, Robert Smithson is the one who most obviously transitioned to the new view of nature as multifaceted and changing. His work and verbal statements are the clearest and most

2. Nature is the flow of change within which humans exist. Evolution is its history. Ecology is our understanding of its present phase.

modern: "We have to develop a different sense of nature; we have to develop a dialectic of nature that includes man."[4]

Yet when asked how he would characterize his attitude toward nature, he reverts to a dualistic world: "But I do have a stronger tendency towards the inorganic than to the organic. The organic is closer to the idea of nature. I am more interested in denaturalization or in artifice than in any kind of naturalism."[5]

Irwin and Smithson have been cited because they are unusually clear in their thinking and in expressing themselves in words. Many artists today struggle in their relationship to nature but have not been explicit about the conflict. In this oppositional relationship of art to nature there are still echoes of the nineteenth-century view of nature as a separate realm from that of humanity; a nature in relation to which people are outside observers, and from which they distance their work. Yet the issue that plagues painters and sculptors is foremost for landscape artists too: whether or not to mimic and represent nature.

But landscape design—as an art—found itself with a countercurrent coming, of all places, from a field which developed from the 1940s to the 1960s: ecology. This development envisioned nature as a gathering of interrelated species, each embodied in a biotope—a region uniform in environmental conditions and in the populations of animals and plants for which it is the habitat—that had reached its climax. In many ways, the idea of "climax" belongs to older concepts of nature that see fixity at one moment in the biotope. The idea of the "natural" embodied in a biotope that had reached its climax came accompanied, for ecologists, by a fierce attachment to the visual mimicry of the "natural," and particularly to mimicry of this fixed biotope.

Though still popular and widely referred to, this idea of "climax" in a biotic community has been abandoned by scientists. Called Clementsian succession, this idea of a stable climax, in which there is no change over time, has been supplanted, by modern ecologists, with concepts of nonequilibrium, which show that most natural ecosystems experience disturbance at a rate that makes a "climax" community unattainable. The newer Gleasonian succession view incorporates a much greater role for random factors and denies the existence of sharply bounded community types. While the Clementsian understanding of succession invited the mimetic reproduction of imagined climax, the Gleasonian perspective does not provide implicit directions to be followed by design, and the art world has correspondingly turned away from the emulation of nature.

Behind this complex dance with mimetism—with efforts to free art from it stepping one way and the insistence on unscientific mimetism by environmental scientists moving in another—lies the nineteenth-century definition of nature, crumbling, but still looming large. As the fixity of biotopes has proven illusory, we now are left with a changing nature. Similarly, on the art side, we are ready to question Kant's view of beauty as a fixed category.

Each art will have to wrestle with its relation to the new understanding of nature as a constantly changing system in which the interconnection of the parts is more important than are the isolated components themselves. How this shift in the understanding of nature will affect its relation to art remains an open question.[6] And this revision of the concept of nature, resulting from the impact of the concepts of both evolution and ecology, opens the door to a similar exegesis of other historical forms.

Scientific evidence ultimately led to ecologists abandoning the model of a fixed biotope, while at the same time, biological evidence came to reinforce the importance of history. François Jacob, who received the Nobel Prize in Physiology in 1965, gives a picture of biological evolution as a sort of molecular "bricolage." Evolution, he says, transforms an ancient system to give it a new function. "Living things are in fact historic structures, they are literally the creation of history."[7]

So our hopes of escaping history are nil; it lies in our very molecules. That said, our only possible escape lies in decoupling the *forms* from the historical functions they served and adapting the system to the new functions, as in the molecular "bricolage."

The last confrontation, the most serious confrontation we have to face after those with history and nature, is between nature and art. It could also be called a battle between ecology and aesthetics.

The world of ecology and its descendant, the world of sustainability—which affects the design professions more directly—have nothing to do with aesthetics. Ecology has considered aesthetics something to be avoided, the imposition of human invention capriciously deforming the natural (which, for ecologists, as for Picturesque theoreticians, needed to be left alone). That early picture has been followed by a tentative new understanding about aesthetics: that the making of something beautiful in fact can be an important aspect of sustainability. Though this has affected ecology's and sustainability's relation to aesthetics, they fundamentally continue to have nothing to do with each other.

If we take the twentieth-century emergence of modern art in conjunction with the nineteenth-century industrialization of the Western world, we could perhaps say that modern art and industrialization had nothing to do with each other. But industry produced such powerful images in its artifacts, buildings, and machines that an architect could sing about the house as a machine to live in, about silos and ocean liners as new forms to use in architecture. Thus architecture developed the aesthetics that have made the modern industrial world enjoyable in some ways that were unforeseen by the English cities of the nineteenth century. No such relation exists with sustainability or ecology. In part, that is because there has been a definite vernacular air about those disciplines, belonging to do-it-yourselfers and sixties' rebels. Their influence on architecture or landscape leaned more to the social and ethical than to the aesthetic. There are no great visual images emerging from sustainability as there were from industrialization. But the support of and the need for sustainability have made designers of all kinds deal with new technology. And not only new technology (photovoltaic panels, etc.), but also a new understanding of what is implied in transforming known artifacts into a new typology.

This could be called its chrysalis stage. The pieces are being transformed; certain lumpy forms are shaping up inside that envelope, and we can see a vague outline and are beginning to feel our way into form. But neither ecology nor sustainability has fed into new aesthetics. Landscape design is the art that engages with all aspects of a sustainable world: elemental forces, materials, humans, and other living beings. Thus it is the responsibility of landscape artists to create the work and develop the aesthetics that will make experiences of a sustainable world highly enjoyable and desirable. The aesthetics of landscape is for the moment a separate agenda. The champions of the agenda of aesthetics, of beauty, are surprised that it can feed into sustainability, but that conviction can in fact come only from the designers who can convert the principles, the technology, and the forms into an aesthetic resolution.

This explains, in part, the lack of artistic quality in all the exhibitions based on the design of sustainable buildings, objects, or landscapes. It is the wrong rubric for aesthetics at the moment.

Given these different, unparallel relations between history and nature and between nature and art, we need to treat them separately. In the design of forms based on the new interpretation of nature, it is critical to uncover the transformations occurring because of this new interpretation, and to make visible the break with the past that it produces.[8]

What follows is a series of examples of pieces that have been reinterpreted in light of our new view of nature and the search for a better relationship between nature and ourselves. Of these examples, the American Lawn in particular has been made to be the leading voice of the section, since it illustrates quite precisely one of the two central premises of this book: the mutually interdependent relationship and transformative power of people and nature. In its eighteenth-century English inception, the lawn reflected the relationship of people and nature as it was at that time. It eventually reached a form that became our American ideal and the basis of an industry and industrial practices. This led to the current need for transforming it into the "Freedom Lawn," as we search for a better model of coexistence with nature. In contrast, the return of historical practices in the forms of hedgerows, sunken gardens, or espaliers illustrates the potential of using past types in new ways and for new purposes, as they are reinterpreted in turn by a new view of nature which assigns these formerly designed features a new value. **3**

Historical Achievements and Contemporary Failures: The American Lawn

As a first example of this redesigning based on a new interpretation of nature and history, and on seeking a better model of the coexistence of humans with nature, let us take the American Lawn.[9]

Your backyard, that third of an acre where you've lounged, played Frisbee, and let your small children crawl, is your private property and nobody else's business. The American Lawn, all thirty-one million acres of it, is the nation's largest single crop, 60 percent of it made up of home lawns like yours, the rest in public landscapes. Between your lawn and those thirty-one million acres lies the new story.

The American Lawn has a notable trait that makes it the perfect landscape to examine. It tells a tale at the very small front-yard-of-your-house scale. And it also tells a tale at the million-acre scale. What emerges from the examination of the relation of each of these scales is that scale itself is what prompts the need for a transformation of the lawn.

The lawn's rise to preeminence as the American landscape first brings us back to the Picturesque and then to the history of its entry into North America.

Though the French had also used lawn (the "flowery Meade" of tapestry) in walled medieval gardens as a place for music and pleasure, the American Lawn is a direct descendant of the eighteenth-century English lawn. More than anyone else, the landscape artist Capability Brown was its creator; in the words of the contemporary landscape artist Ian Hamilton Finlay: "Brown made water appear as Water, and lawn as Lawn."[10] The great inventions that made it Lawn were its scale, sweeping over topography and uniting distant landscapes with its blanket of green, and the contemporary invention of the ha-ha (a dry ditch with a raised retaining wall used to conceal the boundaries of a landscape), which hid hedges or property fences from view and kept vistas open. Thomas Jefferson's notation on visiting one of these English eighteenth-century estates summed it up: "the lawn about thirty acres."

Brown razed villages, gardens, and allées to create, as one continuous space, a countryside without views of anything made by human industry. His work places us in the presence of the eighteenth-century shift in the meaning of nature; humanity is excluded from it, and the ideal landscape is one which contains only the nonhuman, "natural" elements of plants, trees, mountains, and rivers.

The change in scale of this new use of grass in England did not require any feat of engineering. It was an easily created extension of grasses already present, aided by a mild climate with moisture well distributed throughout the year.

The Lawn Comes to North America

When the British colonized the New World, they brought with them their ideas about nature. Cultivated, grazed, and developed over many centuries, the island of Great Britain had no unaltered landscapes left. British landscape design that "improved" a natural landscape in reality only added new artificial dimensions to an existing landscape already highly modified by humans.

Grass played a central role in English agriculture because it sustained sheep and cattle. William Wood, an English traveler, warned settlers coming to New England in the 1630s to seek places where there would be enough grass to feed cattle. In general, grazing land was scarce; domesticated animals quickly ran out of grass, and forestland then had to be cleared to create new pastures. Seed brought from Europe was used, and soon such European plants as bluegrass and white clover, which were adapted to the harsh requirements of pastoralism, began to take over

3. All things in nature are constantly changing. Landscape artists need to design to allow for change, while seeking a new course that enhances the coexistence of humans and the rest of nature.

wherever cattle grazed. By 1640, a regular market in European seed existed in Rhode Island, and within one or two generations these plants had become so common that settlers regarded them as native. During the eighteenth century, European pasture plants, including timothy and fowl-meadow grass and legumes such as red clover and alfalfa, were common on pastures throughout the colonies. Thus the pasture, a mixture of grasses, legumes, and other plants, became a common landscape feature in much of colonial America. Pasture was not only a rural feature but also part of many villages and towns, where it covered the central common.

The lawn, carrying the English connotation of natural landscape with it, became a symbol of prestige in nineteenth-century suburbs. Similarly, New England town centers, the old commons which in the eighteenth century had been the setting for such useful activities as rope making, hay growing, military drills, and town fairs, were transformed in the nineteenth century from bare stamped earth, cultivated fields, or cemetery grounds into lawned and treed parks, now called greens. With this grassy transformation, most of the economic functions of the commons were shifted to other places. At least one American writer, J. B. Jackson, has condemned this transformation of true commons into greens.

In 1830, the Englishman Edwin Budding invented the lawn mower. As these machines became available over the following decades, modest householders could keep their lawns tidily cut without the help of gardeners or flocks of sheep. The well-manicured lawn was now within reach of average citizens. Whether they had an acre or just a tiny patch of land, they could tend it themselves and create whatever image they chose for their surroundings.

The lawn became the symbol of suburbia. It was championed by Frederick Law Olmsted, the famous designer of New York City's Central Park and many suburbs, who viewed the lawn as a sort of community parkland. For Olmsted, the front lawn of a house in a suburb unified the residential composition as one neighborhood, giving a sense of ampleness, greenness, and community.

The curvilinear layout of American residential streets, with houses set well back from the road behind front lawns with informal plantings of trees and shrubs, is a uniquely American residential form, first proposed by and built for an industrialist by the New York architect Alexander Jackson Davis (1803–1892) in his suburb Llewellyn Park, New Jersey, twelve miles west of Manhattan. Andrew Jackson Downing, Olmsted, and others popularized this layout. The plan that Olmsted and his partner, Calvert Vaux, created for Riverside, near Chicago, has become an archetype of this American suburb.

The lawn, since its invasion of the eastern seaboard nearly three centuries ago, has spread to every corner of North America. But the lawn arose in the mild, moist climate of England, while North America is a continent with many harsh climates and an enormous diversity in vegetation and soils, from the extreme winter cold of the northern United States to the hot and drought-prone summers of the South.

Through its success the lawn was commercialized, and through entrepreneurialism it was able to overcome naturally occurring environmental barriers. Not only because it was possible, but also because it was preferred and liked by a mass audience conditioned by a long cultural history, the lawn became the landscape of choice from Kennebunkport, Maine, to Los Angeles, California.

Through this commercialization and geographical extension we see many basic changes. The beautiful greensward developed to high art by Capability Brown was kept mowed by sheep or deer. A variety of species of grass and of other plants such as clover grew in it. The nineteenth century brought the lawn mower, the twentieth century the electric lawn mower. In conjunction with these changes herbicides were applied to kill all but the two or three species of grass that were allowed to grow in lawns, and nitrogen and phosphorus fertilizers were applied to keep lawns at a peak of greenness. In other words, from the 1850s to the 1950s, as the lawn became an industry, it was transformed and became the Industrial Lawn.

The Industrial Lawn

In this transformation, the story of the two scales takes center stage. We now will look at what individual yards do in their thirty-one-million-acre aggregate. From natural, solar-powered, self-regulating, and self-fertilizing ecosystems, they become human-modified ecosystems based on fossil energy, chemical fertilizers, pesticides, and artificial irrigation. The United States in presettlement times had natural ecosystems of evergreen forests in the northern edges and far western states, deciduous forests in the eastern states, grasslands in the middle states, and desert ecosystems in the Southwest. With many different land uses, these systems have changed, but the same conditions that gave rise to them exist today, and if human activity ceased, these regional patterns would eventually reappear. We are now maintaining lawns under a variety of climatic conditions in areas that were once forest and desert. The lawn growing in an area in which it would not naturally occur depends on human management and supplements of fossil energy, water, and chemicals for survival. The use of such supplements affects not only the lawn but also water and other interconnected ecosystems, with direct and indirect effects on the health of many organisms, including us. It is here that actions at the small scale and the large need to be examined.

Fossil Fuels

The machines (mowers, aerators, leaf blowers, weed whackers, edgers) that groom our grass all consume fuel. Most of them have very inefficient two-cycle engines. Fossil fuels are also used in shipping fertilizers and pesticides, as well as in mining, refining, and transporting the materials (mainly nitrogen [N], phosphorus [P], and potassium [K]) needed to produce fertilizers. The use of fossil fuels has serious adverse environmental and health effects. Fuels contribute to the formation of acid rain, ozone, and greenhouse gases, and cause respiratory problems.

Chemicals

According to the Environmental Protection Agency (EPA), a typical annual management program for a homeowner's Industrial Lawn includes four or more applications of a nitrogen fertilizer and ten or more doses of various pesticides. The EPA estimated that in 1984 more synthetic fertilizers were applied to American lawns than the entire country of India applied to all its food crops.[11] Before World War I, nitrogen came from organic sources (guano and other animal manure, and bloodmeal). In 1913, two German scientists learned how to capture nitrogen from the atmosphere—air is 78 percent nitrogen gas—by combining it with the hydrogen in natural gas. This discovery formed the basis of the synthetic fertilizer industry.

The National Academy of Sciences found that homeowners use up to ten times as many chemical pesticides per acre as farmers do. In Connecticut, homeowners use 61 percent of the pesticides applied in the state. And in one year, 1997 to 1998, the number of households purchasing yard pesticides increased from 19.7 million to 24.7 million. The scale of management practices for the lawn is therefore surprisingly large in comparison to what would seem to be much larger-scale ventures, such as the agriculture systems of whole countries. And even a single front- and backyard unit, at its small scale, has connections with the air stream and water of distant ecosystems.

Fertilizers

Nitrogen makes grass grow rapidly; the lush green of the Industrial Lawn is a sign of high growth rates. But too much nitrogen increases the plant's vulnerability to disease, reduces its ability to withstand high temperatures and drought, and discourages microorganisms that are beneficial to lawn health. Some artificial fertilizers can acidify the soil, impeding important biological and chemical processes.[12] When nitrogen fertilizers break down in the soil, nitrous oxide, a potent greenhouse gas that contributes to global warming, can be released in the air. It is one of the gases that act to destroy the stratospheric ozone layer that protects the earth from damaging ultraviolet radiation from the sun.[13]

Pesticides

With the continued use of pesticides, pesticide-resistant strains of the targeted species develop and become increasingly difficult to keep in check. Also, the elimination of one pest may foster the dominance of another. But the unintended elimination of beneficial microorganisms is perhaps the most serious side effect of a pesticide; for example, they may kill off one of the lawn's greatest allies, the microorganisms that kill thatch. But most important, many pesticides persist in the ground and in water for a long time. They can also affect ecosystems far beyond the lawn where they were applied. They may blow off site or be leached from the lawn in drainage water and end up in wells or in streams and lakes where fish and other aquatic species may be affected. One of the most widely used insecticides, Diazinon, kills waterfowl and other bird species. It has been banned by the EPA from use in sod farms and golf courses but continues to be used on lawns. Thus, although this environmental regulation *directly* affects only larger systems (and not the small-scale residential lawn), it does not prevent the indirect spread of Diazinon from individual lawns to those larger systems.

Water Supplies

> *We talk [water] scarcity, yet we have set [some of] our largest cities in the deserts, and then have insisted in surrounding ourselves with Kentucky bluegrass. Our words are those of the Sahara Desert; our policies are those of the Amazon River.*
> —Richard Lamm,
> Governor of Colorado, 1975–1987

In the semiarid plains states, water from the Ogallala Aquifer, which stretches from South Dakota to northern Texas, is being extracted much faster than it can be replaced by natural processes. Water tables have fallen in the Dallas–Fort Worth area and in the Tucson metropolitan area, which is completely dependent on groundwater for its water supply.[14] In the West, lawn watering can account for up to 60 percent of water use. The practice of watering lawns needs to be reevaluated.

Water Pollution

When contaminated with chemicals, water becomes less usable for people and may be destructive to interconnected aquatic systems. Sandy and gravelly soils allow water and dissolved fertilizers and pesticides to move from the surface into groundwater. This becomes particularly serious in areas with permeable soils lying over groundwater aquifers that supply drinking water (Cape Cod, Massachusetts; southern New England; Long Island, New York).[15] High concentrations of nitrates in drinking water can cause birth defects, cancer, and nervous system impairments.[16] Pesticide contamination of groundwater is not as well documented, but it has been detected in water surveys. The EPA considers the commonly used pesticide 2.4-D to be a priority leacher that travels quickly to groundwater. 2.4-D is a component of Agent Orange, a defoliant used in the Vietnam War, and has been linked to cancer and birth defects.[17]

Solid Waste

Yard waste is the second largest component of the waste stream. Three-quarters of it is grass clippings.[18] Clippings are a source of nitrogen and other nutrients, and their removal can result in the loss of up to 100 pounds of nitrogen per acre of lawn per year.

Species Diversity

The Industrial Lawn is a simplified ecosystem in comparison to forests or fields, which contain a very diverse mosaic of plants and animals. It displaces many species. Developed sites house fewer bird species, for example, than the original habitats (though they may contain greater numbers of birds).[19] The spread of the Industrial Lawn and its destruction of native habitats may have a serious cumulative effect on the nation's flora and fauna. More and more species of plants and animals will be restricted to smaller and smaller areas, and larger groups of fewer species will dominate. Twenty million acres of residential lawns and eleven million acres of lawn in public parks and highways already displace what had been a vast amount of diverse habitat for a large variety of plant and animal species.

The lawn holds a central place in the American view of an ideal life. Over vast areas in small towns and suburbs, a spreading green carpet forms a background for living. The well-kept lawn is not only beautiful in itself, but it also provides the setting for the house. In these homes, people feel in harmony with their well-tended plots of land. In the spring, new blades of grass emerge, creating a carpet of green that is a perfect backdrop for the beauty of crocus, daffodil, tulip, azalea, and rhododendron. In summer the world is lush with vegetation, the air perfumed by freshly cut grass. The homeowner is filled with a sense of well-being. Although the season, location, resources, and energy of the residents may vary, the ideal persists. The well-kept front lawns roll down the street, providing open space and beautiful vistas. In this ideal, the grass sward is as pure as possible, mowed two inches high, and free of dandelions and other insidious intruders.[20]

Behind these similar front lawns lie more varied backyards: some contain children's play equipment; others have patios, picnic tables, and barbecue grills; still others have gardens of vegetables and flowers. Here and there is an occasional pool. Evidence of unfinished tasks lies about: a pile of wood half stacked from last winter; a building project, perhaps lumber for a tree house, covered with plastic. Clothes hang on clotheslines. Under all of these activities the lawn rolls on, with bare spots marked by heavy use.

Lawns also have practical merits. Some of the lawn's most beneficial functions are safety- and health-related. In some regions, grass can serve as a firebreak, keeping wildfires at bay. Even before scientists discovered that turf can trap some pollutants and pollens that cause allergies, Walt Whitman called grass the "handkerchief of the Lord."[21] Lawns have great recreational value. They are home to baseball, touch football, badminton, and Frisbee. Grass wears well and provides a cushioning effect that reduces injuries and makes walking, running, and jumping more comfortable. Economics plays a major role in our love of the lawn. A home is the cornerstone of many people's net worth, their primary asset. Great efforts are expended to maintain the home's value; landscaping can add up to 15 percent of a home's worth. Lawns contribute to resale value.

Transforming the American Lawn

Given this interplay of small residential lawns with larger ecosystems, we need to find new, environmentally sounder and healthier ways of designing our lawns. The new lawn—which in our American Lawn book we called the Freedom Lawn—is meant to meet the small-scale aesthetic, environmental, and economic needs of individual homeowners. We need to move away from the use of fossil fuels, reduce the use of chemicals and irrigation water, and increase the biological diversity of our lawns. These changes all represent our increasing understanding of the connection between the small scale and the large. In other words, the lawn needs to be redesigned.

There are two aspects to this redesign. One consists of the concrete changes necessary to obtain desired results in moving from the small to the large scale (that is, significantly reducing or abandoning the use of fossil fuels, chemicals, and water, and increasing biological diversity). The other is the aesthetic, which necessarily will be modified by the new regime. The new aesthetic will not "result" from the application of those changes. It will be the product of the transforming hand of a landscape artist, much as Capability Brown took the existing grasses of England and made lawn out of them. In this first section, I describe only the physical changes. In Part 3, I will deal with the aesthetics.

Specific ways of affecting the problems inherent in the Industrial Lawn may vary, but they all follow the general outline given above. If we take the example of adding a nongrass species such as clover to the lawn, for example, we can achieve two of these goals (reducing the use of chemicals and increasing the biodiversity of the lawn). Clover, which was historically an integral part of lawns, unfortunately has been all but eliminated from modern lawns. Nodules on clover roots contain rhizobium bacteria, which are able to "fix" nitrogen from the air spaces in the soil and convert it into a form that can be used by the clover. When parts of the clover die off, this nitrogen, the most important ingredient in the majority of artificial-lawn fertilizers, is added back to the soil, where it can be used by both grass and clover plants. Adding clover to your lawn thus modestly increases biodiversity and also dramatically reduces the need for chemical fertilizers.

Many people have already moved away from the idea of the "perfect lawn." They plan their mowing to retain patches of naturally seeded wildflowers; they plant ground-cover plants instead of grass; they may replace lawns altogether, with fruit and vegetable gardens. Such actions reveal a new understanding of our relationship to nature, gradually affecting our lawns and gardens.

Landscape forms encapsulate unseen assumptions. The case of the lawn serves as an example. Originally a varied planting of grasses and clover, it was kept short by sheep and deer, which in turn were kept at arm's length from a residence by means of the ha-ha. The eighteenth-century lawn was used to unify large extensions of land, even extending it to the surrounding landscape. The twentieth-century lawn (cultivated from desertic southern California to frozen Minnesota) contains in its smooth velvety greenness just two or three species of grass, managed by gas-powered machines and the application of nitrogen, phosphorus, and great quantities of water. The Industrial Lawn is in fact an industry, an economically successful industry. It was standard in the 1960s to blame corporations for industrial excesses and for fostering consumerism. In the case of the Industrial Lawn, one would rail against the giants of the lawn industry. But we have become more sophisticated in our understanding of these forces. Industries which promote and support sustainability (even if their interests are purely economic) can be financially successful. We have also come to understand that certain attitudes are anti-nature; consumerism is one of them. Thus many of our own activities, as well as the actions of corporations, can be seen as anti-nature. Viewing consumerism as anti-nature puts landscape on the front lines of the battle with large economic forces, which it now has the strength to engage. The blue planet, that early picture taken by the astronauts from outer space, so beautiful and so finite, has become a mythical landscape. Al Gore's *An Inconvenient Truth* has made the public aware of this finiteness and vulnerability, and has revived memories of a sacred Mother Nature. But we should tread carefully in drawing parallels that reinstate past views. Whatever values we attach to this new nature, it is not the sacred nature of our past, since sacrality itself has been transformed and needs to be reinterpreted in modern terms.

Our new concept of nature has transformed the way we look at the lawn, jumping from our front yard to the air, water, and soil around it on a much larger scale, the scale of a city. Freedom Lawns, though ecological, will not be natural landscapes. They will be carefully crafted artifacts that will be natural in the way they work, and will express this in the new forms they take. History and nature have made their presence known in the American Lawn. The shift from Industrial Lawn to Freedom Lawn represents a shift in paradigm, and it does affect the lawn as admired aesthetic object. Beauty is not free of ethics. We can hardly admire the Industrial Lawn when we are poisoned by it. **4**

Retrieving Past Achievements: Hedgerows, Espaliers, Sunken Gardens

Some historical forms that we had prized—such as lawns—have changed into landscapes that we can no longer admire; they have run their course in their present form and demand that we redesign them. Others, however, have been redeemed by time and can assume new roles for the twenty-first century. François Jacob has shown that in biology, evolution transforms an ancient system to give it a new function. Similarly, in some historical landscape types an overlaying of explicit ecological functions makes these forms modern.

Hedgerows

Hedgerows were developed as the linear planting of edges of property, created to define those edges and to keep animals in or out. Many systems were employed for this, such as pleaching or using spiny plants to discourage passage. Their role in the United States was particularly important in the nineteenth century, especially in the Midwest.

Hedgerows appeared in agricultural fields as a result of two forces: the scarcity of wood and the creation of laws governing fences and herding.

4. Landscape forms encapsulate unseen assumptions. To expose them is to enter the economic and aesthetic struggles of our times.

Foraging livestock forced settlers to fence gardens and fields before the first harvest. The dearth of timber in many places, particularly on the western margins of the prairie, led farmers to search for alternatives to traditional wood fences. Although the hedge had attracted interest in the East, it was not until the 1840s that it received public attention as the solution to the fencing problem. By the 1850s, it was used on a large scale in Ohio, Illinois, and Indiana. The planting of hedges, particularly of Osage-orange, became so popular in the 1850s that the *Valley Farmer* coined the term "hedge mania."[22] Territorial legislation recognized the hedge as a legal fence in 1857: "Any structure or hedge or ditch, in the nature of a fence, used for purposes of enclosure which is such as good husbandmen generally keep, and shall by testimony of skillful men, appear to be sufficient, shall be deemed a lawful fence."[23]

Although a wide variety of plants (such as the wild rose and native American thorns) were used, it was the Osage-orange (*Maclura pomifera*) hedge that dominated the prairies. It could be established in three years and had long hard spines which deterred stock from attempting to get through. Of southern origin, it is a small tree that grows to about forty feet in height. It became the favored plant for hedges because it was hardy in northern climates and relatively disease free. The use of Osage-orange plants spread quickly through the Midwest in the 1850s and 1860s, and the decade following the Civil War saw a major increase of these plants in Nebraska and Kansas. By 1871, this kind of hedge ranked with post-and-rail and board fences as one of the three leading types of enclosures in Nebraska. Advertisements for one million of the trees for sale in Baxter Springs, two million in Ottawa, and five million in Bonyshan County—all in Kansas—give a sense of the popularity of the plant, probably encouraged by tax reductions given to farmers who planted hedges.

The use of Osage-orange hedges started to decline after the barbed-wire fence was developed, in the 1880s. The hedge required careful planting and trimming, frequent cultivation, and protection from livestock during its first years. (In fact, many farmers actually built fences around their young hedges.) Hedges also fell victim to prairie fires. Barbed wire required less upkeep and proved a more effective barrier against cattle. Although the Osage-orange was no longer considered the solution to the fencing problem, it continued to be planted until the 1920s, probably because of its lower cost to the farmer.

In addition to their maintenance requirements, hedges occupied large amounts of land and impeded the movement of large, motorized agricultural equipment. Farmers worldwide began to systematically remove thousands of miles of hedges from their fields. In England, a country where hedges once were predominant, the losses have been so great that a law was passed to protect them. In the United States, rates of removal appear to have intensified since the 1970s. But new studies of hedgerows and their benefits are transforming our view of them. These include, as European researchers have found, "the reduction of windspeed leeward of hedgerows to a distance fifteen to twenty times the height of the windbreak, resulting in reduced rates of snowmelt and soil drying; generally, greater water use efficiency by plants' increased humidity, lower rates of evaporation and transpiration; wind erosion decreases, crop increases; and plants exhibiting greater growth. They also provide habitat for wildlife. Hedgerow timber is seen as important in localities deprived of woods. Aesthetic properties—least studied—have emerged in a search in the Netherlands where correlations have been shown between positive public attitudes toward the landscape and the presence and density of hedgerows."[24]

In the United States, the research done by Richard T. Forman and Jacques Baudry on hedgerows has shown their main ecological role to be the deflection of wind caused by the hedgerow, with resulting greater heat and diminished wind speed in the field. By acting as conduits, hedgerows foster wildlife, permitting a variety of insects and small mammals to subsist in acres stripped of all other cover; the hedgerow functions as a lifeline for these species. The animals, in turn, enrich the plant variety of the hedgerow itself, which becomes the depository of a very diverse plant life that is protected from wind, machinery, and desiccation. Hedgerows also serve as

Fig. 42. Newport Garden, Newport, Rhode Island, 2006. Axonometric.

Fig. 43. Newport Garden.

Fig. 44. Newport Garden. Detail of espalier.

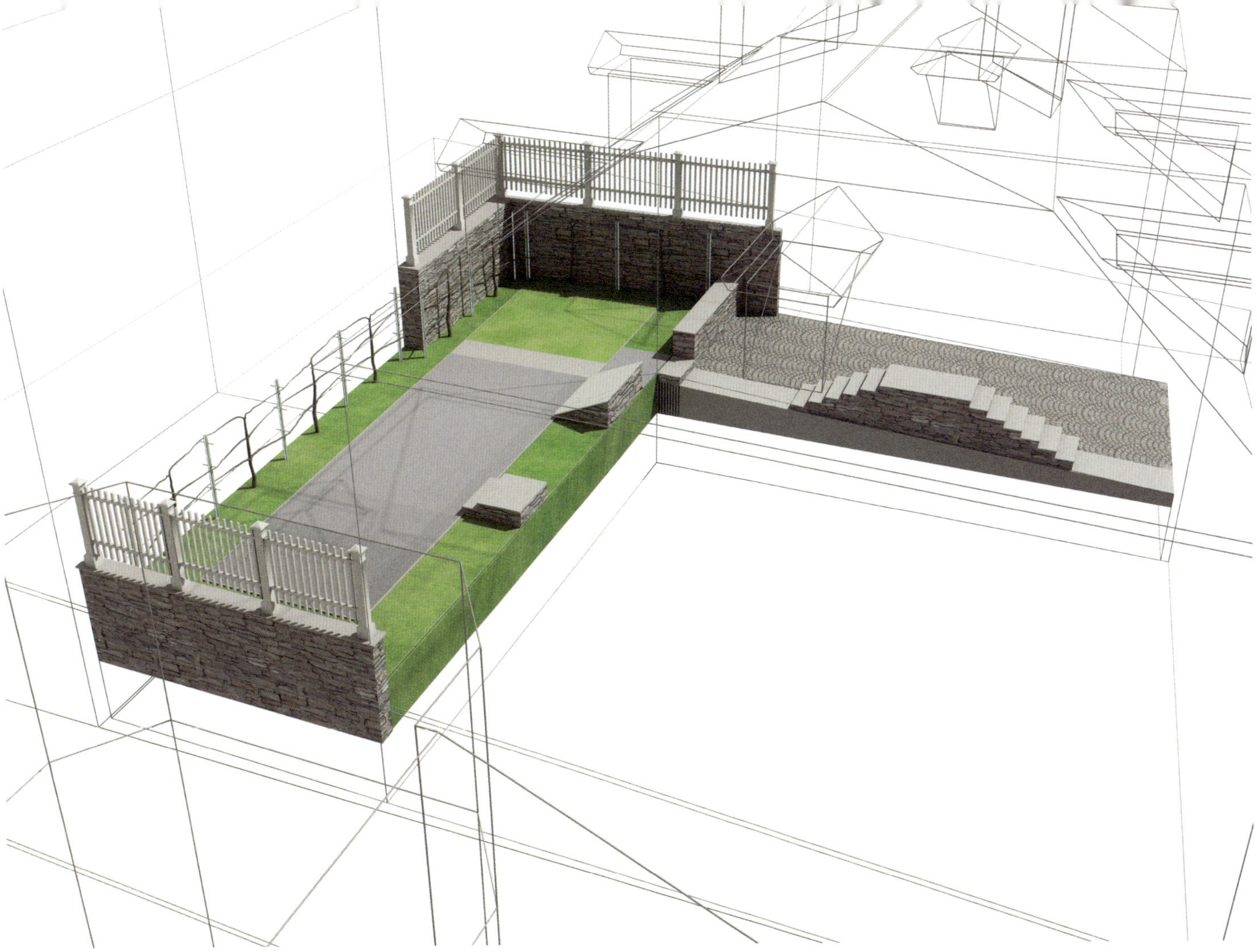

42

43

44

connectors across the landscape, permitting species to escape enemies (though, at the same time, they also serve as conduits for predators), reach another habitat, or escape from a declining one. Particularly in treeless environments, the removal of hedges brings about a decline in landscape diversity, fauna habitat, and shelter, and has a negative impact on crop yield, plant growth, and wind erosion. So, just as the hedgerow seemed to have reached its end in the agricultural world, its aesthetic and environmental qualities have brought it back to life.

The creation of a new kind of park in America—the linear park—presents an opportunity to reinstate the hedgerow, with its new, overt ecological role.

Espaliers

Espaliers, which we associate with the walled gardens of medieval French castles, are a form of miniaturized trees, particularly fruit trees. They are pruned flat against a southern stone wall where they are protected against the wind, and they are kept low, occupying very little space. The warmth accumulated in the stone wall helps ripen the fruit. The space saving as well as the use of passive heat in a masonry wall are both features available for reuse in any modern urban garden, as such gardens are usually walled. We put them to use for espaliered pear trees for a small eighteenth-century urban house in Newport, Rhode Island. The original owner had in fact developed a special pear at this house in the eighteenth century, and the smallness of the garden and its walled character made the use of espaliered trees there an appropriate urban planting (figs. 42–44).

Sunken Gardens

Sunken gardens have a similar function in protecting against wind. In addition, they can serve to drain an area, gathering water from all around and keeping garden plants or a lawn moist and green.

The sunken courtyard at Vassar College—the Frances Daly Fergusson Courtyard, named after the college's former president—gathers the water from a small rise to the south and the two surrounding buildings east and north. Its stone edge serves as a continuous bench, which is heavily used, on its south side, on sunny winter days. Snow gets pushed into it in winter, water runs into it in the spring. But in summer and fall, its green lawn serves as a place for people to gather to watch a movie shown outside the Art Center. It is the aesthetic anchor of a no-man's-land in front of the dormitory to the north and the Art Center to the east, an outdoor place for both of them. This sunken courtyard is backed on the north side by a cedar hedgerow windscreen, adding to the comfort of that southern exposure. Both historical pieces are used in their transformed modern role (figs. 45, 46).

In sum, what we are seeing in these cases is the transformation of some landscapes owing to the change in our understanding of nature and the emergence of a different philosophy for our time, which we have called ecology. This paradigmatic change in our understanding and our new outlook have transformed what we once considered an ideal landscape—our American Lawn—into an example of a destructive relationship with the rest of nature. Given our new understanding, it is imperative for us to make over completely the form, composition, and management of the American Lawn.

In contrast, other historical landscapes, as a result of this same transformation in our philosophy, acquire virtues that turn them into examples of the beneficial coexistence with nature that we now seek. **5**

5. Historical precedents do not support the common prejudice that human intervention is always harmful to the rest of nature.

Fig. 45. Frances Daly Fergusson Courtyard, Vassar College, Poughkeepsie, New York, 2003.

Fig. 46. Frances Daly Fergusson Courtyard.

Transformations: Overcoming the Past 2

The Ecological Transformation of Human-Made Forms

In this section, I will highlight and make visible the break with the past resulting from the cultural shift discussed in Part 1. The creation of a new vocabulary, now emerging, will help in this effort. We do not have a new vocabulary of forms yet—ecological aims and aesthetic ones are still not on speaking terms with each other—but the discussion of form is a separate matter, and will be dealt with in Part 3. When three steps—registering the transformation, creating a vocabulary, and finally creating new forms for it—are achieved, we may be able to make peace with landscape's history and reinsert ourselves in its traditions without being artistically devoured by them.

If we connect the dots between emerging landscapes, we see that we are developing systems that are increasingly in tune with living things. The new outline of landscape, architecture, and city is still blurry, but a general framework can be discerned. It would be easy to label what is emerging as a movement from the artificial to the natural, from heavy, nineteenth-century industrial systems to green, ecological ones. But that would be an oversimplification. We are inventing new structures that are closer to living ones. They are constructed systems which, while they take their cues from natural processes, do not emulate preexisting forms of nature.

While the natural materials and management of the Industrial Lawn have been transformed, the resulting Freedom Lawns still attempt to fulfill functions similar to those of their predecessor. What I describe next shows much more radical transformations, which begin to make landscapes on the scale of cities and put old human artifacts to new uses.

Examples of such redesign and transformation are presented in the following sections: old canals and railroads into linear parks, underground drainage infrastructure into stormwater parks, asphalt rooftops into green roofs, parking lots into rain gardens, floating heavy docks in rivers into lightweight public structures.

Landscape first registered the start of this metamorphosis in the early 1970s, in Seattle, with Richard Haag's Gas Works Park, in which the rusted pieces of an old gas plant were kept as an integral part of the new public park into which it was transformed. Later came Peter Latz's Landscape Park Duisburg Nord, near Essen, Germany (1995). More recent still is the Water Purification Park in Seoul (2002), which retains the old water plant's industrial ruins as a register of the past. These new developments still echo the Picturesque period, which made much of ruins, with their timeworn aesthetic, as an element of the landscape. But the intention in these new works is different. This decaying industrial framework and the new types of spaces generated by it result in places that are unlike those derived from a typical public park design.

First, the *general* characteristics of each of these emerging landscapes will be discussed. Then a project in my office is described as a specific example. These two aspects are presented separately in order to keep the individual interpretations of a project from interfering with the landscapes' description, since they are new members of the landscape family, many of them too new to be fully recognizable or describable.

Many contemporary landscape issues have been addressed in recent writings. However, these issues have mostly been treated on the general, grand scale, only occasionally accompanied by examples of what has actually been done in practice. This text breaks down the scale to look at very specific emerging landscapes and then gives a close-up of a specific project. This has the virtue of moving the text and the work away from the general and making everything concrete. This is not an accidental choice, nor merely an organizational strategy; it is an attempt to move landscape work away from large-scale diagrams and bring it down to a middle scale, where specific design is necessary and becomes visible. It is there that it achieves concreteness and can be examined and evaluated. The changing scale of landscape design today is little noticed. Though both large and small scales will always play a role in design, it is the middle scale that achieves the balance of concreteness and contextuality. The approach to this subject therefore comes out of the intellectual structure of this book. Scale is the very essence of work in landscape. The specificity of the examples given in this book redirect attention to the middle scale and to concreteness, both of which are absent from most exegeses. **6**

6. Shifts are taking place before our eyes. Landscape artists and architects need to give them a name and make them visible. Aesthetic expertise is needed to enable the transforming relations between humans and the rest of nature to break through into public spaces.

From Green Corridor to Thick Edge: The Linear Park

Converting a railroad corridor to a linear park results in an essential transformation of a past artifact. Though linear parks and other new landscape forms take their structure from the past, they have risen to the level of new typologies. They mark the beginning of a new landscape agenda. The example of an abandoned railway line made into a linear park or greenway will serve—as did the American Lawn, in Part 1—as the poster child of such ecological transformations.

This kind of transformation is not what it may first appear. Some members of the public consider the linear park a "greening" and the return to nature of an industrial mechanized corridor, where coal- or oil-driven engines polluted a strip of land for hundreds of miles. But the reality is more complicated. It is true that the making of the rail line into a greenway often involves planting trees along its edges and removing railroad ballast. But in most cases, the removed ballast is unfortunately replaced by asphalt, making the corridor surface impermeable and thus ecologically a loss. Whatever vegetation is in place or is added to this trail generally has little in common with the original vegetation; it is not a return to the plant life that was there before the railway. What will grow on this line now will be vegetation that flourishes along edges. There will be many invasive plants that prosper in these situations, and the animal life will also be edge species. The greenway will contain plants changed by having survived decades of application of herbicides (to keep railroad lines clear of vegetation) and by having endured diesel oil and coal emissions. As a corridor for mass transit, it could also be considered to have been a greener artifact than the resulting pedestrian and bike greenway, though its function as a space which permits people to walk and bike does enhance the quality of human life.

Metamorphosis is taking place before our eyes, and we are essaying a new vocabulary for what is emerging. We are taking an old cultural artifact, the product of a heavy steel and iron industry, and reverting to a hybrid system; we are taking rigid industrial systems that overpowered and separated themselves from the living systems surrounding them and allowing life to infiltrate them and transform them.

Linear parks are dynamic rather than static; they are not peaceful retreats but ways. A huge network of outworn and defunct transportation systems and public-utility corridors—canal lines, railroad lines, waterfronts, abandoned ports, utility rights-of-way—is being converted into open public space. That they have become recognized shows their success; they have exceeded and moved on from the artifact that generated them—the railroad corridor—and have spread to anything that can take a linear format.

The large-scale abandonment of railway lines across the United States gave rise to the creation of these linear parks, or greenways. The possibilities of this new form have not yet been fully explored. More appropriate to our times and culture than the traditional central urban parks of the Olmsted era, the linear park differs from them in many ways. Nonetheless, this new park, like those of the nineteenth century, continues to embody our civic ideals; today's greenway has sparked the first truly widespread citizens' movement concerning public space since the great park era of the 1830s to 1860s, eliciting the same broad-based grass-roots idealism and support as the nineteenth-century urban parks did. This movement has spawned citizens' organizations that support various individual conversions of old infrastructures to new parks, as well as national nongovernmental organizations (NGOs) such as Rails-to-Trails; it has also become a strong base for another NGO, the Trust for Public Land, which has been brought in to negotiate land acquisitions from the most challenging of clients, the railroad companies.

The main characteristic of this new public space, the linear park, is above all the creation of a dynamic set of connections rather than a destination. It responds to a new stage in our thinking about transportation and to the peripatetic spirit that has long characterized American life. The linear park opens pathways to diverse neighborhoods and new recreational spaces and experiences of nature; it invites exploration of alternate modes of transport and of cultural resources. It weaves connections between city and suburb, suburb and country, and nature and culture, and among people of different origins, ages, or sexes. It is an answer to the increasing cultural isolation and physical separation in which we find ourselves.

Linear parks are the twenty-first-century parks par excellence. Their implications are dramatic: for a relatively small amount of money, these narrow green corridors can reconnect parts of a city, weaving themselves through it, spreading themselves democratically to reach all areas. They can be attached to streams, rivers, or shores to provide soft edges and restore floodplains. And they function as pathways for people to travel on foot or bicycle, not as ancillaries to an avenue of cars. Though the idea of the linear park is less than twenty-five years old, it has the potential to remobilize our life in cities, encouraging pedestrian movement.

There are many other positive effects of greenways. They can foster a community of businesses along their edges, so that neighbors can once again walk, bike, or skate to the store for a loaf of bread or a bottle of aspirin. They can also provide critical migration corridors for animals through urban areas. They are active landscapes, which can introduce open, green space to various parts of the city; intensify topographic features, rivers, ridges; offer a soft surface capable of absorbing rainwater; and let people escape the car-dominated hardscape.

The transformative power of linear parks comes from the connections they are capable of producing. Up to now, linear parks have developed without arms, as straight ten-to-fifteen-foot-wide strips along the path of an abandoned railway, canal, or utility corridor. But linear parks can also become links (either as permanent paths or as one-day street closures) to museums, to bakeries, to marathons, to concerts, to state parks, to political rallies. This modest caterpillar with the capability of becoming a centipede is a landscape that can actively change a community: greening, invigorating, and connecting.

One of the chief values of the linear park is that it addresses the problem of socioeconomic separation to which the suburb contributes. Greenways, which accommodate movement on foot or bike, might be possible restitchers of the urban fabric, joining urban centers and suburbs to one another recreationally and culturally, providing the continuity of a common space. The linear park enhances the character of all the neighborhoods it connects. It might provide an outdoor activity for people in a medical or child-care facility, or offer space for educational and aesthetic activities for children, teenagers, or the elderly. In other words, an interplay can be achieved between continuity and locality, in response to the specific needs and characteristics of each neighborhood it transverses. In this way, the linear park can offer many different experiences.

In a time when open land is being voraciously consumed by suburbs and unending construction, the linear park extends a continuous living and healing linear public tissue. It is a habitat corridor that fosters life rather than expanding and isolating suburbanization, a continuous path through city, suburb, and farmland. Along greenways, the direct human experience of the landscape, which had often been lost in the industrial age, is recaptured. It is not simply a modest tweaking of our concept of the park but a major reconstitution of the way we use space and time and of how we view transportation. We cannot yet imagine the consequences of this transformation. By converting these corridors into havens for pedestrians and cyclists, we are no longer relegated to the sidewalks along highways but become the shaping force of the corridor, free from all machines other than those powered by our own energy.

This new park system, with human motion at its heart, promises to be economically productive. The linear park energizes areas around it, just as the railroad and highway before it did. Though it invites dense development along its edges, we have the opportunity to think about how we wish to implement and direct that growth. The linear park can increase land values and attract premium residential areas around its perimeters, just as nineteenth-century parks did. At the same time, however, the continuity and length of these corridors also lend themselves to a variety of commercial and institutional uses. Moreover, there is a political potential in these parks, as new avenues to community empowerment.

The originality of the linear park is to be expressed, not buried in ideals and agendas of the past. I think that it is not too idealistic to propose that clean energy sources be used to build greenways; that linear parks should be drained, planted, built, and maintained to restore a healthy environment; that they thus become reliable refuges in which plants, animals, and people can thrive. We can, in these modest strips of land, create a blueprint for the life we wish for ourselves.[1]

One valuable aspect of linear parks is that they stem from local initiatives. It requires a group of motivated citizens to band together, pay for a regular newsletter, and pressure local government to acquire abandoned corridors of railroads and canals. This is often a slow process. In the case of the Farmington Canal in New Haven, Connecticut, it took more than fifteen years, and progressed bit by bit. In the case of New York City's High Line, ten. These projects shepherded by citizens' groups, moving gradually but persistently, are a lesson about American society's potential for action.

This new landscape at city scale has already entered the urban fray, putting citizens' associations, politicians, railroad companies, NGOs, and state DOTs in one jousting arena. The conflicts and their resolution are not to be taken for granted. Though the citizens' movement has been successful in many instances in obtaining the land from the railroads, there have been many compromises: the land in most cases is simply being banked for new public transportation systems. Also, the majority of these projects receive external funding ($1 million a mile), which has meant that only their use has been transformed; no aesthetic language has been developed for them as a new modern typology. The work of transformation usually consists in making a narrow band—typically fifteen to twenty feet—of asphalt pavement with some markings or signs at road crossings, thus creating paths for bikes and pedestrians. For a landscape's new typology to succeed, landscape artists need to enter a battlefield of competing interests and experiment with alliances to shift economic interests toward it.[2] These struggles and partnerships are not only with client groups but also with others who have the various types of professional expertise needed to create a new typology. The economics for linear parks have kept them from developing a landscape aesthetic that reveals the new sustainable relations between humans and nature. They still speak the old language of suburban "nature" trails, echoing an old relationship with nature.**7**

7. High visibility, multiple alliances, and public support are critical to new landscape genres that portray our present.

Farmington Canal, New Haven: The Master Plan

The main idea behind the master plan of this linear park was to make it a series of distinct sections responding to the conditions of the parts of the city surrounding it, not just a homogenous ribbon applied generically. By modest moves, it could modify projects in progress along its length, becoming a spine on which to hang them. The linear park could also reconnect parts of the city, thereby making it work better—all by means of this narrow strip of land moving through it.

We authored the master plan for the nine-mile section through New Haven and Hamden of the now-abandoned railroad and former canal, which preceded the railroad. The canal was started in 1825, abandoned in 1839, and then bought up by the railroad. The New Haven/Hamden section of the railroad was abandoned by 1982. We worked for a citizens' group, the Farmington Canal Rail-to-Trail Association, founded by New Haven and Hamden residents and chaired and led by the New Haven activist and ecologist Nancy Alderman.

The Farmington Canal is not a return to nature, yet it is nonetheless a return to a more biologically diverse corridor. A new entity will thrive here, a somewhat hedgerowed tree corridor with diverse weeds and urban trees, both usually invasive, creating a landscape that is neither industrial nor independent of human intervention: a hybrid that results both from the conditions of the site and from our interventions to make it a sustainable and beautiful public space.

The conversion of the Farmington Canal, first from a canal to a railroad and, more recently, from a railroad to a linear park, shows quite clearly the new hybrid entity which has emerged. A forest has sprung up since the railroad abandoned the line, making the below-grade section quite beautiful. That forest is not the maple-oak-beech mix typical of this area and that still surrounds some parts of it. Nor does it contain any chestnut trees, which were very common when the canal and railroad were built (in the 1820s and 1850s) but which by the 1890s were decimated by a blight. Rather, it is predominantly a forest of Norway maples. These are invasive trees which take over and stamp out native maples, but which can take much more abuse and resist edge conditions better. The Norway maples, the last trees to lose their leaves, light up the greenway with their very late fall yellow color, making an unusually beautiful space at that time of the year.

As previously noted, the linear park is a new prototype of open public space. In this particular project a great amount of research was devoted to understanding the possibilities of a twenty-five-foot-wide corridor, which might eventually extend to as much as eighty-four miles, since the railroad line runs north to Northampton, Massachusetts.

Our commission from the Farmington Canal Citizen Association, for a first conceptual presentation of the New Haven section, was followed by two grants, one from the NEA for work on the second section of the Farmington Canal, in Hamden, and another from the Carolyn Foundation for further work on the New Haven section.

The result of all these ideas became an exhibition at the Museum of Contemporary Art (MOCA) in Los Angeles, curated by Elizabeth Smith as part of a show of fifteen new U.S. urban projects, called *Urban Revisions: Current Projects for the Urban Realm* (1994). In 1995, the exhibition traveled to the Canadian Center for Architecture, in Montreal (figs. 47–51).

Farmington Canal, Yale University: The Malone Engineering Center

In the master plan, we saw this section of the abandoned railway, in New Haven, not simply as a trail, but rather as a new prototype for public open space, since it starts in downtown New Haven. The master plan created a linear park made up of discrete segments. In the Yale section we were able to design and build one of those segments.

Our master plan included a proposal for a light-rail connection from the Yale section of the line to the New Haven railroad station. It would have served Yale well, since the midpoint between the Humanities Campus and the Science Campus occurs at the

Fig. 47. Farmington Canal Greenway Master Plan, New Haven, Connecticut, 1995. Existing site, summer.

Fig. 48. Farmington Canal Greenway Master Plan. Existing site, fall.

49

end of this below-grade section of the corridor. Very much like the Dinky, at Princeton, it could have met the New York and Boston trains and delivered people to the heart of Yale in a painless manner. However, in the years between the presentation of our master plan and the design of this section of the line, the possibility for a light-rail connection was lost when an FBI building was constructed right where the railroad track (which had been placed along the canal) separated from the other railroad lines. That made it impossible to have a public transportation system going through the building's lower basement level, as we had proposed. There are rumors that the FBI may move out, which would free the site from security considerations; such an idea would then be worth reviving.

We also sought to develop a complex planting strategy to manage the stormwater and make this section a display of northeastern forest. We wanted to recognize the Farmington Canal as a pathway that influences the evolution of plant communities around it and promotes biodiversity. The plan ensured that breaks, or short discontinuities, did not occur within the habitat of the site, thus preventing the isolation of plant and wildlife species. Through selective plantings, a continuous wildlife corridor was created, providing native wildlife with the food and shelter necessary for their healthy survival. Scientists have found that the creation of wildlife corridors can even help prevent the extinction of species.

We improved the site's ability to manage stormwater. Alongside the Engineering Center we designed a combination of planted terraces and energy dissipators. Near the inlet pipes, these specially designed plantings help to channel and delay surface runoff and direct it toward a vegetated swale along the canal where the water is filtered and absorbed. This swale, a rain garden, has become a mix of planted grasses and wildflower volunteers that were brought as seeds by birds or the running water itself. These plants also act to control erosion. Porous paving was used for the hardscape on the site, reducing both runoff volume and velocity.

We focused on using concentrated nodes of limited planting. More than 50 percent of the open area of the site has been planted with native or naturalized vegetation. The planting strategy mimics the natural distribution of the canopy, based on its sunlight/shade tolerance, thereby strengthening the existing natural patterns and making connections to the surrounding area.

This first piece of the Farmington Canal, on Yale-owned land in downtown New Haven, currently serves as a trail head and is already heavily used by students, professors, and staff of the university as the departure point for the rest of the nine-mile section to the north. Another Yale-owned section, to be added to the Farmington Canal as of 2009, is under design in our office. With this new section, the Farmington Canal Greenway will become one of the first of these twenty-first-century parks to reach a downtown area and fulfill an urban role (figs. 52–55).

Fig. 49. Farmington Canal Greenway Master Plan. Light rail proposal.

Fig. 50. Farmington Canal Greenway Master Plan. Proposed constellation-viewing device.

50

Fig. 51. Farmington Canal Greenway Master Plan. Model of New Haven showing Farmington Canal.

Fig. 52. Farmington Canal, Yale University, Malone Engineering Center, New Haven, Connecticut, 2006.

Part 2   40

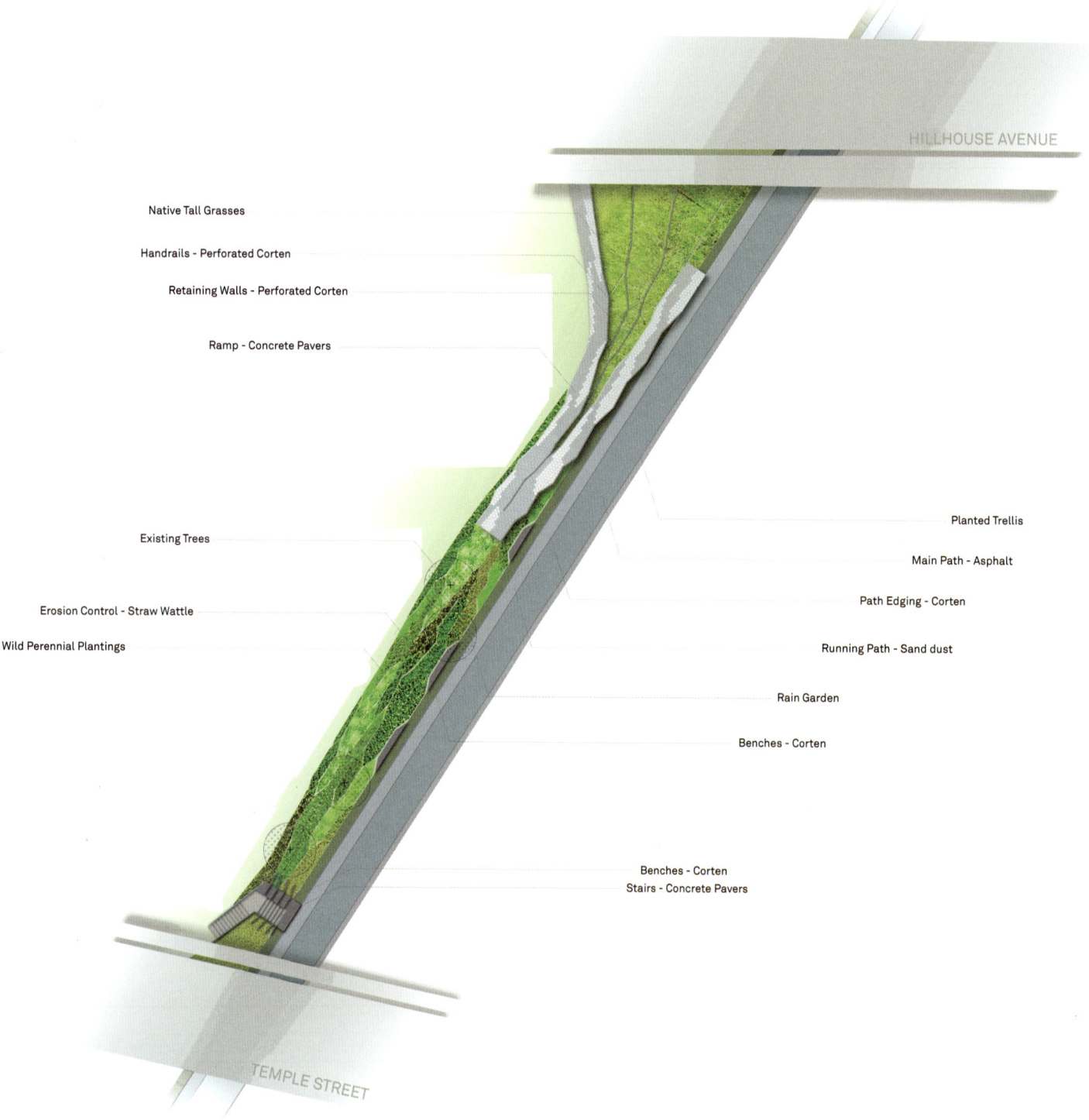

Native Tall Grasses
Handrails - Perforated Corten
Retaining Walls - Perforated Corten
Ramp - Concrete Pavers

Existing Trees

Erosion Control - Straw Wattle
Wild Perennial Plantings

Planted Trellis
Main Path - Asphalt
Path Edging - Corten
Running Path - Sand dust
Rain Garden
Benches - Corten

Benches - Corten
Stairs - Concrete Pavers

HILLHOUSE AVENUE

TEMPLE STREET

53

Part 2   41

Fig. 53. Farmington Canal, Yale University, Malone Engineering Center. Plan.

Figs. 54, 55. Farmington Canal, Yale University, Malone Engineering Center.

The Gwynns Falls Trail Master Plan, Baltimore

In this project, a valley with a polluted stream and a railroad was designed as a trail along the stream, establishing connections among the diverse neighborhoods along its path.

The Gywnns Falls Trail master-plan project was a response to community interest in restoring the Gywnns Falls stream ecosystem, which had been damaged by industrial pollution, illegal dumping, and neglect. The master plan drew public attention to the stream and its watershed by outlining revitalization strategies, which included educational activities for area public schools and annual public celebrations. The design team consulted with citizens from sixteen neighborhoods, seven Baltimore city agencies and departments, and forty-seven public and private organizations and institutions.

The trail has seven separate segments running through various geographic and cultural areas of Baltimore. The proposals were developed to respect the particular terrain, vegetation, and cultural context of each trail segment. The master plan was a comprehensive study, outlining recommended designs for trail routes, safety features, signage, planting schemes, ecological restoration, and management of historical features. In addition, the master plan explored ethical and environmental procedures for its design and construction, eliminating the use of pollutants. This practice could help generate jobs for the surrounding communities and could be integrated into their educational activities.

The Gwynns Falls Trail plan was built upon an earlier vision created for open public space in Baltimore. In 1902, the Baltimore Municipal Art Society commissioned the Olmsted brothers to design a master plan for Baltimore parks. Completed in 1904, the Olmsted Report recommended that the city acquire three principal stream valleys to protect the watershed from future development; it also envisioned a network of stream valley parks. Though only partially implemented, the Olmsted Report was a starting place for our evaluation process for urban open space because of its understanding of parks as an integral part of cities.

The master plan, finished in 1995, was followed by a complete restructuring of the Department of Parks and Recreation and the Department of City Planning, as well as the election of a new administration. Years later the trail was built, ignoring the master plan. However, the plan in itself has survived as a source of ideas, and it was placed in the archives of the University of California, Berkeley, at the university's request. We have received several calls from different Baltimore agencies that would like to implement the master plan provisions.

The Baltimore master plan illustrates some of the issues involved in working with public agencies. At one level, it was our first experience in crowdsourcing—working with a multiplicity of neighborhoods and agencies (parks, water, art). Ultimately, the Parks Department and the Baltimore Percent-for-Art Program, as well as the Trust for Public Land (TPL), an NGO, ended up being our clients.

The main interest of the Parks Department's director was obtaining funding to upgrade the trail, which overlapped one of his parks. Since parks receive very little money in American cities today, and since the park was a part of the trail, his position was understandable. The Percent-for-Art money allowed the selection of a designer whose fees would come out of 2 percent of the total budget. We put together a group which included an artist, an architect, a civil engineer, and a local historian. In this crowdsourcing experience with the professional team, we learned useful lessons for later work. It was a relatively successful collaboration.

The TPL was interested in having the entire trail built with the money allotted (about $15 million, or $1 million a mile), which was inadequate for creating a master plan for a linear park that was establishing new parameters and intended to restore a polluted stream. The design did succeed in establishing an ambitious set of parameters. But the reorganization of the Department of City Planning and the transfer of the director of the Parks Department orphaned the project. A minimal asphalt-paved trail was built later.

Crowdsourcing, both professionally and with public neighborhoods and agencies, is valuable to landscape projects. But the real aims of the agencies, politicians, and/or funders involved need to be clearly understood (figs. 56–63).

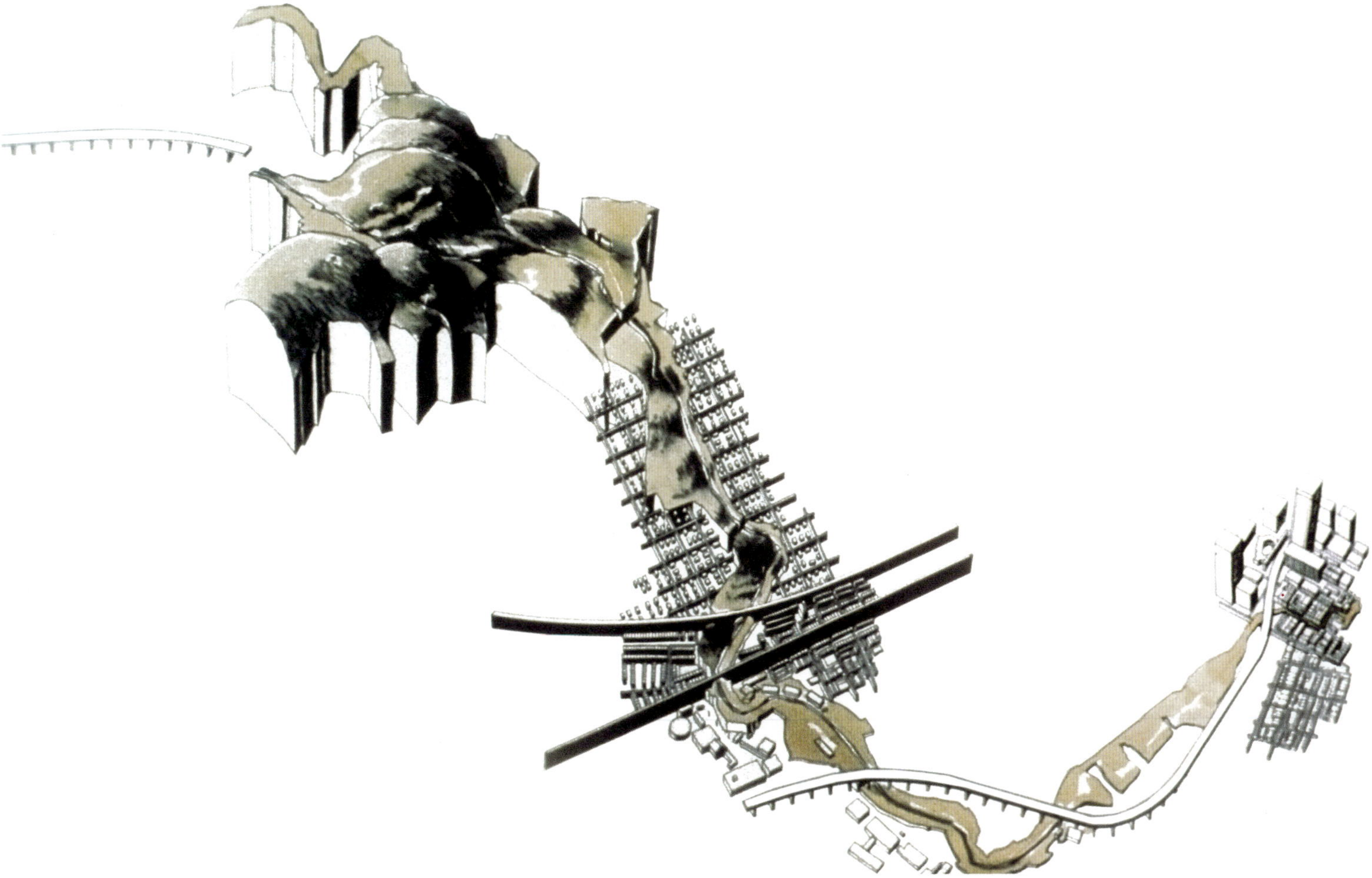

56

57

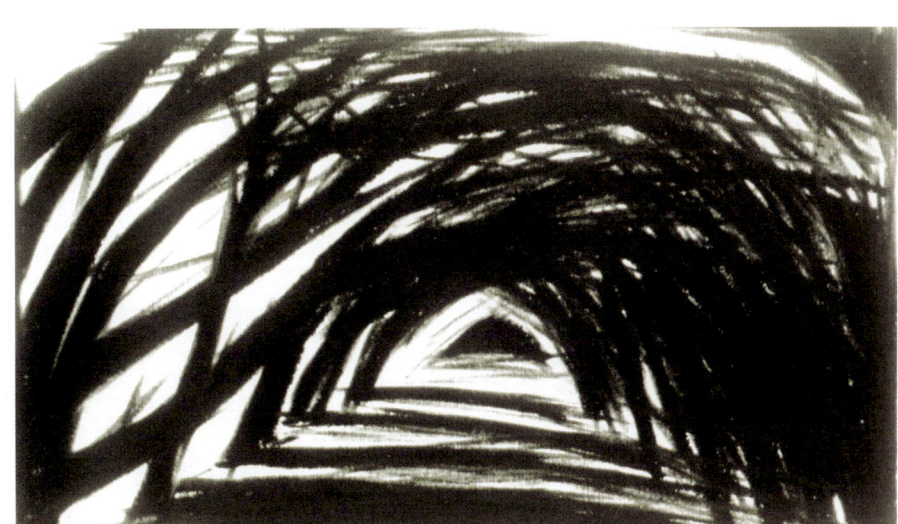

Fig. 56. Gwynns Falls Trail Master Plan, Baltimore, 1995. Axonometric.

Fig. 57. Gwynns Falls Trail Master Plan. Charcoal rendering of Osage-orange trees.

58

59

Fig. 58. Gwynns Falls Trail Master Plan. Photocollage showing reuse of abandoned objects.

Fig. 59. Gwynns Falls Trail Master Plan. Charcoal rendering of entrance.

Fig. 60. Gwynns Falls Trail Master Plan. Ink drawing showing reuse of abandoned stoops.

Part 2   46

61

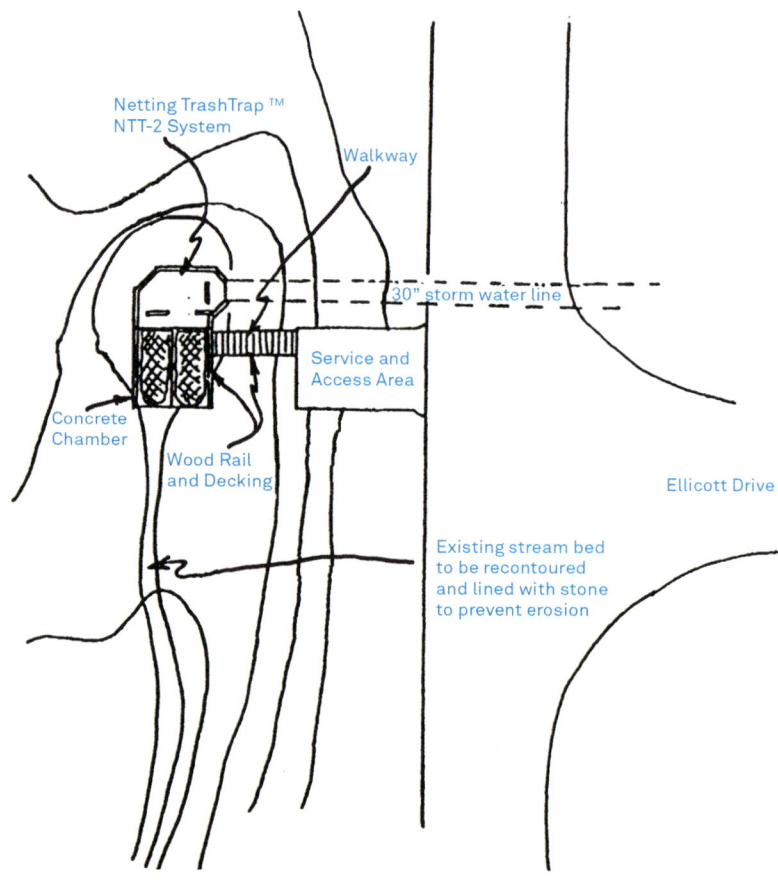

62

Fig. 61. Gwynns Falls Trail Master Plan. Model.

Fig. 62. Gwynns Falls Trail Master Plan. Diagram showing cleaning device for river.

Fig. 63. Gwynns Falls Trail Master Plan. Drawing showing reuse of abandoned objects.

The High Line, New York

The High Line is a good example of the public interest in linear parks. We were one of five teams selected to compete for the design of the High Line, a 1.5-mile abandoned elevated railroad in Manhattan. We formed a team with Zaha Hadid's office, Skidmore Owings & Merrill (represented by Marilyn Taylor, then a partner), MDA Architects (an architect out of Hadid's office with a New York office), Arup, and several arts organizations (Creative Time, Public Art Fund, The Kitchen). We did not win the competition, but we were able to integrate a complex and disparate team incredibly well. Had we won, we would have been able to carry out an unusual integration of engineering, architecture, energy sustainability, urban design, and landscape. It was a good example of the use of crowdsourcing.

The attention devoted to this 1.5-mile elevated railroad track is a perfect illustration of the current interest in these corridors; twenty years earlier, it would have been torn down. As is the case with most linear parks, it was the result of the efforts of a citizens' group. Two enterprising men, Robert Hammond and Josh David, and the group they formed, Friends of the High Line, worked with New York politicians and found donors to support the project. In just five to seven years the group was able not only to save the High Line, but also to bring about the beginning of the work on its renewal as a public corridor and public space. Its success in the face of complicated New York City politics and commercial interests, which overwhelmingly favor money-making enterprises, says something about the intense interest in this landscape genre, the linear park. In this case, it is a space that is even more elaborately constructed than that of a typical railroad line, since it is a steel structure rising high above the ground. The fervor about the possibilities as public space that even this short 1.5-mile el has produced can be explained only by the public's sophisticated understanding of it as a new twenty-first-century space, the linear park.

Our own idea for its use was a double-sided corridor with arms extending outward on weekends and evenings. It was to be made into a micro-grid for the West Side (employing hydrogen energy technologies), not only supplying the power for its own needs, but also serving as an emergency power source for surrounding buildings. It would have had a gradient of planting: greenest at the north, less green at the hub, most active at the south. With the help of Arup, a gradient of noise and quiet was measured along the line to determine where tranquil pools of space should be placed. A study of sun and shadow did the same, to indicate where sunny spots in winter and cool spots in summer could be created. The line was conceived as a place to set people in motion, vertically and horizontally.

This competition was won and is being built by Diller Scofidio & Renfro Architects with Field Operations Landscape Architects. It is a good example of the work of other firms on these new types (figs. 64–71). **8**

Fig. 64. The High Line, New York, 2004.

8. Landscape—through new landscape elements—enters the city and modifies our way of being in it.

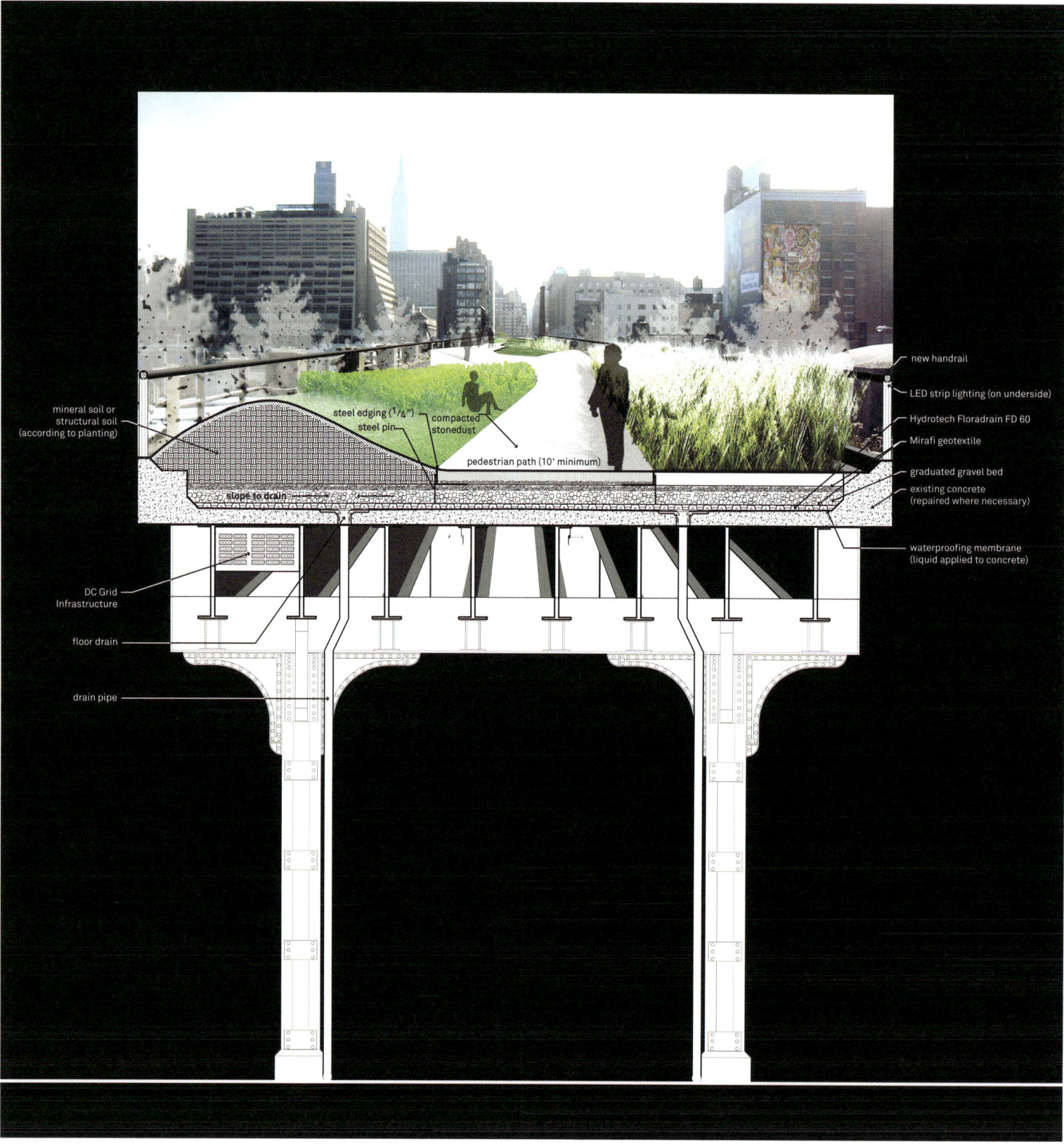

Fig. 65. The High Line. Section.

Fig. 66. The High Line.

Fig. 67. The High Line. Conversion of existing gas station to hydrogen station.

Figs. 68–71. The High Line.

69

70

71

From Roof to Fifth Façade

Green roofs are landscapes that can change a city. Although they are created individually and independently, the sum effect of hundreds or thousands of modest roof gardens atop many buildings could reduce a city's "heat island" effect (the accumulated heat from paved and roofed surfaces), help dispose of urban runoff from storms, and establish many small, pleasurable oases in a landscape usually dominated by hot, tarred surfaces.

With their black tar roofs constantly exposed to the sun, cities soak up great amounts of heat, increasing temperatures both day and night, as stored heat is slowly released after sunset. High urban temperatures also make smog conditions worse. Roof gardens can give shade while their plants absorb carbon dioxide, release oxygen into the air, and cool a city down. The shade of a single tree with a fifteen-foot canopy can lower the temperature under it by three to four degrees Fahrenheit. This cooling can become even greater as moisture evaporates into the surrounding atmosphere. And the cooling effect is further enhanced when the leaves cool down at night, allowing them to absorb more heat the next day. Computer models created by the Lawrence Berkeley National Laboratory, in California, show that a city with hundreds of roof gardens could reduce the urban temperature by as much as five degrees Fahrenheit. Germany and France already provide incentives for creating roof gardens; closer to home, Seattle is considering such a move as a simpler and cheaper solution for disposing of urban runoff. In Chicago, Mayor Daley has a $1 million experimental rooftop garden atop City Hall.

The large acreage of a city makes the disposal of rainwater a problem during heavy storms. The sudden rush of enormous volumes of water pulls pollution off paved surfaces, through drainage pipes, and into rivers. As a river's volume increases, so does the speed of its currents, eroding and flooding the riverbanks and tearing vegetation from its sides. As a city grows, so does the volume of water it must dispose of, along with the size and cost of the drainage system and the devastating effects on the rivers and streams that receive all the water.

By contrast, when rainwater falls on an unpaved, nonurban site, it is absorbed. A planted surface stabilized by roots, stalks, trees, and composed material breaks the impact of the falling water, slows it, and gives it someplace to go. Though some water will run off, it will move slowly. Some of this water returns to the atmosphere through evapotranspiration, some trickles through the earth into the water table (being filtered as it moves), and some runs off into rivers and streams.

Roof gardens can have a very similar effect (though there is no route from a roof to the water table). The more rooftop plantings there are, the less water reaches the paved ground, storm drains, and beleaguered urban rivers. The greener rooftops are, the less heat is absorbed (and released) by a city. And roof gardens also create attractive, healthy environments where once there were only hot, black tar roofs.

Greenways and green roofs are very different landscapes. One is a large-scale urban intervention, existing on the ground for everyone to use. The other is an individual act, the transformation of one piece of private property into green space. Yet both are active landscapes, with the potential to transform our cities by regenerating natural cycles within an urban fabric that has lost them. Ultimately, this makes for healthier cities and healthier people.

Green roofs, like Freedom Lawns, allow individuals to take action. The fact that Stuart and Alan Suna, of Silvercup Studios, and Donald Gratz and Roberta Brandeis Gratz, of the Gratz Company, wanted to install a green roof and make it visible to the thousands of motorists crossing the Queensboro Bridge daily was the driving force for this change. They believed in its benefits, and they wanted to make that change visible to others. It is this high visibility in a city, not only from a bridge but also from any tall building, which makes the green roof into a *fifth façade* and a candidate for good design. The green roof and the Freedom Lawn declare that you as an individual can bring about change. They embody the ecologists' credo: "Think globally, act locally."

Although individuals may create green roofs on their own, there is also the issue of the aggregate. A city with many green roofs has a landscape for dealing effectively with the urban heat island. Encouraging a massive adoption of this landscape requires setting a variety of economic forces in motion: tax abatements for creating green roofs, tax assessments for excessive water sent to the public drainage system (a practice in Germany), new ways of accounting the costs to the city of constructing new drainage structures in comparison with those for a passive system that additionally reduces the heat island effect. (One challenge to implementing such changes is that the accounting for infrastructure occurs in a longer timeframe than politicians' short terms in office.) An added incentive for a citywide implementation of this landscape is the opportunity it provides to develop a local industry for green roofs. This is an arena that landscape is now entering, but as in the case of linear parks, it has yet to develop the economic muscle to produce convincing results. Our green roof projects give an indication of the enormous efforts we made, with the help of granting organizations, to create two such landscapes. Although the efforts were not commensurate with the results (the costs were too high per square foot because green roof contracting and technology in the United States were new at the time), they were justifiable as pioneering projects with high visibility.

Four green roof projects are described below, starting with a theoretical one, which led to the realization of two of the others. The study for Long Island City takes the small-scale green roof and its achievements to the large scale of an entire city area, demonstrating its additive possibilities. These scale shifts are the spinal cord of our work in landscape and the most creative area of the discipline. The other three projects are Silvercup Studios, Gratz Industries, and The Solaire.

Long Island City, New York

The development of ideas about green roofs emerged from a theoretical proposal for Long Island City, Queens, New York, to examine what could result if the idea of individual, privately owned green roofs were applied to an entire city area.

Such a study is not just a matter of examining things at a larger scale; rather, it requires looking at the small and the large at the same time. The examination of the large scale is then coupled to a very detailed design at the small scale. In the 1960s and 1970s, under the influence of the Scottish landscape architect Ian McHarg (1920–2001), the realm of the very large scale was introduced to landscape, to the field's benefit. His book *Design with Nature* was valuable in observing natural processes as the basis for design. Its limitation was that it addressed so large a scale that it became the basis for master planning and strategies of location but did not truly engage with design. In retrospect, perhaps one could say that it did not shift scales enough to require an engagement with the specificity of design.

Today, though the greater geographic scale is still important, work at the middle scale is what matters most, forcing landscape into design. Though a planning approach still influences landscape design, landscape work itself has moved more firmly into form-giving.

From the first exploration of a small green roof for Earth Pledge, an ecological organization, came the idea of examining how individual units would work in additive fashion in an entire area of New York City. We chose Long Island City because the prevalence of "pancake" buildings there (low buildings with a very large footprint) meant that green roofs would make more of a difference.

The Long Island City story was made into a PowerPoint presentation and a booklet. The presentation of these ideas in public forums resulted in two Long Island City commissions, Silvercup Studios and Gratz Industries (figs. 72–77).

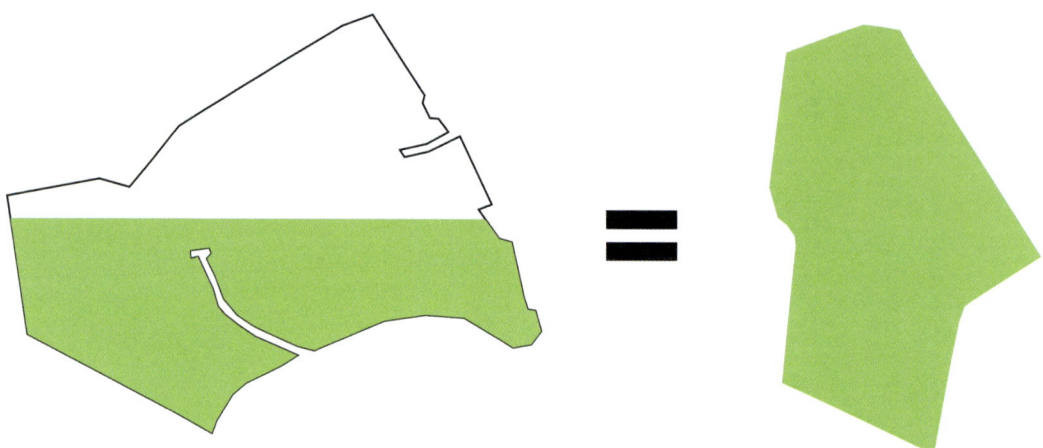

Green Potential Area in Long Island City=Area of Prospect Park

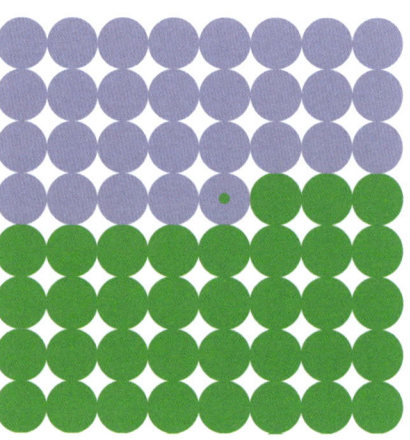

55% Greenspace Potential

Total Possible Green Area: 26,678,743ft² (55%)
667 acres

Fig. 72. Long Island (Green) City, Long Island City, Queens, New York, 2002. Study.

Fig. 73. Long Island (Green) City. Study of potential for green roofs.

Part 2   57

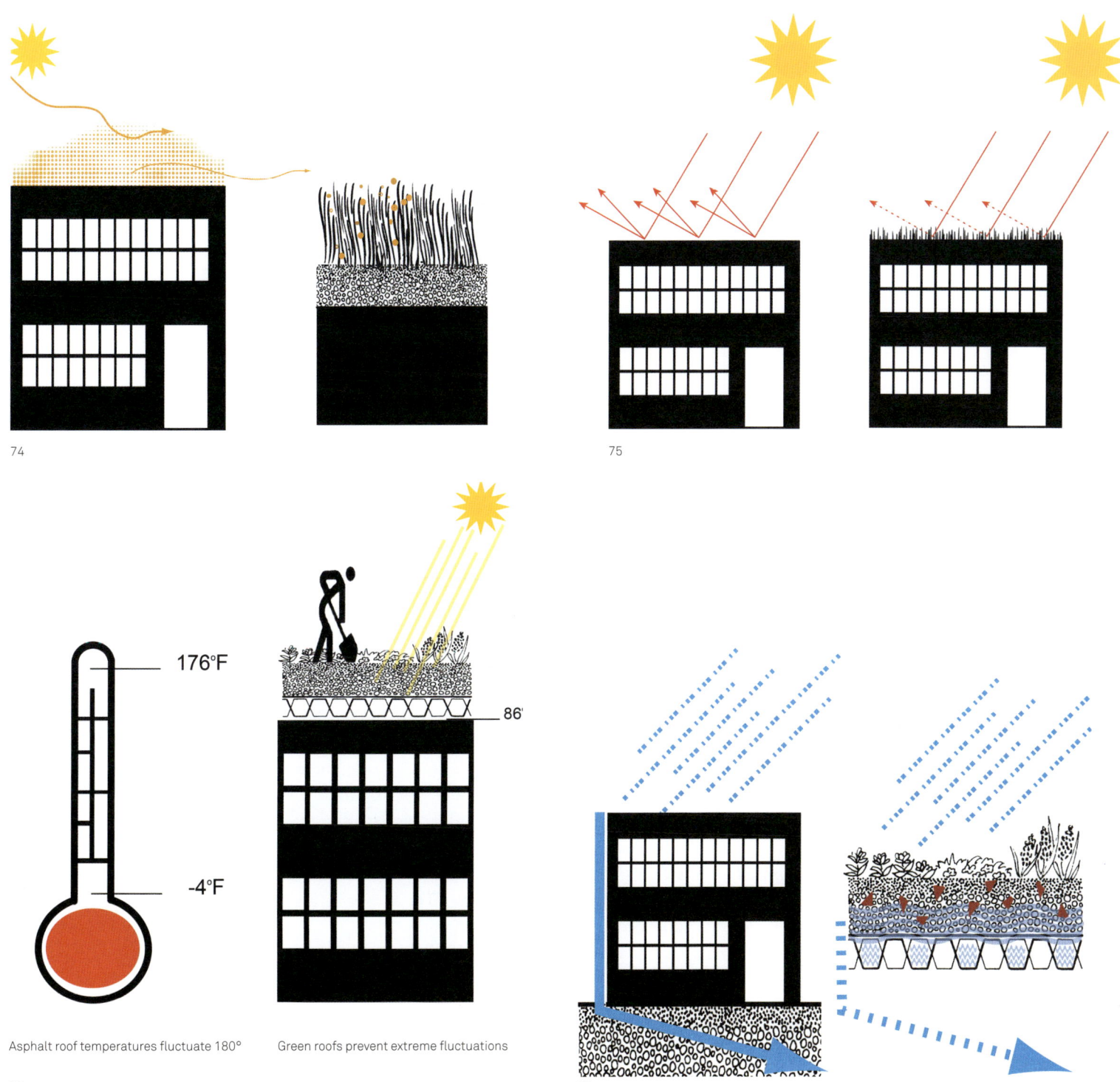

Asphalt roof temperatures fluctuate 180°   Green roofs prevent extreme fluctuations

Figs. 74–77. Long Island (Green) City.
Diagrams showing benefits of green roofs.

Silvercup Studios, New York

Grants were written to fund the creation of two demonstration green roofs in Long Island City. Although not all of the funding was fully in place, both projects—for Silvercup Studios and Gratz Industries—had sufficient financial commitments to move forward.

Because we had to justify every expense, we set out to build the most economical and the most sustainable green roof possible to serve as a prototype. This meant we would be designing a minimal vegetated layer, or extensive green roof, that would require very little maintenance and little or no irrigation after the first growing season. Because of weight-load considerations, only a shallow depth of planting medium could be used (three to three and a half inches), which also meant that we couldn't mound the soils to work with topography. Sedums are among the few plants that thrive in such shallow depths of mineral material and that can survive under the harsh solar and wind conditions found on an urban roof.

Although these economic, structural, and horticultural restrictions limited our design possibilities, we still believed that it was important to create a green roof that had some visual impact. Our larger goal for this project was to help promote the green roof industry in New York City and to encourage the mayor's office to offer incentives for the creation of more green roofs. An unexpected image on a roof can capture the interest of the general public. We didn't want the roof to look like a science experiment, nor did we want it to appear as if plants had colonized the roof on their own (as they had on top of the High Line). We wanted the plantings to convey a clear intent, something that would lead the thousands of commuters who pass by Silvercup everyday to ask themselves what thirty-five thousand square feet of plants were doing on the roof. Our hope was that seeing this vegetation integrated into the architecture of the buildings in this industrial neighborhood would lead some people to develop an interest in green roofs, whether or not they understood the benefits of such a landscape. Funding for a monitoring study of the Silvercup Studios green roof was written into our original grant proposal so that we could have actual data, analyzed by environmental scientists, to present to city officials, business owners, developers, and the general public.

The challenge was then to come up with a design that would not involve significant additional material and labor costs beyond those that might be incurred by a very minimal green roof installation. We began thinking about how to use the plant palette to create varied patterns. We worked with Ed Snodgrass, of Emory Knoll Farms, to come up with a list of twenty sedum types and varieties that would do well on this particular roof. Our pattern would highlight the variety in these twenty sedums by using their different leaf colors (from bright chartreuse to a blue-gray green), textures (ranging from pebblelike leaves to taller stalks with wider leaves), and bloom times and colors (yellow, pink, and white blooms from spring through fall). In this way we would create a picture constantly in flux through the seasons and over the years, as some sedums thrived and took over where others weren't quite as successful.

To allow Silvercup Studios greater flexibility to reconfigure the green roof at a later date and to test an alternate way of building a green roof, we decided to use a modular green roof system. These modules, made from recycled plastics, measure roughly four feet by four feet. They lock together by footpads and form a continuous planted surface. By using them, we already had a gridded, flat plane to work with. Using an early idea about pixilation, we began to design patterns for Silvercup Studios that were based on textiles, with linear blocks running vertically and horizontally that would break off at certain points and form larger geometric groupings.

Since this planted field would be constantly changing, we decided to have a static element to contrast with the plantings. For that, we chose to use brightly colored outdoor fabric that would be stretched over empty modules. The addition of the fabric panels also saved the project money, as stretching the mass-produced material over empty modules was less expensive than filling them with sedums. Of course, using materials in an atypical way on a project can always lead to some problems. We first specified a

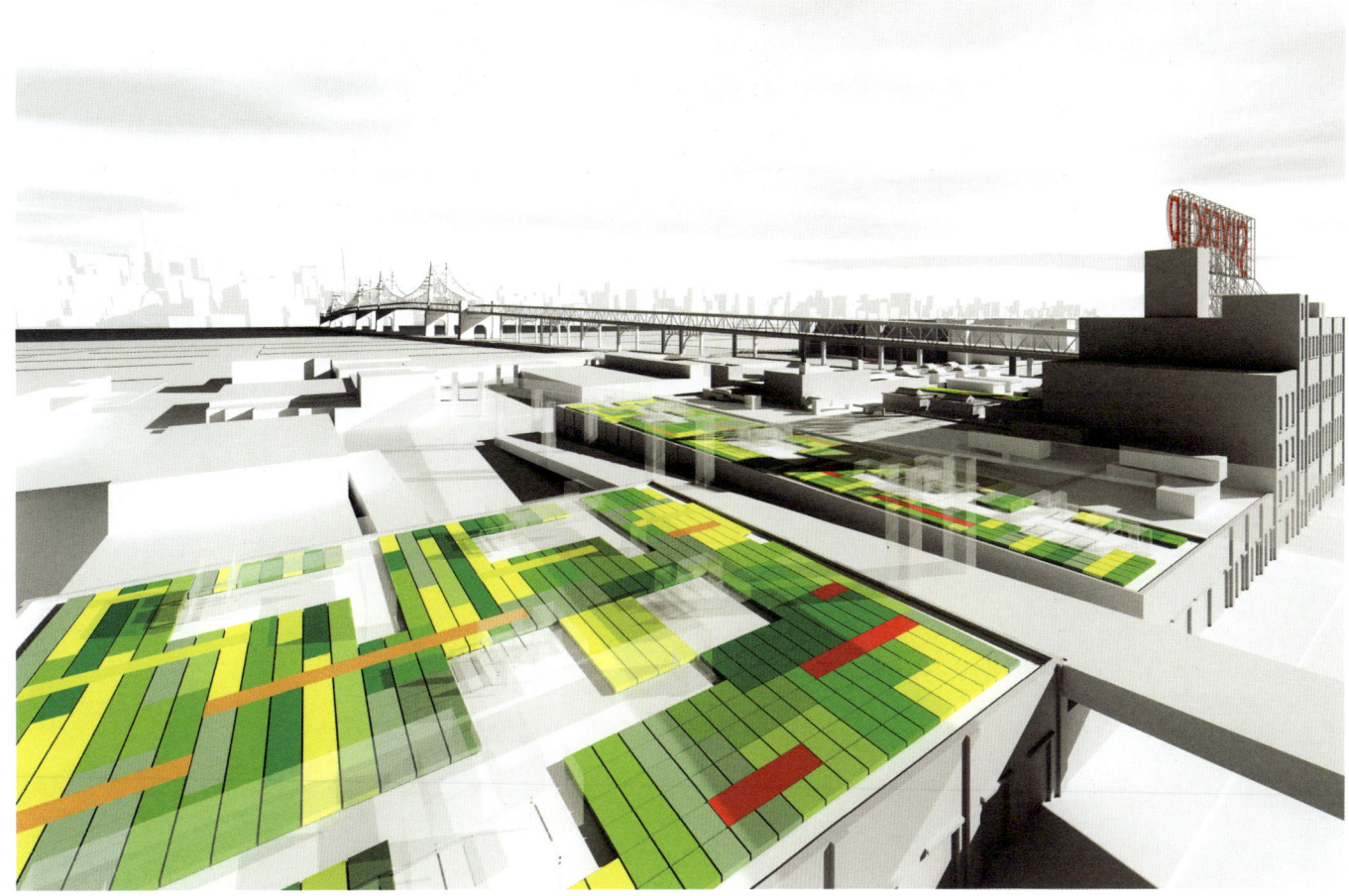

Fig. 78. Silvercup Studios, Long Island City, Queens, New York, 2005.

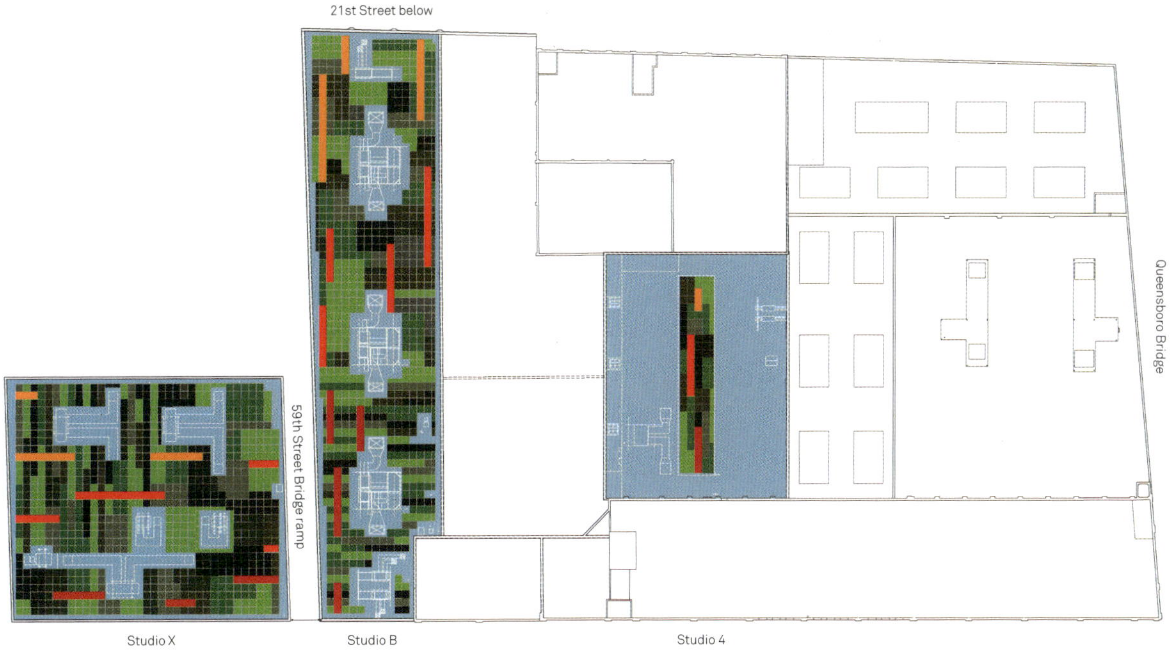

Fig. 79. Silvercup Studios. Plan.

Figs. 80–81. Silvercup Studios.

Fig. 82. Silvercup Studios.

Figs. 83–85. Silvercup Studios. Installation of green roof.

83

84

85

cotton awning material that was supposed to shed rain water. However, no matter how tightly the canvas was stretched, we had a problem with water pooling on it, so that material was replaced with mesh (in the same colors) that would allow the water to flow through.

Having good documentation of the project is another way to promote the green roof. We were able to hire a professional photographer to shoot the entire installation, beginning with the off-site preparation of the modules. We will continue to photograph the roof as the sedums grow and cover the entire surface of the modules.

The Silvercup monitoring project was set up by Green Roof Initiative and Earth Pledge, using Campbell Scientific equipment. The computer programmer for the project was Blue Dot, Inc., the local representative for Campbell Scientific, recommended by NASA Goddard Institute for Space Studies, at Columbia University. Given the scarcity of specific data, we thought that measurement of the effects of a minimum green roof in New York City would be valuable. We are proceeding in the same way with the Gratz roof and will have that data in a year. The comparison will provide data for two New York City roofs that are close to each other, one using an integral system (Hydrotech), the other a tray system. The resulting temperature data on Silvercup is very precise, the data on water management less so; but the performance of all the parameters measured was higher than expected (figs. 78–85).[3]

Gratz Industries, New York

A demonstration project for "Long Island (Green) City" was installed in autumn 2007 on the roof of Gratz Industries, a well-known metalwork manufacturer. Balmori Associates teamed with the Pratt Institute Center for Community and Environmental Development (PICCED) and submitted a proposal, "Manufacturing Green," to the New York State Energy Research and Development Authority (NYSERDA) to help fund this new green roof, a monitoring project led by NYEI, and an educational outreach program about green roof technology.

NYSERDA awarded the funding and, with it, an approximately eleven-thousand-square-foot green roof has been designed and built. Thousands of people will be able to look down onto this rooftop landscape from the elevated train and the Queensboro Bridge (though it will not be accessible to walk through).

Divided into four equal quadrants, the basic design for the roof is an overall grid pattern. One of the quadrants will be kept without plantings for a year in order to gather comparative data on tar roof versus planted surfaces. After a year, this quadrant will also be planted with sedums. A variety of sedums and herbaceous plants were chosen and arranged to achieve highly contrasting squares within the grid, utilizing the plants' wide range of textures, colors, and different bloom times. With each season the grid pattern will change. Balmori Associates' design for this roof was influenced by both color field paintings and the pixilation of enlarged computer imagery (figs. 86–88).

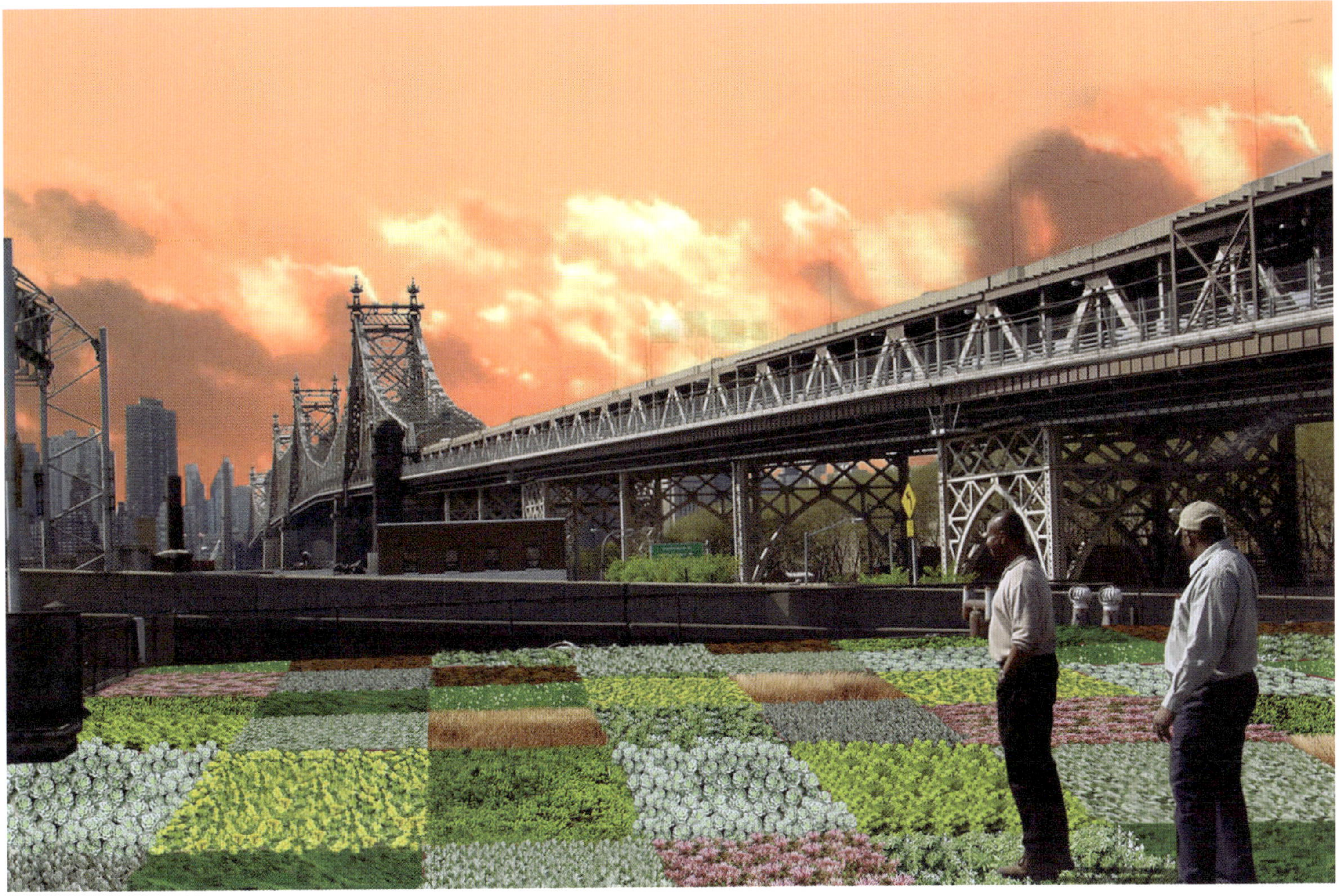

87

88

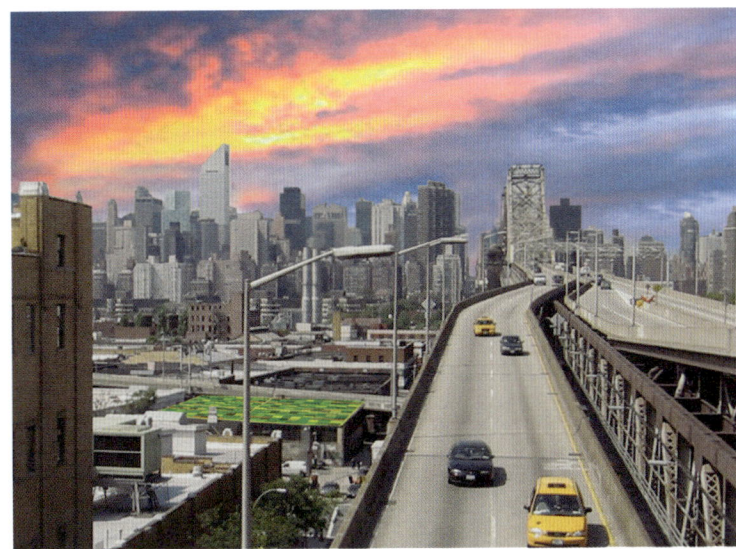

Fig. 86. Gratz Industries, Long Island City, Queens, New York, 2007. Plan.

Fig. 87. Gratz Industries.

Fig. 88. Gratz Industries.

The Solaire, New York

The Solaire, a residential tower in Battery Park City designed by Pelli Clarke Pelli Architects, has two types of green roof: an intensive, accessible green roof garden of about 5,000 square feet on the nineteenth floor and an inaccessible, extensive green roof of about 4,800 square feet on the top (twenty-eighth) floor. The two green roofs were integrated into the hydrological systems of the building. Excess water not absorbed by the vegetation or growing medium is collected and drained into a cistern in the basement. There the water is filtered and reused, in combination with treated gray water collected throughout the building, to provide water for Teardrop Park (directly behind the building) and to irrigate the intensive roof garden as needed. Nature's principles of reuse, storage, and adaptability are thus brought into the building. The Solaire represents the first step toward urban smart development, uniting architecture, landscape, and the urban setting into a sustainable system.

People can enjoy spectacular views of the Hudson River as they sit or stroll on this intensive green roof. Four large stands of bamboo, visible from street level, organize the roof layout. Stone pavers for walkways and seating areas were laid directly on the growing medium, which supports a lush carpet of groundcovers and sedums. Vertical aluminum screens planted with honeysuckle and ivy are placed around mechanical and other utility structures, which help integrate the growing space with the mechanical equipment, rather than hide it. Through evapotranspiration, these plantings create a microclimate on the roof that is several degrees cooler than the surrounding rooftops.

The extensive green roof on the top floor is an inaccessible installation planted with a variety of sedums. It is visible from adjacent buildings, a fifth façade of flowering green, which absorbs stormwater runoff, insulates the building (reducing the amount of air-conditioning required in the summer and the amount of heating required in the winter), cleans the air of pollutants, and produces oxygen. Together with the intensive green roof on the nineteenth floor, the plant materials and growing medium will absorb at least 75 percent of rainwater.

The building won a gold LEED (Leadership in Energy and Environmental Design) rating and received New York State's Green Building Tax Credit. Balmori Associates' design was given an Award of Excellence by Green Roofs for Healthy Cities in the category of intensive residential design in 2004, and in 2002 the Solaire was one of five projects selected by the U.S. Department of Energy to represent the nation at the International Green Building Challenge in Oslo, a conference for sharing information on sustainable design for buildings. Other awards for this green building included being named one of the AIA/COTE Top Ten Green Projects in 2004, and the winner, in the Multi-Use Residential category, of the Environmental Design and Construction Magazine Excellence in Design Award, also in 2004 (figs. 89–91).

89

Figs. 89, 90. The Solaire, New York, 2003. Nineteenth-floor garden.

Fig. 91. The Solaire. Detail of twenty-eighth-floor garden.

Green Roofs in a City's Context

All these green roofs, and others under construction, are in New York. All have a role as fifth façades; they can be seen from above from other buildings or from the Queensboro Bridge. The technology that makes them possible and the plant suppliers have both evolved considerably since we first started. As with any new design element, it is only just developing. A green roof or fifth façade is planar; it may take on a third dimension, but it is as if a surface of paper had been modeled into a sculptural form. The delineation of a pattern on such a surface will prevail over the volume. Its significance grows when seen in the context of a whole city. Even a concentration of green roofs in one particular zone can have a marked effect on the quality of the air and the urban heat island, just as a large park does. In addition, green roofs provide habitats for both insects and birds that need to be reintroduced in the city (figs. 92–97).

From Ditches to Rain Gardens

A ditch is, first, a form of depression in the land where drainage water is collected. But in its transformation into a modern landscape it is modified through planting. The higher humidity of the depression favors this, and the selection of plants which can be submerged or semisubmerged furthers its ability to gather water, clean it, slow it down in big storms, and reuse it if needed, by collecting it at the rill's end. It is particularly well suited for draining parking lots. Our rain gardens for the parking lot of the Botanical Research Institute of Texas, in Fort Worth, do just that. Because it is an institution for botanical research, we intend to make the rain gardens an area of botanical display that announces to visitors that they are at a botanical institution the moment they park.[4]

The transformations described so far apply locally to relatively small areas—a roof or a narrow corridor—though their reach and extension can be citywide. The next sets of cultural artifacts are at a larger scale (ports, suburbs), and they can yield results that go beyond a particular artifact. These transformations involve dealing with larger patterns, including patterns that may not be visible and patterns that vary over time.[9]

9. New landscape elements can become niches for species forced out of their original environment.

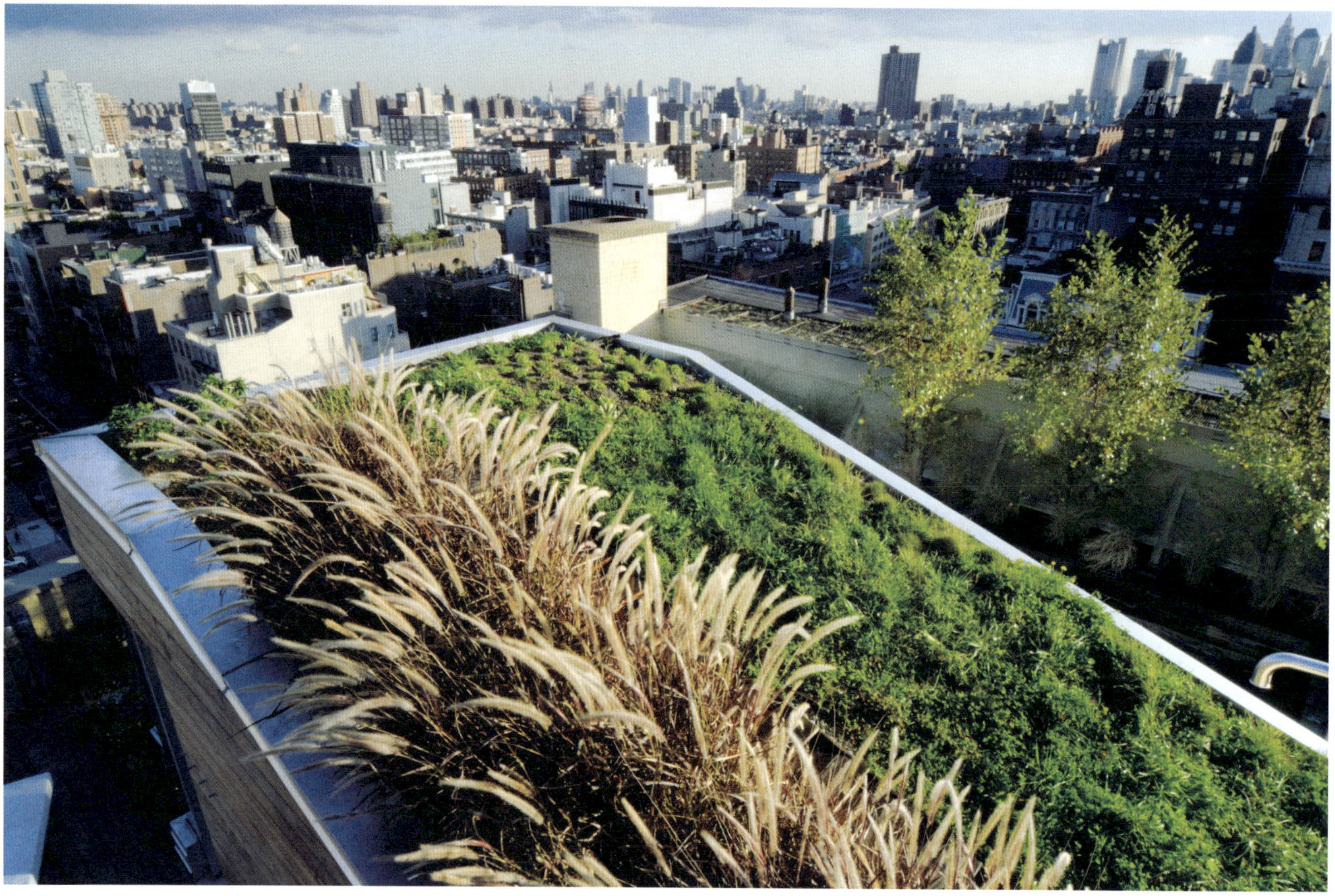

92

93

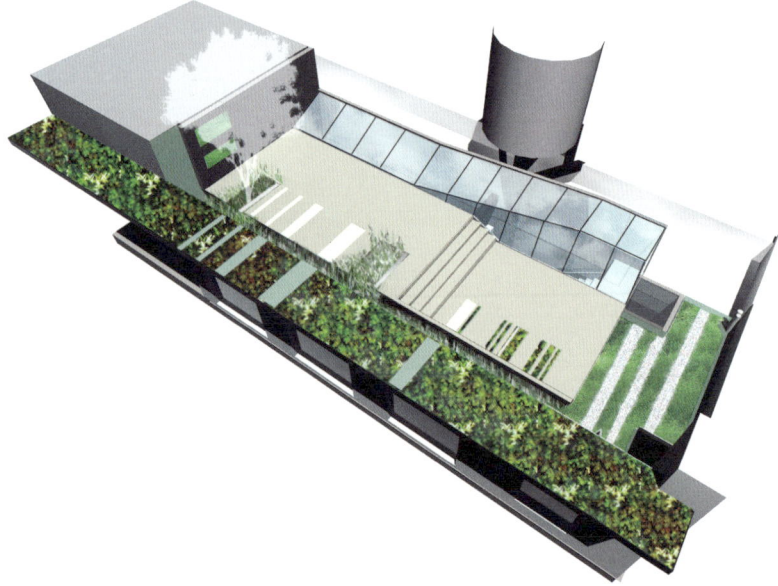

Fig. 92. Broadway Penthouse, New York, 2007.

Fig. 93. Broadway Penthouse. Axonometric.

Fig. 94. Loews Miami Beach Hotel, 2006. Plan showing green space and fiber-optic lighting.

Fig. 95. Loews Miami Beach Hotel. Alternate scheme.

96

Figs. 96, 97. 240 Central Park South, New York, 2007.

Botanical Research Institute of Texas, Fort Worth

A parking lot seems an unlikely place to begin the design of a new building and landscape. But a study of parking on the five acres of the Botanical Research Institute (BRIT) led to reconfiguration of the site and the incorporation of a joint parking area for BRIT and the Fort Worth Botanic Garden on an expanded twelve-acre site. Landscapes cannot be considered in isolation. They are part of a watershed, which means, literally, that water runs in a particular direction on any given site. Any effort to oppose that takes work and money, and many times doesn't succeed.

It is therefore important to consider a landscape's context on a larger scale. To do that, often we get into a small plane and fly over a site to see what surrounds it, and to discover what the implications of these larger connections are for the site. Whatever we do on the site, conversely, may affect what is around it.

BRIT's landscape, when viewed at this scale, is part of the corridor of the Trinity River. When you look at it together with the Botanic Garden, which adjoins it, you see how odd the discontinuous band between them is. The continuity of landscapes has been found to be important for the health of the larger systems in which they are located, and the BRIT project should be looked at in those terms.

At first, the vast space required for parking (358 spaces) presents itself as a huge, budget-consuming problem. But if the parking lot is seen, along with roofs, as part of an active stormwater management system and research field, then together they become an ecological working system—not just a problem to be solved, but something to delight visitors as soon as they park. The water collected from roofs can be stored in a cistern and reused for supplying a pond and for watering plants in a drought, and the roof, in addition to being a collector, can also be turned into a research plot.

The client, BRIT's board, and the architect for the new building, Hugh Hardy, encouraged us to connect the two institutions as much as possible, both physically and visually. The board was able to persuade the city to allow the city-owned land between the two institutions to become a joint

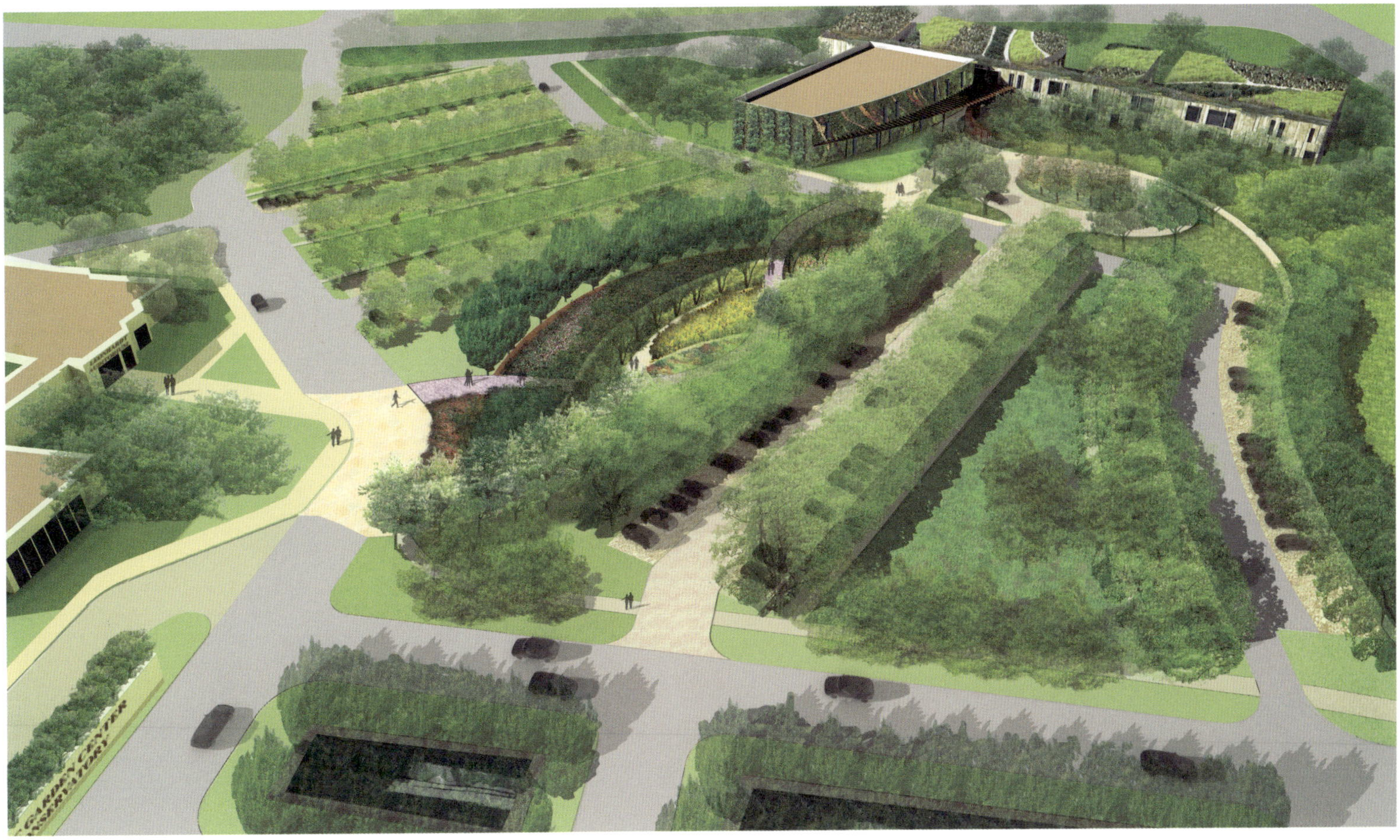

99

100

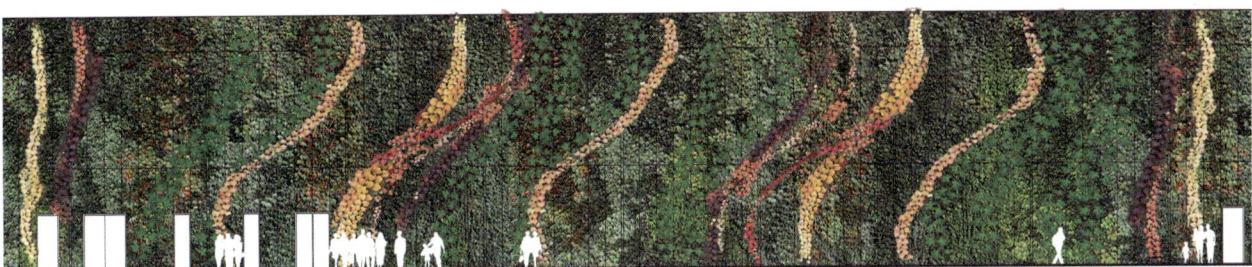

Fig. 98. Botanical Research Institute of Texas (BRIT), Fort Worth, Texas, in progress. Plan.

Fig. 99. BRIT.

Fig. 100. BRIT. Planted wall treatment.

parking lot for both. We were then asked to redesign the existing parking lot of the Botanic Garden to make a seamless composition. Given the extreme and constant heat and the continuous presence of the Texas sun, shade became paramount. Water management was next in importance in this project, since droughts are followed by torrential rains in this area, and water then needs to be contained and, ideally, stored for drought-period reuse.

This parking lot will serve water- and shade-management purposes. But, above all, it will join the two institutions. And—even more important—it will not be a throwaway experience, with visitors arriving at the Botanical Institute only after leaving the parking lot. Rather, people come to a special botanical ambit the moment they enter the lot. The heavily treed shady cover and the densely planted, water-gathering rills that line each parking aisle were designed for precisely this purpose. Getting into the parking lot and getting out of the car are designed as the beginning of the botanical experience.

But the most important experience of BRIT, in addition to the parking lot botany, is the main entrance, which unites the Botanical Research Institute to the Botanic Garden. This consists of a major display of plantings based on "systematics," a type of research that is the core mission of BRIT. BRIT describes systematics as research seeking an understanding of evolutionary relationships among species—in other words, looking at species not as fixed entities but as evolving systems. There are also studies looking at the coevolution of plants and animals. The botanists are therefore studying evolutionary relationships among groups of plants. These relationships are inferred from information about plant structure, chemistry, or genes. BRIT works with structures at the specimen level. BRIT's study of the systematics of north central Texas led to identifying five groups of plants for their main entrance: Asteraceae, Cyperacieae, Poaceae, Rosaceae, and Verbenaceae. Though tied directly to BRIT's mission, they are also an extension of the design strategy adopted for the parking lot.

The central pedestrian corridor joining the entrance to BRIT to the entrance to the lecture hall at the Fort Worth Botanic Garden has all been intensively planted based on the systematics of these five northern Texas plant groups. Of the five, two groups predominate: Poaceae (or grasses) and Asteraceae.

So this wide avenue, with different routes of winding paths, displays the actual mission and classification of plants according to the BRIT model, a display of plants according to new principles. Moreover, they represent something more profound, which informs the ideas pursued: the lack of fixity in all of the materials of a landscape and the lack of fixity in species as evolving systems (figs. 98–102). **10**

10. The new view of plants as groups of interrelated species modifying each other, rather than as separate and fixed, exemplifies fluidity—a main motif of landscape form.

101

102

From Drainage Pipes to Stormwater Parks

Water is the issue of our day. Scarcity of it, flooding by it, pollution in it—these are constantly surfacing as problems to be solved. Many of the projects here revolve around controlling water and using it in different ways. Green roofs save water, reuse it, evapotranspirate it, hold it back in peak storms. Rain gardens reuse it and filter it through the earth, feeding into groundwater. Abandoned ports, which we will look at further on, release a waterfront to a city's public, with the resulting opportunity to include water in a city's life in ways that accept its fluctuations. The nineteenth century introduced sewers into cities; the sewers also served to drain urban streets. As the growth of cities, paved surfaces, and roofs increased, so did the volume of water in sewer pipes, so that now, in the twenty-first century, any large storm produces an overrun of water, resulting in sewage overflow entering streams and oceans. In addition, the sudden volumes of water increase water speed, erode river edges, flood, and pollute.

Removing drainage from sewer pipes solves many of these issues and helps prevent sewer overflow. But it does not solve the problem of peak storms' sudden discharges of large volumes of water into rivers. That overflow can be removed from underground drainage pipes by creation of an open water system on grade and acquisition of land for it, which in turn offers the opportunity to include green public space around it. This is more easily accomplished in suburbs than in cities. The result is a body of water that runs along vegetated edges. When a certain water level is reached, the system reverses itself to fill depressions that hold water until peak storm levels are past. The water is then cleaned as it passes through the vegetation. And the river benefits from not receiving too much water at once, or too swiftly, thus preventing flooding and eroding edges. Increased biodiversity is an additional benefit of the creation of the green park and the water's presence.[5] The Prairie Waterway, in Farmington, Minnesota, is an example of such a transformation.

Prairie Waterway/Park Place, Farmington, Minnesota

This waterway has a dual purpose, providing drainage for a new development of nearly five hundred homes while creating and functioning as a public space. We proposed an open water-drainage system to replace the usual underground pipeline. Dubbed "Park Place" by local residents, the ninety-one-acre park has now become an integral part of the community, not only as a part of the infrastructure, but also as a public amenity. It provides an environmentally sound solution to the issue of flooding in a flat plain with a high water table and peak storm volumes that empty into the Vermillion River, a tributary of the Mississippi.

The Issue and the Site

The project's task was to deal with the added volume of water that suburban development produces from the large impermeable surfaces of its new roads, roofs, and roadways. This water, dumped all at once into rivers (in this case, the Vermillion River first and then the Mississippi), produces sudden floods that erode riverbanks and can harm plant and aquatic life. The Farmington waterway functions successfully as a drainage project, as was shown in the recent peak flooding years of 1998 and 2001, when the Mississippi River remained above its floodplain for at least three months. The public space, a park, was made part of the drainage solution.

The area near Farmington is completely flat. In winter months the temperature often dips to well below zero. A slight, glossy covering of snow reflects the low winter sun. Around the site, a few farmhouses are surrounded by acres of fields of dry cornstalks standing in the snow. On the edge of the planned development, a north-south road bisects the rural terrain. On the opposite side is the agricultural town of Farmington, which has a population of 12,500.

Farmington is about twenty-five miles northwest of Minneapolis, close enough to the nearby urban area to create a high demand for housing. Rod Hardy, director of the Sienna Development Corporation, proposed building a development of some five hundred houses over ten to fifteen years, with approximately

Fig. 101. BRIT. Detail of planted wall treatment.

Fig. 102. BRIT. Rendering of entrance through systematic planting beds.

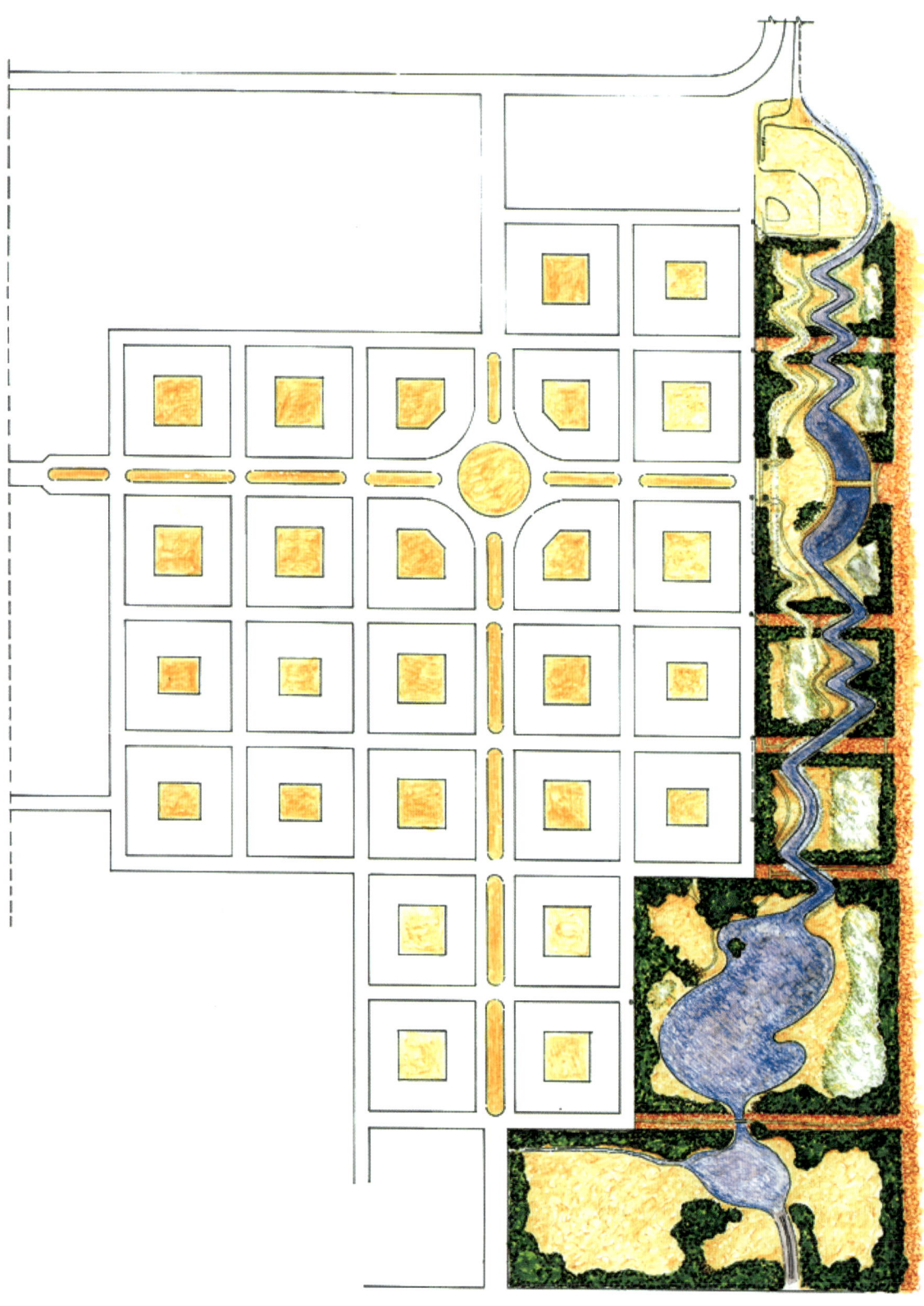

Part 2   81

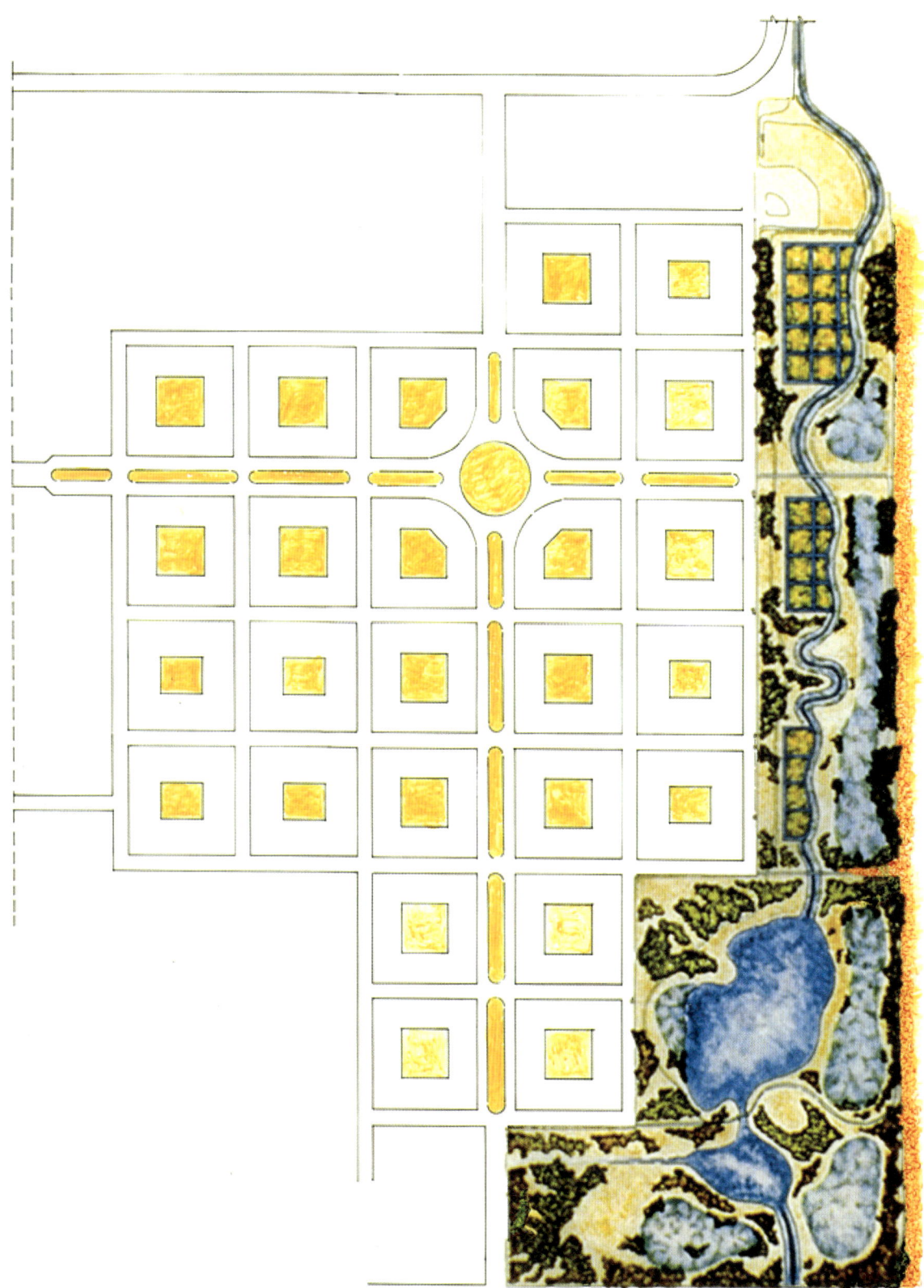

Fig. 103. Prairie Waterway/Park Place, Farmington, Minnesota, 1996. Selected scheme.

Fig. 104. Prairie Waterway/Park Place. Alternate scheme.

one hundred seventy houses in the initial phase. In 1993, several months after the summer of the worst flooding of the Mississippi River in twenty-eight years, William Moorish, director of the Design Center for American Urban Landscape at the University of Minnesota, proposed to the town that our office design a different kind of drainage system for the planned Farmington development (which the town had not approved at that point). The developer's initial proposal was standard, directing the increased runoff into a single pipe that would empty into the Vermillion and continue on into the Mississippi River, about twenty miles downstream from Farmington. But since this proposal was made right after the 1993 floods, the Farmington town board was willing to consider a new approach, despite its understandable reluctance to try something new and unproven, and despite the fact that such a slow-down system of managing runoff would probably require using more land than a development corporation would want to purchase.

On the other hand, if the area around the wetland system became public space, an amenity for the whole town, it could be justified. Happily, the small farming town had a capable town planner, Lee Smick, who supported the idea. My colleague at Yale University, the hydrologist Paul Barten, was added to the project team as a counterpart to the developer's civil engineers, who had already proposed the standard system.

The town of Farmington made the development of an innovative drainage system a condition for approval of the housing development plan. The town planner supported the idea of a stormwater park throughout the lengthy approval process. The town board, composed mostly of local farmers, did not object but expressed some apprehension over the need to buy land exclusively for the water system. The land was purchased with city money recovered through taxes paid on the property once the houses had been sold (tax increment financing). The taxes were established by the town as the developer's contributions to needed facilities, but the city also had to buy additional land beyond the development to allow access for the water to flow to the Vermillion River.

The Design Process and Landscape Aesthetic
We presented two schemes for the surface water-drainage system to the Farmington town board and the developer. The first scheme, which the town board and the Sienna Development Corporation much preferred, made the waterway a naturalistic stream (fig. 103). The second scheme, which we preferred, created a series of interconnected geometric ponds

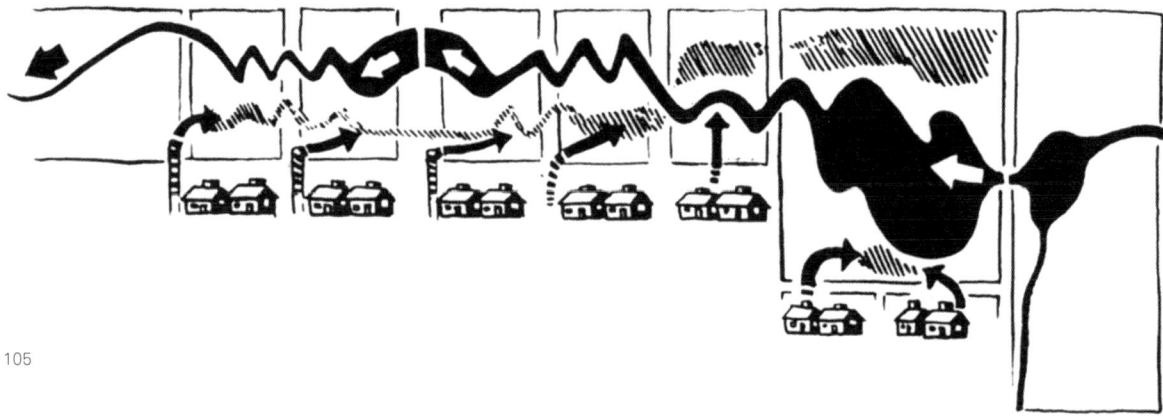

Fig. 105. Prairie Waterway/Park Place. Diagram showing water flow.

Fig. 106. Prairie Waterway/Park Place. Diagram with three views.

that cleaned and retained the water, based on the system used in cranberry bogs (fig. 104). The town board and developer raised objections to the gridded bog system, claiming that it seemed unnatural. Here, though this is an artificial drainage system, we again encounter the eighteenth-century Romantic landscape idea of the "natural." Because it is important in any new work to find an aesthetic appropriate to it, the use of a well-known, human-created system, such as the time-tested system of cranberry bogs, seemed appropriate to the site and the project requirements. The city board rightfully expressed an aesthetic preference. We accepted it, because convincing the town and the developer to accept an open drainage system at all was in itself quite a step forward. Yet this choice unfortunately encourages a misreading of the drainage system by its future inhabitants. It hides the reality that the drainage is the result of a deliberate and courageous choice to use land for the sake of filtering water. A new aesthetic, making such ethical choices visible and enjoyable, is needed.

The development's layout and architecture were completed before we were engaged. We did request, and obtained, a few modifications to reduce stormwater runoff. Streets were narrowed, driveways shortened, and a depression was made at the center of each block to collect the rainwater running off the roofs and lots. These areas at the center of each block were to be thickly planted with trees (for example, red maples) that can survive with roots in standing water for part of the year. Through evapotranspiration from the foliage, these trees would get rid of the water in these depressions.

Planting turned out to be the most troublesome part of the project. Basically, neither the developer nor the city had sufficient funds for the trees for either the center of the blocks or the public green space created by the new water system. We proposed several inexpensive solutions, including gathering seeds from local vegetation and then having schoolchildren plant those seeds as part of their science curriculum. We also proposed that the town board contact the Minneapolis Department of Transportation to request permission to reuse plants that were being removed to widen roads, after discovering that there was just such a project not too far from the site. But to no avail: a cover of winter rye was put in to control erosion the first year at the center of each block, and eventually the town implemented a ten-year plan for investing $10,000 a year a year in small trees. As of this writing, nine years of planting and growth (largely of willow, hackberry, plum, and ash trees) have taken place.

106

107

Figs. 107–109. Prairie Waterway/
Park Place.

108

109

The Stormwater Park

The parklike landscape for the growing town of Farmington consists of a riparian waterway, a civic lawn on an axis with the downtown area, and playing fields. The wetlands associated with this urban waterway provide a recreational component for those interested in observing wildlife or using green public spaces. In addition, of course, they store stormwater. The form of this landscape is revealed through the rise and fall of water levels during and after storms.

In addition, two older housing developments to the south of the new development in Farmington, known as Castle Rock and Henderson, are served by the drainage system. Their stormwater enters the pond at the southern end of the Park Place site. (Basements in both older developments had previously flooded every spring.) This pond reduces the velocity and turbulence of the stormwater and settles out the coarser particles of sediments. From there, the water continues to a larger pond that is surrounded by an aquatic bench of emergent wetland plants, ten to fifteen feet wide and six to twelve inches deep.

The channel leaving the pond has the sinusoidal curved edges produced by running water. The channel also slows the water, allowing it to become cleansed as it moves through the vegetation. The great porousness of the local soils means that groundwater rises and falls quickly during and after storms. Under these conditions, the great width of the channel, which varies between 80 and 110 feet, helps to reduce the velocity and scouring of the waterway. The vegetated, expanded streambed traps particulates and takes up nutrients.

The mitigating wetlands to the north temporarily store the higher groundwater, but only in one-hundred-year events is the berm between the wetland and the channel breached. On September 15, 1998, just as the construction of the drainage system was completed, a one-hundred-year flood took place. The drainage system worked exactly as it was supposed to; the berm was breached, and the mitigating wetlands stored the higher waters.

Then in April 2001, as the Mississippi River again flooded large areas, the drainage system prevented substantial flood damage to the immediate area.

Some local residents are completely unaware that the waterway/park system that they enjoy for recreation is also responsible for solving the stormwater and drainage problems that would likely have occurred without it. Here is where false aesthetics—those of another time and with another meaning—serve us badly. It is critical that our aesthetics reveal the newness of the design so that its users understand what these forms have wrought (figs. 105–109).[6] **11**

11. Nostalgic images of nature are readily accepted, but they are like stage scenery for the wrong play.

Inscribing Urban Forms in the Larger Geographical Context

Studied on a city scale, wet soils, marshes, winds, and currents can throw past failures into relief and suggest new alternatives. Our first suburbs, like downtowns, have decayed. Our derelict, polluted urban marshes and our ruined urban beaches are now attractive to developers again and are being studied as areas for renewal. In this section, projects covering these city areas are discussed as examples of approaches to a new urbanity.

Examining Humboldt, an early suburb of Minneapolis, reveals a pattern of decay and abandonment due to subsurface conditions. It shows a clear relation between vacancy and a subsurface of wet soils where streams run underground.

In Arverne, close to John F. Kennedy International Airport, on New York's Long Island, we see a pattern of groins undoing a long stretch of beaches, the pollution of marshes, and diminishing protection from dunes. Marshes, dunes, levels of water, and wet soils—these all speak to both the need to examine the urban treatment of those areas and the need to study the physical environment in which they are set. What has come to light in some cases is a pattern of building that was ill advised; houses were constructed on inappropriate sites and quickly lost their value. Their backyards were flooded or frequently muddy; their basements were often flooded or constantly damp. This subsurface condition led to a pattern of house abandonment.

Shorelines are particularly delicate environments. Efforts to urbanize or reurbanize them are now afoot all over the world as water edges are being rediscovered. Usually lined by train tracks, highways, or the remains of ports, or overbuilt in ways that have destroyed the very water edges that were sought in the first place, shorelines are places where geographical features are particularly important.

Sand dunes are a valuable component of some shorelines. Their importance is highlighted in the case of two projects: Arverne and Qing Huang Dao, in China. Ian McHarg was the first to make a case for dunes in shoreline sites. The more we learn about them, the more we understand both their fragility (to human traffic) and their nearly miraculous plasticity and strength, allowing them to provide protection from storms. They are mobile elements when given enough room, which is nearly impossible in urbanizing schemes. Our projects called for fixing them in place with grasses, building boardwalks to be used as the only paths across them to respect their fragility, and forming them in two lines to preserve their effectiveness. In both projects these guidelines were described in great detail. The sand dunes were also used for their character; they are beautiful forms and, well used, can make a haunting and lovely shoreline.

At the same time, very urban and nongeographic liberties can be taken. Establishing areas that contrast with what is expected on a shoreline can provide a series of landscapes which run the gamut of local flora and geographical formations, from dune boardwalk to lawn (Freedom Lawn), or, as in the case of Qing Huang Dao, include a completely foreign, imported element (European grasses and clover). In other words, inscribing urban forms into the larger geographical context does not mean submitting to a dictatorship of that geography. Certain features, such as dunes or wet soils, can provide a strategy and a character for an urbanization that benefits directly from either avoiding building on them (wet soils) or using them (dunes). But the diverse mix of other landscape elements makes for a rich, new urban space. We are, after all, constructing a new natural environment that is neither wild seashore nor country stream, but a piece of city which uses the basic conditions only as a point of departure.

Larger geographical forces—tides, currents, winds—enter the design arena in larger projects by the water. Each formidable in scale and effect, they are all forces that can be put to work in shaping a design. The abandonment of old ports worldwide has opened central areas in cities to reconsideration. The same issue is confronted in each of those locations: the edge between water and land is one where geographical elements weigh heavily. There may be fluctuations of water levels of forty feet throughout

Fig. 110. Humboldt Avenue Reinvestment Study, Minneapolis, 1996. Plan showing surface wet soils.

Fig. 111. Humboldt Avenue Reinvestment Study. Plan showing buried wet soils.

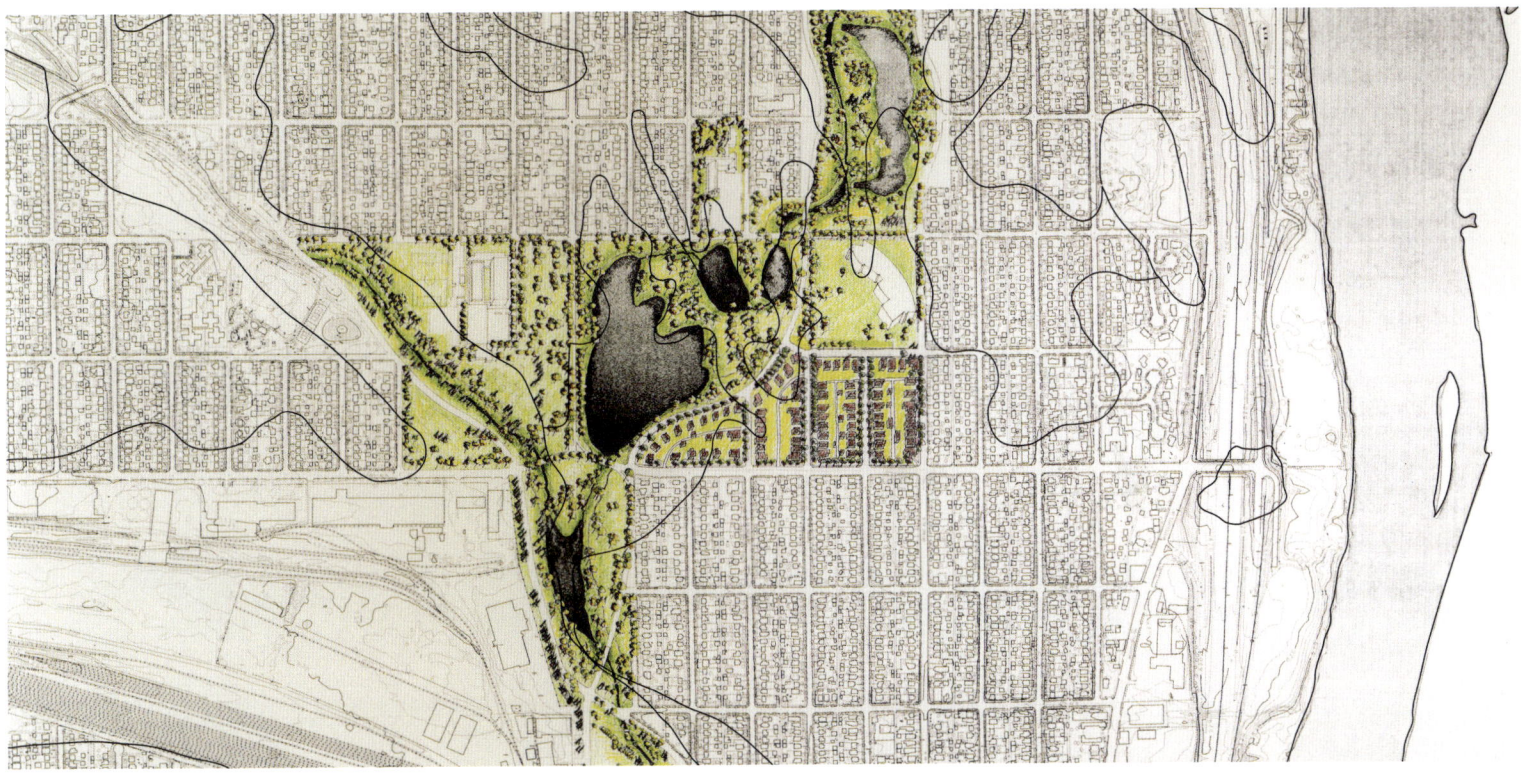

110

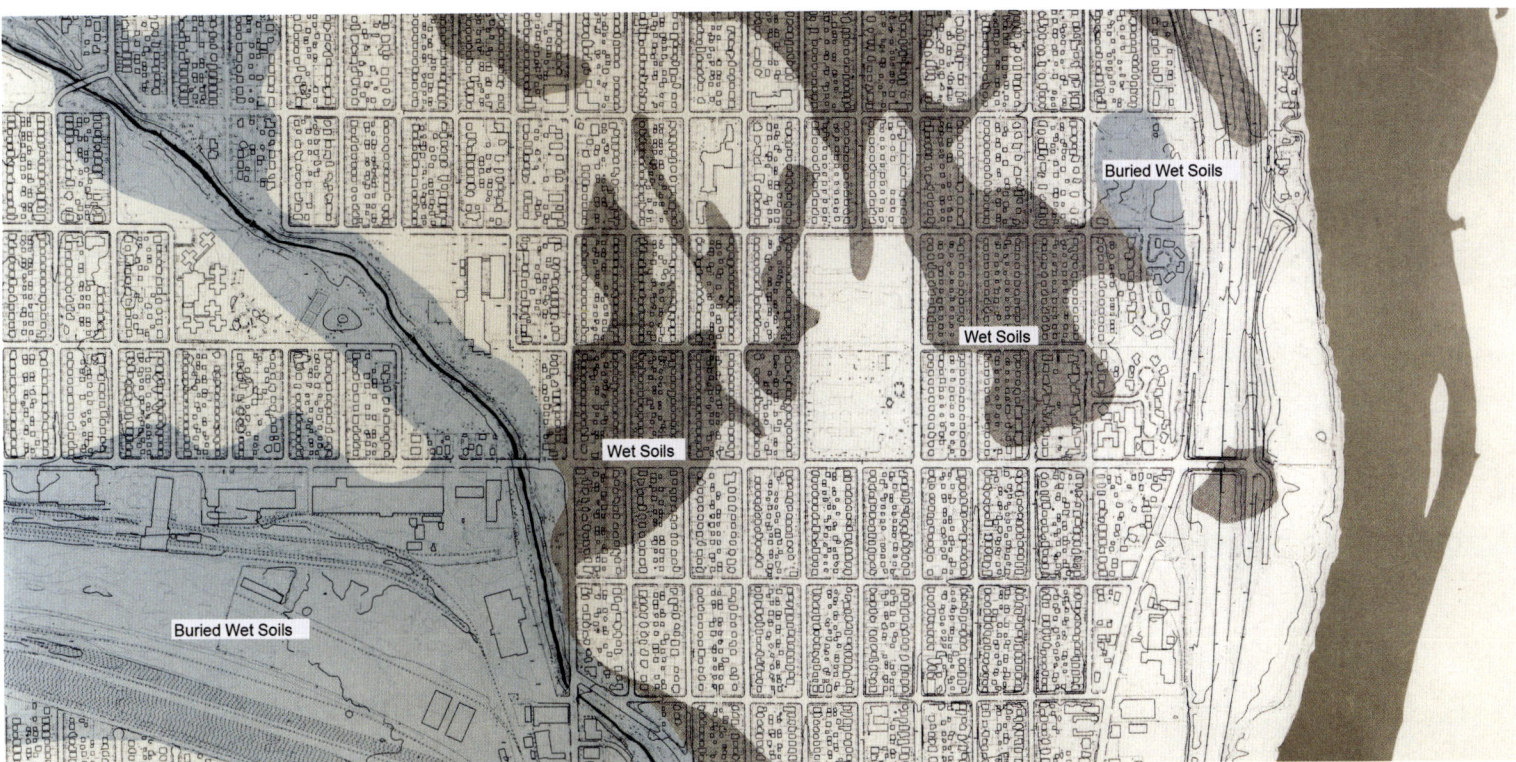

111

the year, or erosive currents, or constant desiccating winds. As in the case of sand dunes and wet soils, these elements can be the basis for a design strategy. **12**

Humboldt Avenue Reinvestment Study

This project spreads over the northern residential edges of Minneapolis and its first ring of suburbs in Hennepin County, an area with deteriorating and abandoned housing. It has a diminishing tax base, with younger people moving farther out to new suburbs, leaving older residents left trapped behind. A surprising discovery was made: the worst of the housing had been built on wet soil.

As a multidisciplinary team, we presented a proposal for the area's reconfiguration. Our own contribution to the major site issues and their solution is presented here. It is an example of how to inscribe urban forms in larger geographical contexts—in this case, an urban insertion over a subsoil condition which made for an unsuccessful suburb.

The solution we propose is removal of the housing on wet soil. A linear park by a stream will be created on those lots, and water resurfacing from the wet soil will join the stream nearby. At the same time, some new lots will be created for housing with contemporary amenities along the linear park's edge. These modest interventions will clear spots for small villages to spring up along the linear park waterway, slowly renewing the area over twenty-five years (figs. 110–113).

The modern form of the linear park is used to renew this troubled first-ring suburb. But it is the geological substrate of wet soil that reemerges to give a direction to this new urban form.

12. In his *History of the Modern Taste in Gardening* (1780), Horace Walpole writes that William Kent "was the first to leap the fence and show that the whole of nature was a garden." Today landscape has leapt the fence in the opposite direction, to the city, making it part of nature.

Part 2   92

Fig. 112. Humboldt Avenue Reinvestment Study. Detail of proposed layout.

Fig. 113. Humboldt Avenue Reinvestment Study. Axonometric section.

Arverne, New York

Arverne was a Yale project (fig. 114). A run-down residential beach area in Long Island was being considered by New York City for new residential development. The Architectural League invited five universities to put forth ideas for a presentation to developers, who were to bid on the site.

Princeton, Columbia, Yale, City College, and CASE (a housing research group from Holland) were invited. Dean Robert A. M. Stern asked four of his colleagues at Yale (the architects Deborah Berke, Peggy Deamer, and Keller Easterling, as well as me) to create a scheme for the site. The five proposals were exhibited at the Architectural League. But they ultimately had no effect on the developers' proposals, which were typical developments with a few minimal nods to sustainability.

The one hundred acres of the Arverne site sit on a sandbar, a fragile landscape easily breached. Ideally a sandbar has a profile of two lines of dunes. Arverne currently has only one line of dunes. If the site were to be developed further, another line of dunes could be created, along with a boardwalk bridge across them to keep people from trampling the delicate grasses that keep the dunes in place. Another aspect of the surrounding landscape also affects Arverne's development: the rising water levels caused by global warming (9 inches over the twentieth century, and a projected 23.5 inches over the next fifty years; fig. 115).

Arverne, on the edge of a floodplain today, will then itself become a floodplain. Its buildings must be raised. A continuous green belt along its northern, Jamaica Bay, side—through which the floods flow into the site—needs to be created; it would help absorb, detain, and store floodwaters. Arverne also suffers from the declining health of Jamaica Bay, whose marshes have one of the richest biota in the United States, but are disappearing. One contributing cause is the amount of nitrogen entering the bay; another is sewage overflow from an old and overtaxed combined drainage and sewage system (figs. 116–118).

Our design for Arverne's landscape responds to this context. Deterioration begins when the impervious surface of a watershed exceeds 25 percent; our site has been designed to have only a 14 percent impervious surface. Second, the water that collects from drainage passes through vegetated swales, which clean it before it enters Jamaica Bay. Third, that landscape and its sewage systems—originally created for nineteenth-century cities—are due for a revision. **13**

13. Existing urban spaces can be rescued from their current damaging interaction with nature.

114

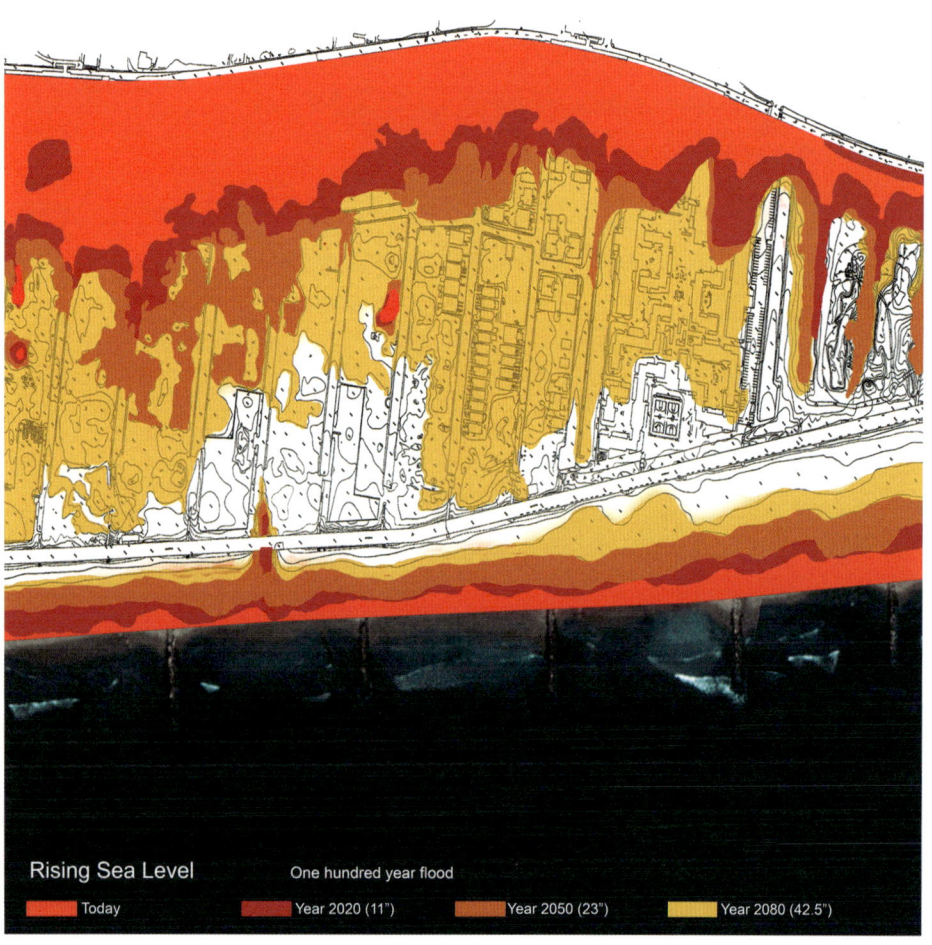

115

Fig. 114. Arverne, New York, 2001. Watercolor of proposed new dunes.

Fig. 115. Arverne. Diagram showing rising sea level.

Fig. 116. Arverne. Photomontage plan.

117

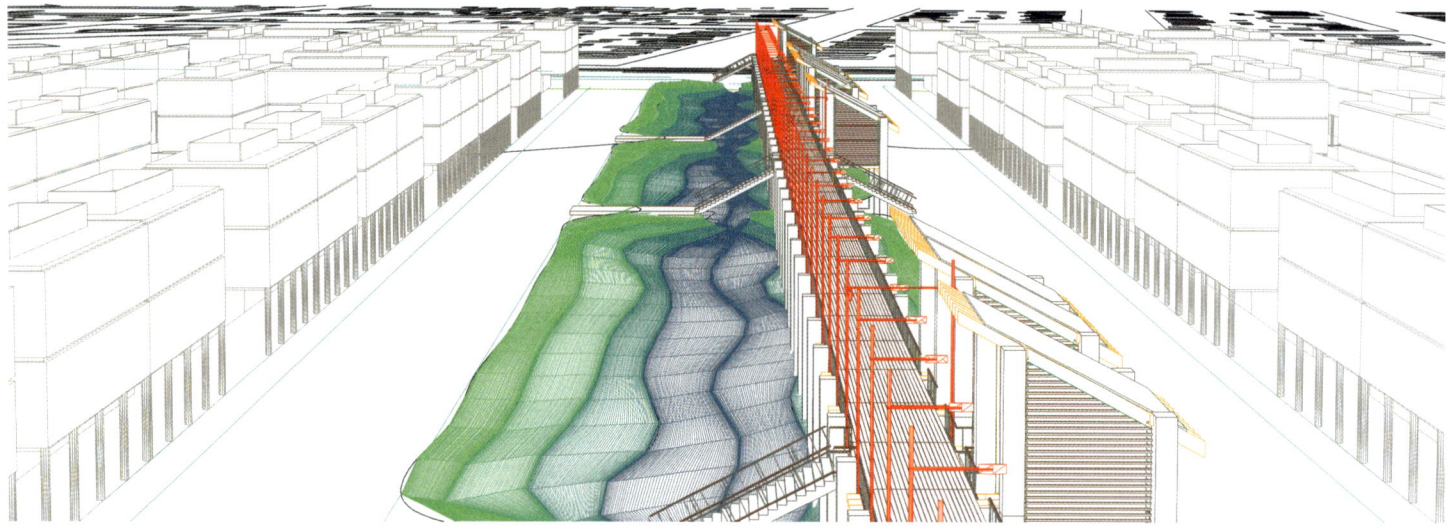

Fig. 117. Arverne. Rendering of retail pier.

Fig. 118. Arverne. Rendering of new boardwalks over dunes.

Qing Huang Dao Park

This project was our entry in an invited competition of five. Although we did not win, the strategy we used has been important to later work. Juxtaposed landscapes, extreme in their differences, some indigenous, some foreign, have been jumbled and mixed to produce intense experiences. They allow for very different kinds of activities and appeal to a wide variety of senses—smell, sight, touch.

The Qing Huang Dao landscape is a very big site at a very exclusive location: 11 million square feet directly on the sea, a prime location 175 miles from Beijing. It will be transformed into a recreational area housing a wide range of sports facilities. The park offers outdoor as well as indoor activities and incorporates cultural and shopping facilities. As the site is immense, it is preferable to have multiple developers and contractors work on it. Therefore, we have created a master plan that divides the site into different zones and parcels. Each of these works independently and is focused on one theme. A system of paths, a walking promenade, and a running track separate the individual parcels and are the basis for exploring the park.

Each parcel houses a building and a unique program. All buildings are integrated into the landscape, preserving spatial continuity. The landscape itself is also specialized, as each parcel is a distinct ecosystem with its own plants and building arrangements.

The basic functional idea places a diverse range of sports in equally diverse landscapes. The landscape employs a strategy of ecological zoning through which parcels are woven together with active recreational programming—by a network of paths and architecture and by the ecological concept of a landscape mosaic. The image of the entire site reads as one landscape but it contains very different landscapes within each part of the mosaic.

The landscape mosaic is composed of six ecological zones: tidal marsh, dune prairie, meadow, red-pine forest, oak woodland, and finally a purely urban landscape of lawn and hard surface. Each landscape is made manifest and linked by paths and trees. Some of the elements of the mosaic are part of the existing local ecology. Others are nonnative and artificial (for example, lawns). Moving among them creates the feeling of being in a number of very different places, so that the site seems much larger and its programmatic potential is maximized.

The division of the parcels and landscape mosaics can take many forms. What we are presenting is not a fixed plan, but one of many possible variations. This flexible arrangement allows the program to change and develop over time.

The contrasts between program and landscape in each parcel enliven the mosaic and create unique public and private spaces, such as a spa in the marsh and a campground in the dunes. The parcels and the landscape mosaics are an innovative model of landscape design and development.

The entrance to the park is from the north side, off the parking area. From there a green lawn surface raises up to a level of twenty feet before dropping down to level zero again. This will guide visitors toward the sea and give them an overview of the park. From here they will decide where to go and which parcel to explore (figs. 119–121).

Part 2   101

Fig. 119. Qing Huang Dao Park, Qing Huang Dao, China, 2004. Plan.

Fig. 120. Qing Huang Dao Park. Diagram showing various planting ecologies.

Fig. 121. Qing Huang Dao Park. Marsh.

121

Accommodating Natural Processes in Cities

Imagine being able to put a Central Park in the center of an already built-up old city. That is the scale of change that the abandonment of ports in cities allows.

The change to container format for cargo has forced many old ports in cities to relocate, making central parts of cities on the water available. Ports and their facilities have become fewer and bigger, no longer able to function where they had been. These areas, though sited downtown and active in the past, were never considered places to go to unless you were going to board a ship. Ports were tough, industrial places and considered unsafe.

But what is critical to this transformation is that it puts the natural functions of water, ignored when these areas were ports, inside cities. It makes ecological processes and events (previously present in the city only in parks) visible, and gives urban dwellers a new opportunity to reconnect with nature. The interest in being on the water, of observing its rhythms, of being able to experience it directly, has made these spaces valuable real estate and an attraction to those who share the increasingly common desire to have access to "nature," particularly in cities. The transformation of these areas is an opportunity to reconnect the city to the water and to other parts of itself; it is an opportunity to design a powerful edge, an ecotone (the area where two or more distinct habitats adjoin) where land meets water. And this edge is the opportunity for new design. In this section we address approaches to the renewal of past artifacts—in this case, ports. In Part 3 we take up the aesthetics of this encounter of water and land.

The nineteenth-century engineering approaches to rivers—damming, channeling, straightening, using hard revetments along the banks, making levees, and so forth—all were implemented in attempts to give the river a fixity which it never had. The new approach to this ecotone, where land and water meet, is one of working with a flexible system in between the two; in some cases returning them to the sinusoidal curves that water forms, in others, perhaps, softening the edges. The key is to create a wide band of public space that works with both river and land. The band's design and construction attempt to approximate the changes in the life cycles and dynamics of streams. This is the essence of the current transformation of these industrial artifacts.[7] **14**

14. Landscape artists can reveal the forces of nature underlying cities, creating a new urban identity from them.

Parque de La Luz

Because the entire port at Las Palmas, on the main island of the Canaries, is to be moved, a competition was held in 2005 for a project to reincorporate the site as part of the city. We teamed with Pelli Clarke Pelli Architects against four other firms (Rafael Moneo, Nicolas Grimshaw, Ben van Berkel, and Kazuyo Seijima + Ruye Nishizawa). We were asked for a comprehensive scheme for the abandoned port, with a new large marina, city hall, museum, and commercial facilities. The area would be joined to the city by burial of a dividing vehicular artery. Our team won. The judges cited the concept of the extension of the green zone, with the botanical garden and floating islands, as the determinant in their decision (fig. 122).

The size of the site, its central position, and its location on an island far off the African continent make this a project that operates on a very large scale. Ocean currents and hot winds carrying sand from the African desert are large geographical forces at work on the site. In addition, there are strong tides and long periods without rain. This forced us to use the very limited palette of plants that can survive under the extremely dry conditions of the island.

The Botanical Garden of Las Palmas has made a virtue out of the lack of water and contains an extraordinary collection of halophytic plants, which we made the backbone of the scheme. Many of them are indigenous to the Canary Islands.

Our design focuses on transforming the nineteenth-century infrastructure and rethinking the civic possibilities of this area while making the most of its sea edge. Like most ports, its rigid, straight-lined geometry creates many dead spots that accumulate flotsam. Piercing existing piers, we proposed a system of water circulation that uses the current to clean the water trapped in the port by making it move through plantings introduced on the edges. Separate channels at opposite ends of the marina directed flow-through currents toward the center of the marina. This diminished future costs by protecting the bulkhead structures from water erosion.

The narrow band of interface between sea and land was created to improve the quality of the water by filling the straight angles of the bulkhead, which would normally accumulate sediment, to create floating islands of vegetation. These bands of vegetation were in direct contact with the daily changes of the tides, forming diverse biological communities that contribute to the health of the water by oxygenating it and absorbing pollutants.

The surface of the park was mounded to produce three systems of circulation, protecting visitors and vegetation from dry northeasterly and easterly winds. Each path was planted according to its distinct ecosystem and corresponding plant community: halophytic plants in the coastal zone, vegetated dunes in the center zone, and thermophytic forest farther in. The gray water of the project's new buildings was gathered for irrigation. The design of the many small shore pavilions around the basin was based on the effects of the prevailing easterly wind, suggesting forms distorted by its action. The hills, along with the distant line of the wharf and the pedestrian bridge, created a continuous undulating scene.

The park created a remarkable postcard image of Las Palmas for the boats coming in to anchor in its marina.

The political party of the mayor of Las Palmas, who launched this project, lost the last elections, and the opposition party now governs the Canaries. Since projects in Spain generally are attached to political parties, this change has made it more difficult for the project to proceed, even though, as we know from the experiences of more than a century, real estate constructed around a park acquires an immense added value (figs. 123–129).

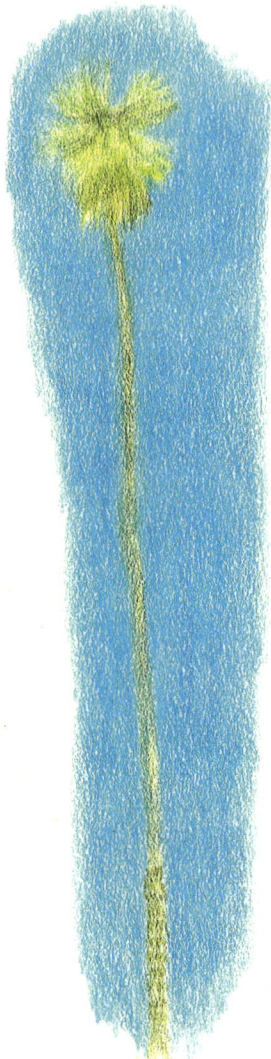

122

Fig. 122. Colored-pencil sketch of palm tree as inspiration for Parque de la Luz.

Fig. 123. Parque de la Luz, Las Palmas, Gran Canaria, Spain, 2005. Plan showing proposed ground contours.

124

Fig. 124. Parque de la Luz. Photocollage showing proposed connectivity port/park and city.

Fig. 125. Parque de la Luz.

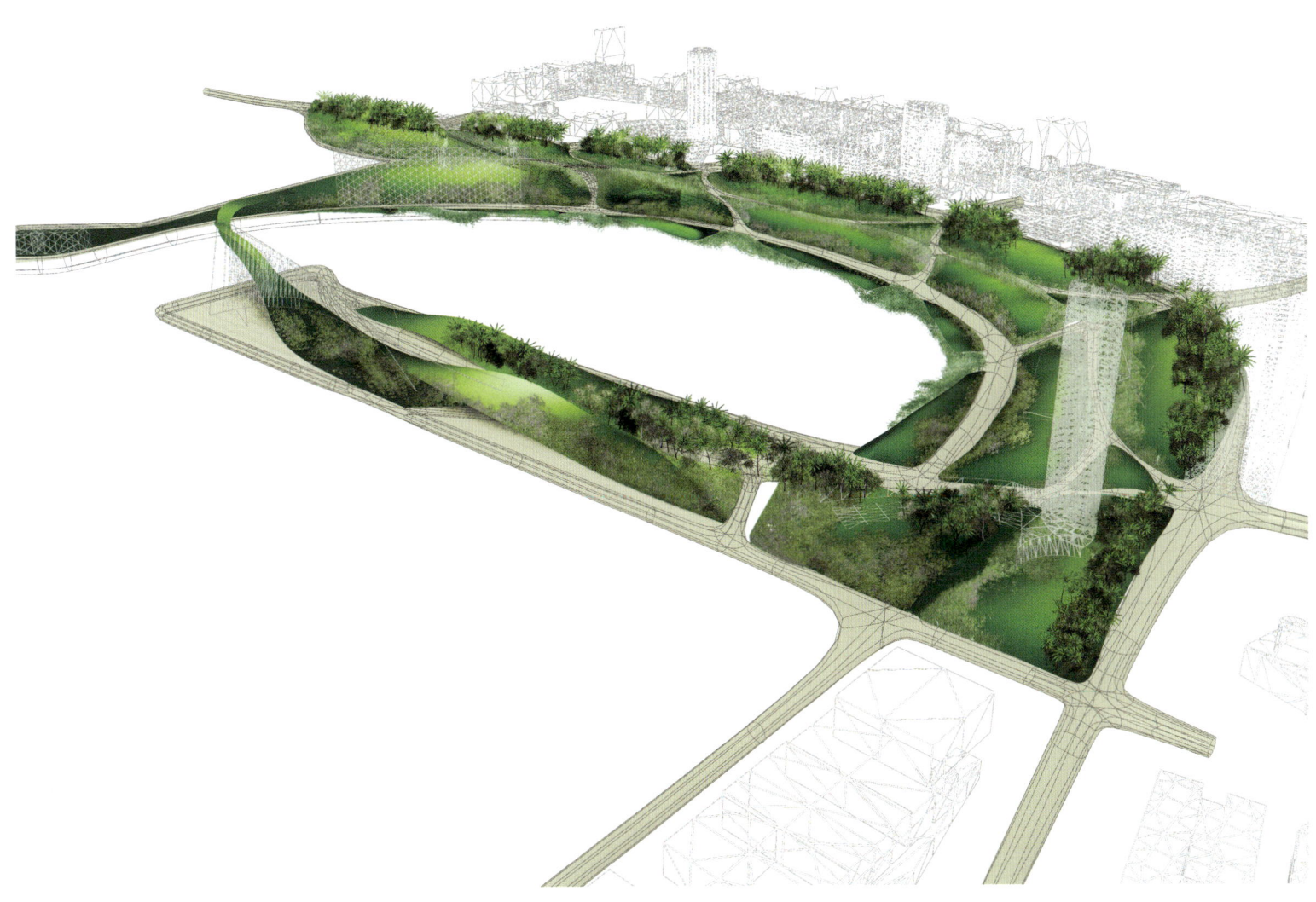

126

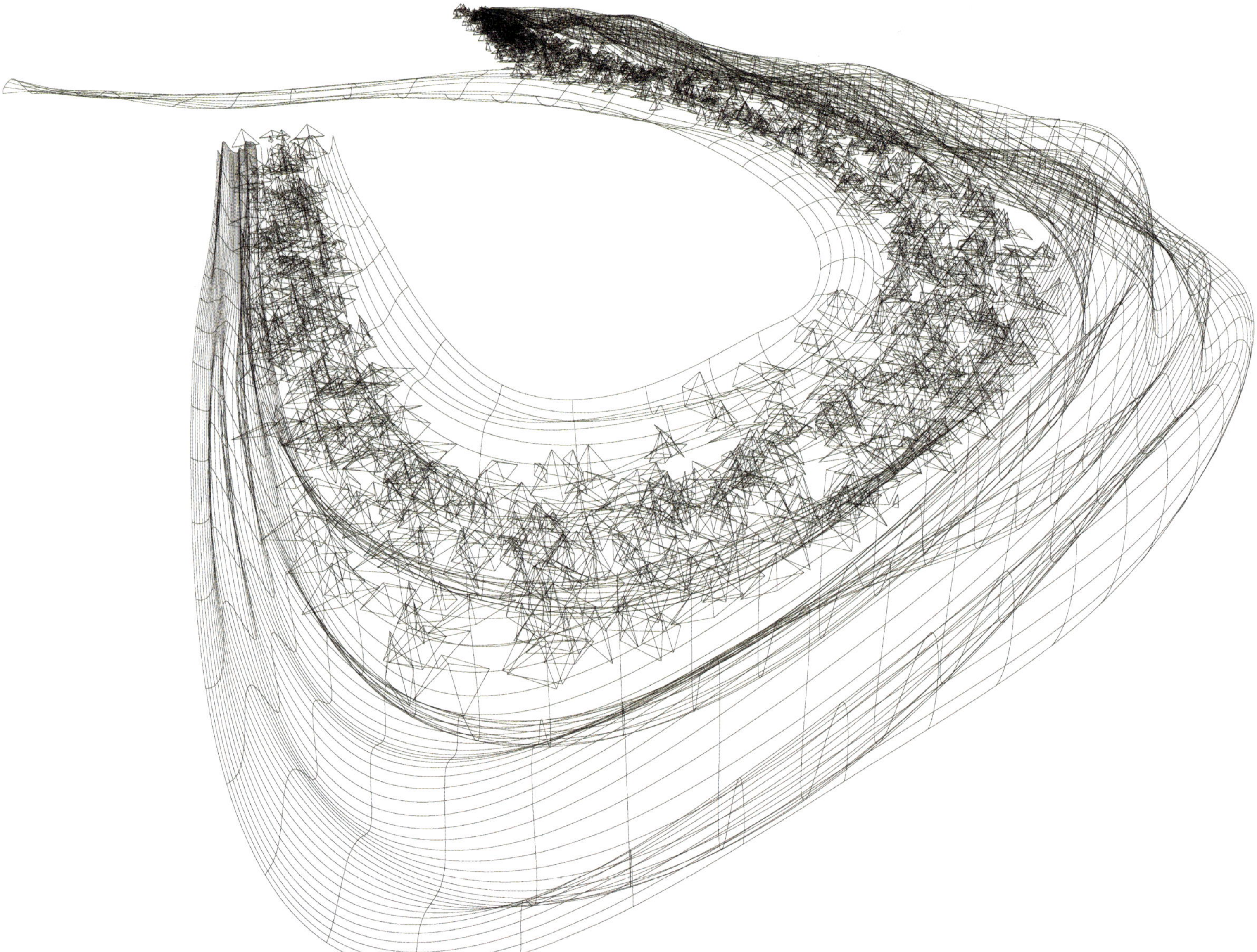

127

128

129

Fig. 126. Parque de la Luz. Sections.

Fig. 127. Parque de la Luz. Wire-frame volumetric study.

Fig. 128. Parque de la Luz. Sections.

Fig. 129. Parque de la Luz.

Memphis Riverfront: Beale Street Landing

Begun in 2003, this project was our first encounter with the Mississippi River (fig. 130). It was the result of an international competition won by the architecture firm RTN, which had proposed a public space comprising a café, a ticket booth, a series of "trays" looking out on the river, and a floating pier for Mississippi tourist boats. Some of these trays would be covered with water in spring, when the river runs high. The architects asked us to create programs, plantings, and public spaces adaptable to the changing water levels. We developed a scheme of interpreting these trays as islands of public space, and joined them by bridges; we terraced the areas around the trays and connected the terraces by steps and a ramp.

The project—on which construction began in 2007—was seen as a waterside public venue and the grand finale to Beale Street, the famous boulevard in Memphis, where blues music was born and still holds sway. The waterfront would provide space for those who played in the many venues along Beale Street to hold public concerts and festivals. The islands and terraces would accommodate audiences for large events. The islands were developed as lightly programmed public space shaded by trees. One was dedicated as a concert area for players and a small group of listeners or dancers. This music island, used mainly at night, has a hard, treeless surface.

Water was the first and most important determinant of the design; the second was shade, essential in Memphis' blistering sun and heat. The changing water levels provide the opportunity to plant each island according to how often it is under water. The lowest level, most often under water, could be left to develop vegetation from volunteers—material, seeds, and twigs brought by the river. A few willow twigs could start the process by providing something to slow the water down and catch additional material. The second level could have plants that can endure being submerged for less time, and so on. The specific choices for plants for each island level were calculated risks in this inevitably varying land-versus-water environment.

The design creates a riverside place that—far from being self-explanatory, as a functional building or space would be—creates a sense of the unexpected that demands interpretation. It will be the privilege of local users and visitors to construct a narrative that makes sense of this place, highlighting the variegated action of the river and the flow of music history in Memphis.

The great spectacle of this project comes from its being a multifaceted artifact transformed with each change of water level. This is a public space defined by the waters of the Mississippi, and is part of them, a first step toward working with a new concept of nature and the thick edge (figs. 131–134). **15**

15. Landscape can create meeting places where people can delight in unexpected forms and spaces, inventing why and how they are to be appreciated.

Part 2 114

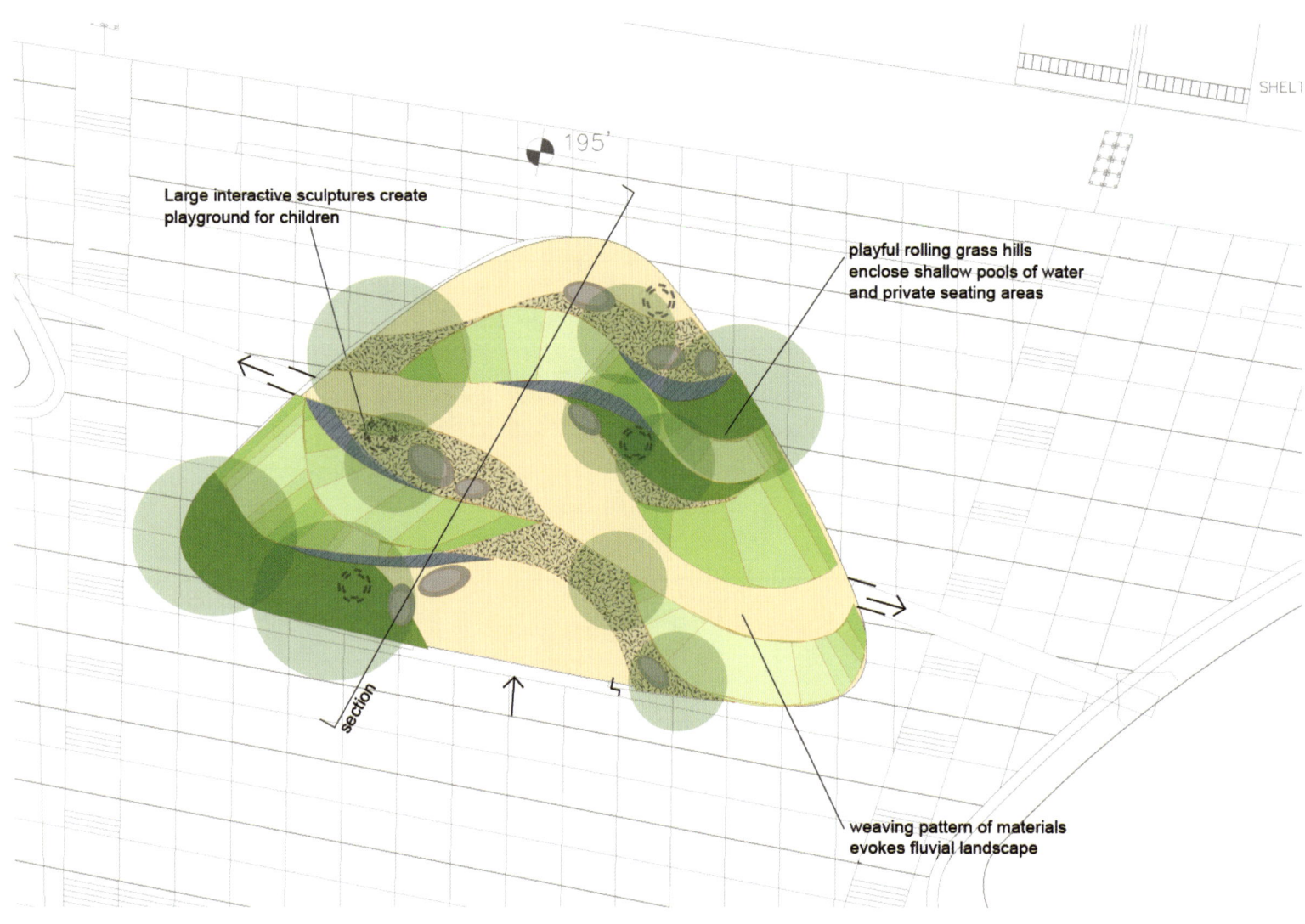

Fig. 130. Beale Street Landing, Memphis, in progress. Plan showing occupiable tiers.

131

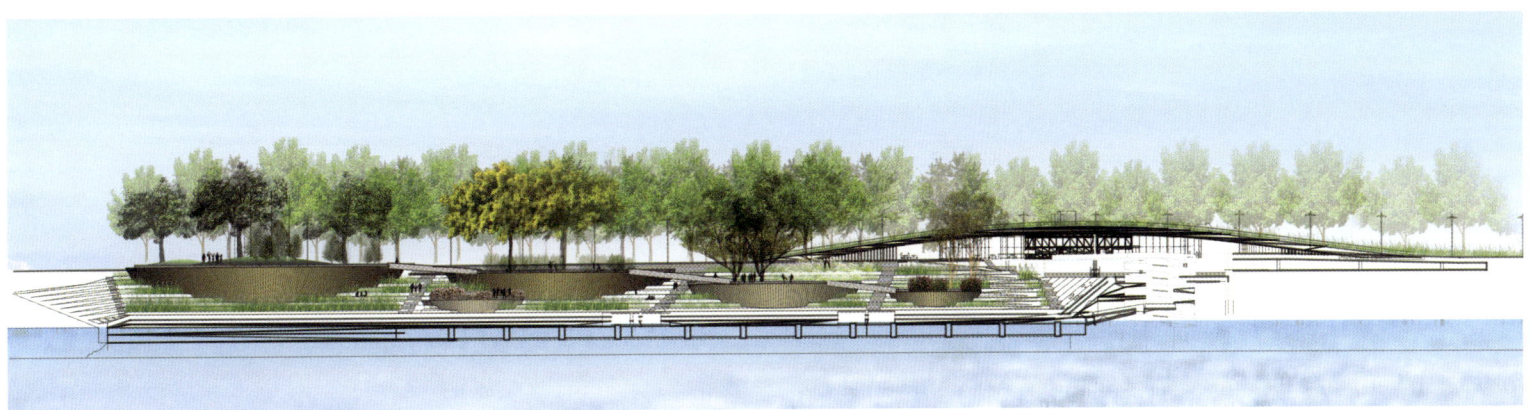

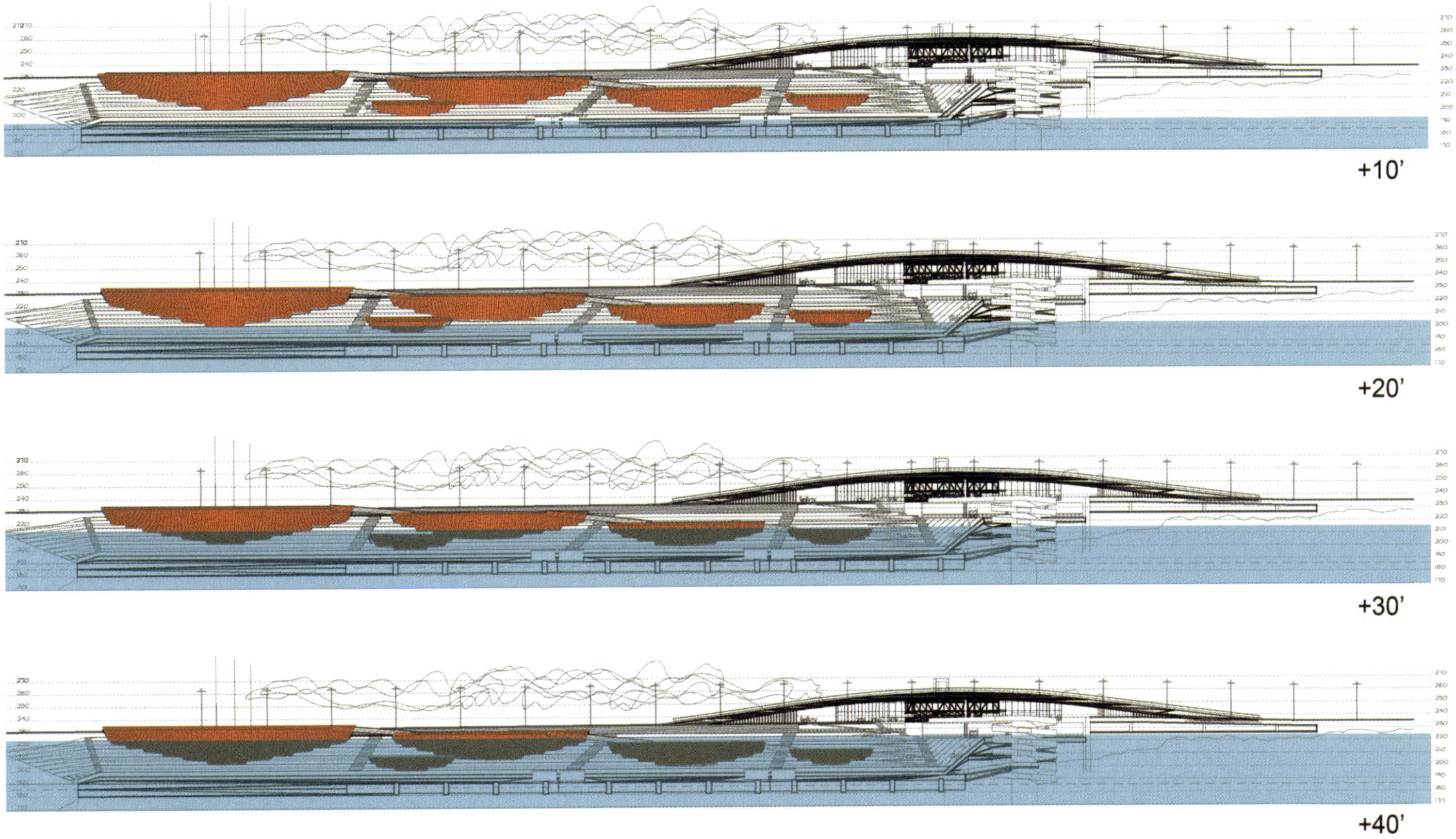

132

Fig. 131. Beale Street Landing. Elevation.

Fig. 132. Beale Street Landing. Elevation showing changing water levels.

270
260
250
240
230
220
210
200
190
180
170

133

gathering
viewing
wetland garden
children's play
event seating
performance
wetland garden

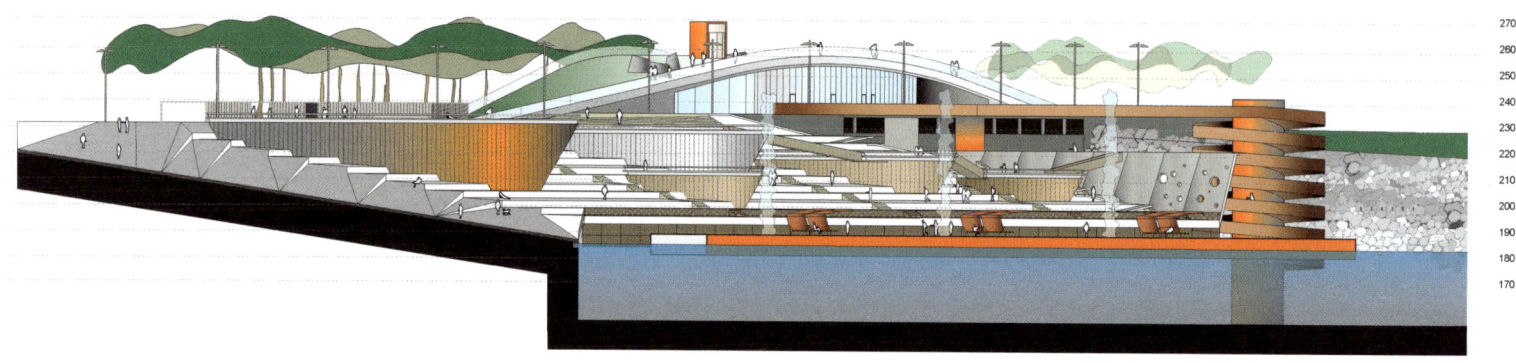

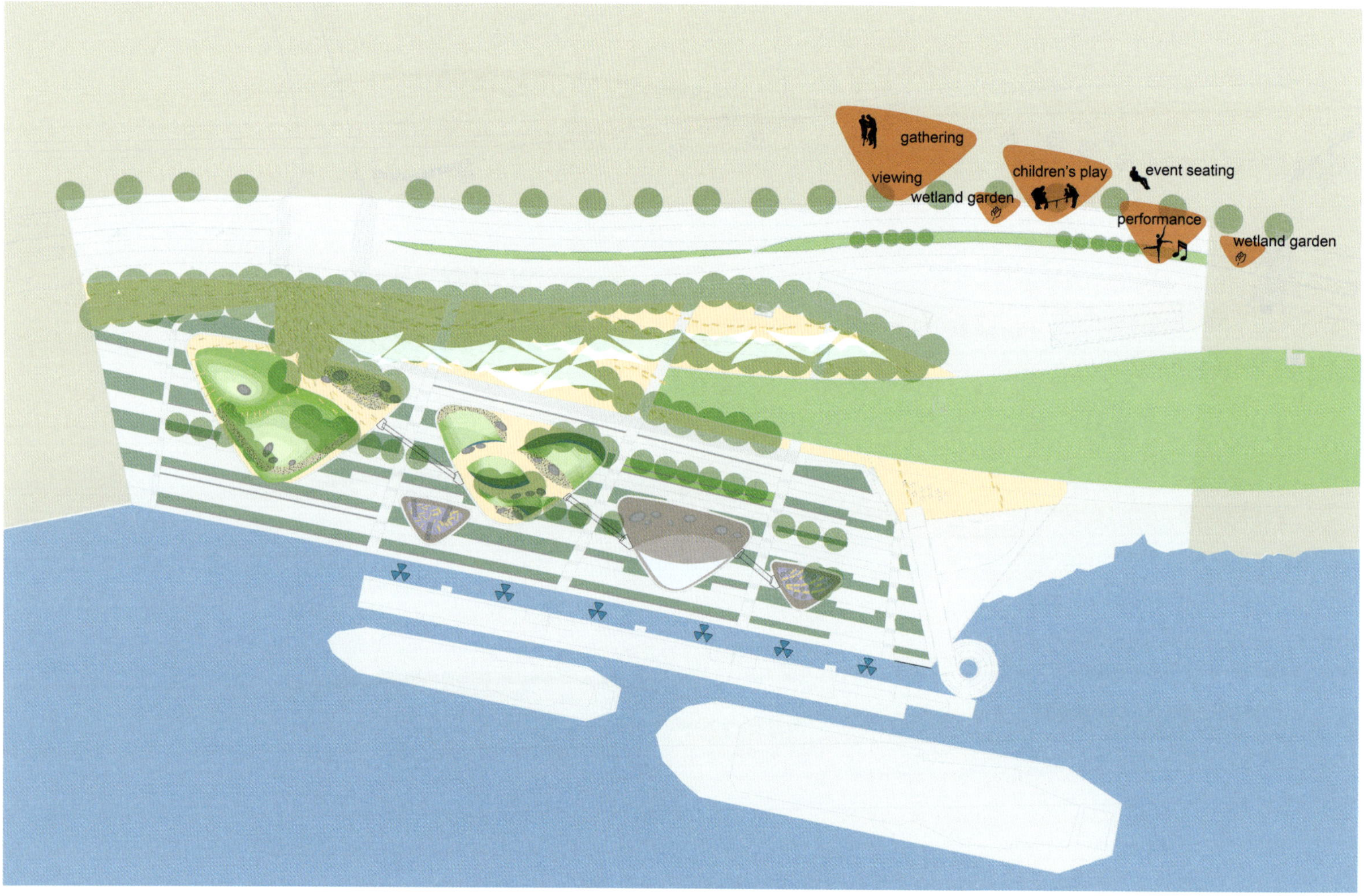

134

Making Temporary Landscapes

Temporary landscapes are appearing because our understanding of ecology has made us more sensitive to and interested in change—nature's essential trait. Temporary landscapes touch on two inherent aspects of landscape: the constant changes in living material (linear) and in annual conditions (cyclical). Although not immediately obvious, motion is also a dimension of this temporality. Two kinds of motion are implied: that of a spectator passing through a landscape (and I believe no landscape can be understood without considering this) and that of the landscape itself (for example, a river rising and falling). Smithson's Floating Island, a landscape traveling around Manhattan, is another instance of this second kind of motion.

Of course, all landscapes are temporary; everything around us is. Even houses rise and fall. But there are different degrees of temporality. Some landscapes are temporary by design: the viewing fence around Ground Zero, which will be removed when the construction planned for the site is completed, for example (figs. 135, 136); or the temporary landscape built on a derelict site in Brooklyn, until the site is used for another, more permanent, project.

Still another aspect of temporality is how quickly a designed landscape disappears when it ceases to be used. Landscape's fragility is enormous; fewer historical landscapes have survived than historical buildings. Preserving landscape is a much more difficult enterprise, because it is constantly changing; unlike a building, a landscape is not a fixed entity. **16**

Though each of the three projects described here had a quite different aim, they were intentionally designed to have only a very brief life. This clearly defined end exposes landscape's temporality and enlarges it to take over the project.

Landscape as an art is not just three-dimensional. It has a fourth dimension, which is time. The relation of landscape to time goes even beyond the cyclical or the linear: landscape is always in the process of becoming. It exists in time just as we do, and only in time can we capture it. Time's most difficult dimension is the challenging concept of the world of nature—and ourselves in it—as one in which all the parts are constantly changing.

The category of temporary landscape has a special place in the work of my office because it accentuates time as a design factor, making that most essential of landscape traits more obvious and visible. After spending part of the twentieth century decrying landscape's relatively unfinished status vis-à-vis architecture, and the concomitant absence of the inauguration hoopla that marks the completion of architectural projects, we must now celebrate the constantly changing environments set in motion with the creation of a landscape. That continuous transformation is one dimension of its temporality. Another is that this ever-changing scenario makes it an art of performance. Put it on stage and roll it off. Make it for a night, week, month. Take a bow and go.

It is this latter dimension that occupies a favored niche. It appeared all by itself when I designed a landscape for *A Midsummer Night's Dream* in Central Park's open-air Delacorte Theater, in the summer of 1982, for Heidi Landesman, the set designer. This sort of project is pure play—fast, fun, and like a new toy to enjoy. All of our temporary projects have had this as their dominant quality. Being ephemeral makes them light and joyful. And then they are gone. Their short lives, the faster process of designing them, makes them stand apart, separate from the other projects in the office and in this book.

Fig. 133. Beale Street Landing. Elevation and section.

Fig. 134. Beale Street Landing. Plan.

135

136

Fig. 135. Viewing fence surrounding World Trade Center site, New York. Model.

Fig. 136. Viewing fence surrounding World Trade Center site.

16. A landscape, like a moment, never happens twice. This lack of fixity is landscape's asset.

Smithson's Floating Island, New York

Minetta Brook, a public art organization under the leadership of Diane Shamash, and the Whitney Museum of American Art, presented the project called *Robert Smithson's Floating Island to Travel Around Manhattan Island*. Although not realized during Smithson's lifetime, the island was built on a thirty-by-ninety-foot barge—landscaped with earth, rocks, native trees, and shrubs—towed by tugboat around the island of Manhattan. The design was based on the only drawing he left behind for this project. The fabricated "island" was on view from September 17 to 25, 2005, visible to millions of residents, commuters, and visitors along the Hudson and East Rivers.

Smithson, a major figure in the cultural landscape of the 1960s and 1970s, developed the concept for Floating Island in 1970—the same year he created his best-known work, the ambitious earthwork Spiral Jetty at Utah's Great Salt Lake—but his efforts to realize the project then were unsuccessful. Probably an homage to Frederick Law Olmsted's design of Central Park, Floating Island offers a displacement of the park—itself a man-made creation—from its natural habitat. When the barge finally made its trip around the island of Manhattan, New Yorkers had a chance to see a reimagined fragment of their island floating by.

We were brought in to make the project a reality by constructing a landscape on a barge. The temporal quality of the project was a good match with our interests, as was the fact that it was a landscape in motion. The basic earthy details of making a park out of a barge appealed to us, too. Nancy Holt, the artist's widow, came in at each stage to see that Smithson's idea was interpreted correctly. The hardest part turned out to be that the project, planned for spring, was delayed until fall because of the slow pace of fundraising. As a result, there was considerable shedding of (colorful) leaves from the Floating Island's trees over the week that the barge traveled around Manhattan. We made sure that everybody understood that this was part of the lack of fixity inherent to landscape and that there was the possibility that no leaves whatsoever would be left by the end of the week.

Floating Island was presented in conjunction with a retrospective of the work of Smithson at the Whitney. He remains a central influence on contemporary artists and on my own work (figs. 137–143).

Fig. 137. Concept for *Robert Smithson's Floating Island to Travel Around Manhattan Island*, 1970.

Fig. 138. *Robert Smithson's Floating Island to Travel Around Manhattan Island*, New York, 2006. Planting plan and contour section.

Overleaf:
Fig. 139. *Robert Smithson's Floating Island to Travel Around Manhattan Island*.

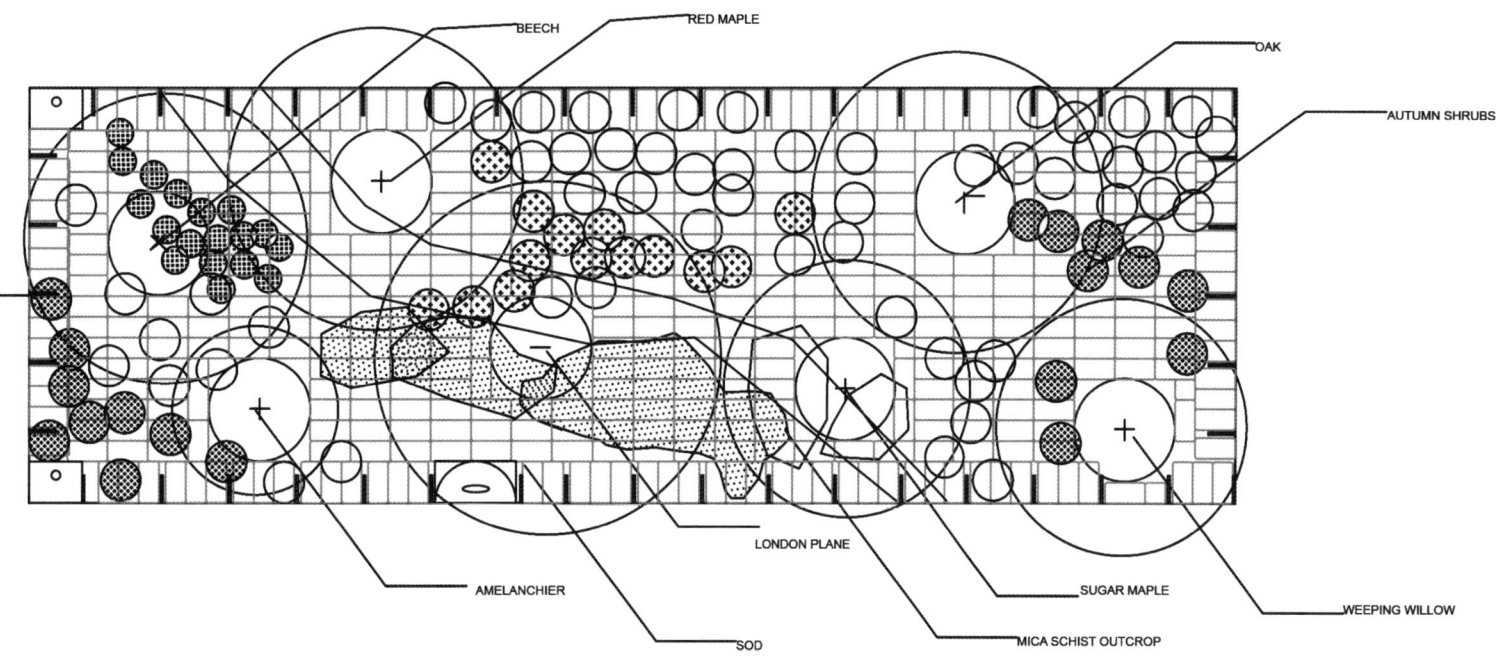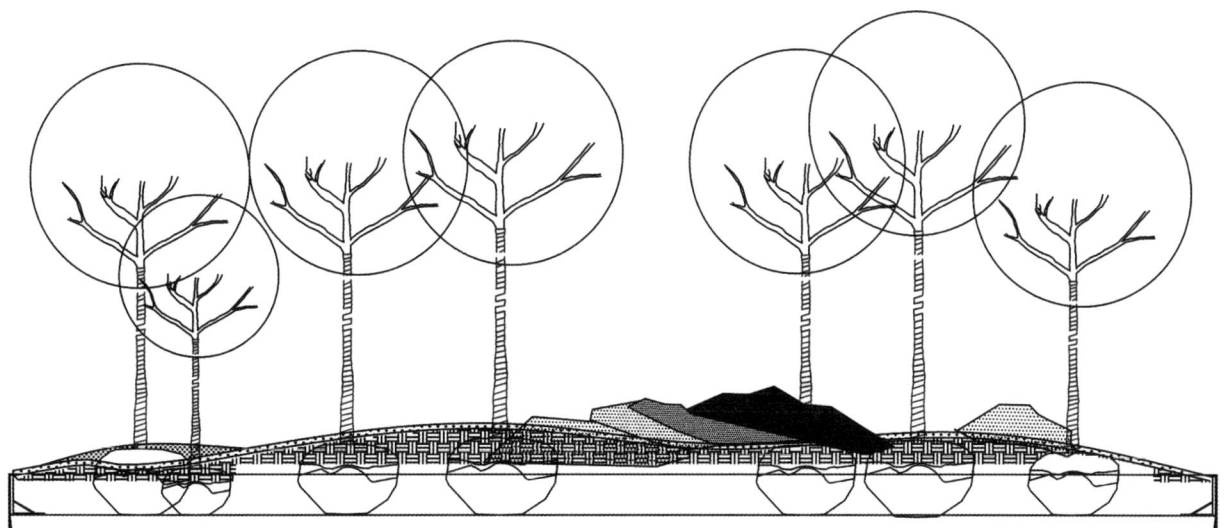

140

Figs. 140–142. Robert Smithson's Floating Island to Travel Around Manhattan Island.

Overleaf:
Fig. 143. Robert Smithson's Floating Island to Travel Around Manhattan Island. Rendering (as part of an initiative to reinvent ways of representing landscape).

141

142

Skid Rows, Queens Museum of Art

Skid Rows was a submission I made, together with Brian Tolle, to a competition, organized by the Queens Art Museum, for the creation of a two-acre urban garden; altogether, ten artists were selected for the project, which was to be a collection of gardens as an expression of contemporary art (fig. 144).

Our first impulse was to think of ways to make the space truly public, something that people could participate in. A spectacle? A witnessing of the making of it? That was the start. We also wanted it to be fun for us and for others. When we came up with planting as an event, beer and hamburgers followed. Tolle and I took turns careening and doing donuts around Queens Botanical Gardens in a truck dropping seeds and "drawing" a flower garden that would blossom into a trail of red poppies and yellow tickweed in time for an exhibition called *Down the Garden Path* opening later that summer. The final form of the garden derived from the loops and tracks laid down randomly by us as drivers of a red 1991 Chevy Silverado pickup truck. Through his hybrid performance and earthwork, we planted an unusual flower garden—and a work of public art.

We didn't go about this by saying that we were going to join our respective arts, sculpture and landscape. We work in different media. Though landscape too often is confused with horticulture or ecology, it is a topographic art. But it is distinct from sculpture as an art, and we each held our ground.

Ecology is embedded in our project: planting without plowing. Plowing can be seen as destructive, breaking the soil's structure and resulting in soil erosion. Therefore, we used direct seeding instead. The ecology here enabled us to come up with new forms. We started by looking at vehicles commonly used for planting, such as tractors, and retrofitted similar seeding equipment to a second-hand truck. Putting flowers on the chassis was the final touch. And we researched seeds (poppy, tickweed, and cosmos) that would provide strong lines of colors for the planting.

We both had fun with it. The driving was a lark; we carried spectators who wanted to go through the rough ride with us. Neither of us had a preconceived notion about how we would drive and what patterns we would make. I thought in terms of landscape patterns and "parterres de broderie"; Brian thought about line drawings in the history of art. The visibility of the lines of planting occurred both at eye-level

144

145

Fig. 144. Skid Rows, Queens, New York, 2005. Detail from exhibition animation.

Fig. 145. Skid Rows.

and from above, since the proximity of LaGuardia Airport made the planting pattern visible to those in planes.

For Tolle the idea was in large part born out of off-roading and cutting donuts. We talked a lot about the conflict between having a good old time and protecting the environment. We fused our concerns to create a vehicle that would satisfy both aims at the same time. In pairing urban garden and rural planter, we had lengthy discussions about high versus low culture and the negative perceptions of each by the other, of the aesthetics of the beat-up truck as opposed to the elegant lines of the planting.

Once I began driving, I saw that making curves was easy and that the more that curving lines cut across each other, the richer the pattern became. The wheels of the truck felt each ripple of the land. Every slight rise or dip registered. I felt the totality of the field and the relations among the trees; it was like dancing in a field defined by trees, with the definitions constantly changing as I moved among them. The high came from having a directionless field rather than a road before me.

With a more critical and distant view I can see that, though we created Skid Rows for the fun of it, the project also seemed to be just right in terms of landscape in two important dimensions. Motion is landscape's most critical dimension. In spite of the lengthy history of landscapes being designed as landscape paintings—that is, from a fixed point of view—landscape has four dimensions, not just three, the fourth being time, as mentioned above. In landscape, displacement through space and time is essential.

In sum, Skid Rows transformed the meaning of many known activities. It made the planting a public event. It turned an object (a garden) into an action (planting). It transformed the transgressing joyride into constructive action. That action took on an unfamiliar form, direct seeding (rather than plowing), and so established a new possible model for sustainable seeding. In May 2008, Brian Tolle and I performed Skid Rows for the opening of Mildred's Lane, an artists' colony in Pennsylvania (figs. 145–148).

147

148

Figs. 146–148. Skid Rows.

Urban Meadow, Brooklyn, New York

For this temporary landscapes lab, we worked with XS Space, the studio of one of our former designers, Julie Farris, who had investigated abandoned spaces in New York. We put together a simple proposal: grassing an eight-thousand-square-foot rectangular urban space with two kinds of Freedom Lawn, one a mix of grasses and clover, the other a mix of grasses and wildflowers. A few flowering trees complete the planting of this rubble-strewn lot (fig. 149).

The densely populated community in which this project is sited had no open space until this first landscape opened, in the summer of 2008. It was made possible by some private funding and the backing of the New York City Department of Parks and Recreation. Two large signs at the entrance to the space enumerate the environmental effects of greening it. We asked Columbia University's Center for Climate Studies to quantify these benefits, and they gave us data on the site's increased capacity to absorb stormwater runoff, offset carbon emissions, and create a cooler microclimate. This information was placed on the site as a way of making its positive impact explicit.[8]

Though it was initially conceived as a temporary landscape, the project had such enormous support from the community that the Parks Department adopted it under the auspices of its Community Garden "Green Thumb" program. Now that it has been designed and installed by our office and XS Space, the park will be maintained by local residents (figs. 150–153). **17**

17. We can heighten the desire for new interactions between humans and nature where it is least expected: in derelict spaces.

149

150

151

Fig. 149. Urban Meadow, Brooklyn, 2008. Detail of first planting.

Fig. 150. Urban Meadow. Site before design.

Fig. 151. Urban Meadow. Plan.

152

153

Fig. 152. Urban Meadow.

Fig. 153. Urban Meadow. Final recovered community space.

Straddling Borders: Jordan River Peace Park

Peace Parks are sites that include land on both sides of a disputed border. They are emerging in Africa and Asia, perhaps because many new nations came into being on those continents during the twentieth century. New nations spend much of their first century of life settling borders. New borders are fungible. A Peace Park is a new landscape form, made by war and mired in politics. Its emergence creates an area where people with agendas that transcend conflict can meet and work together.

Peace Parks bear the mark of their time. They spring up mostly when nations are young and relatively weak, allowing a transnational entity to emerge.[9] Ecological NGOs most often initiate them.

Another mark of their time is that they carry an ecological agenda: to become a conservation zone, a kind of sanctuary, particularly for local flora and fauna decimated by war. Even mortal enemies share a goal of protecting a nation's ecology. Therefore, Peace Parks, whatever else they *can* be, play significant roles as ecological conservators and peaceful intermediaries.

A proposed Israeli-Jordanian Peace Park provides a concrete example of this new landscape. The area was set up as a Trans-Boundary Protected Area in the Israel-Jordan Peace Treaty of 1994. The NGO Friends of the Earth Middle East (FOEME), led by its creator Gidon Bromberg, obtained a memorandum of understanding between local government authorities for the park. When Bromberg was a World Fellow at Yale, he asked the Yale School of Architecture for a short on-site design effort to get it started. Israeli, Jordanian, and Palestinian professionals joined us. This is a report from the front.

We walked the site and worked together for four days. The temperature hovered around 100 degrees. There was only an outside privy on the work site. The group worked well together and received enthusiastic support from the mayors of the surrounding towns, two Israeli and two Jordanian.

The 750-acre site for the Peace Park has a barbed-wire fence around it and a Jordanian military force on it. Mines have just been removed. Its bordering rivers are depleted and sewage-laden. But the site is on the Jordan River in the Great Rift Valley, where the continental plates of Asia and Africa meet. It is also where the Jordan and the Yarmouk Rivers meet, and where ancient texts place the gates of the Garden of Eden. It is on the largest migratory course for birds flying from the tip of Africa to northern Europe, and the wetlands that were on this site serve as a respite for flocks on their journey.

Our proposals for the site included looking for a geothermal energy source in the Great Rift Valley; collecting the sewage from the four surrounding towns (now emptied into the Jordan) and using a low-tech system (for example, Eco Machine) to clean it anaerobically, transforming the sewage water into gray water; creating a lake in the Peace Park, where plants finish cleaning the gray water, which supports the migrating bird population; converting the ruins of workers' housing into eco lodges and using them as a model for sustainable local housing; leaving an abandoned dam as an industrial ruin in a river and wetland park; and changing the existing water-intensive agriculture to arid agriculture. It is only a beginning.

Never has a landscape been so much a part of the warp and weave of politics (figs. 154–157).[10] **18**

Fig. 154. Jordan River Peace Park, Israel/Jordan/Palestine, 2008. Remnants of Roman bridge on site.

18. Emerging landscapes are becoming brand-new actors on the political stage.

Fig. 155. Jordan River Peace Park. Map showing major bird flyway.

156

157

Fig. 156. Jordan River Peace Park. Map showing water crisis in region.

Fig. 157. Jordan River Peace Park. Map showing the Rift Valley.

Conclusion: Searching for the Present

The importance of the city in contemporary landscape design has been mentioned throughout the text, but it took time for the projects in the office to become more city-centric. The city became the main object of our work gradually, as it became clearer to us that even the smallest projects—a lawn or a green roof—became much more revealing when envisioned on a citywide scale. When Herb Bormann, an ecologist and a colleague of mine at Yale, was conducting research on acid rain, he found that the watershed (a divide separating two water catchment areas) was the geographical unit that revealed the presence of acid rain.[11] His example led me to search constantly for the appropriate scale in which to work. The city is the unit in which most contemporary landscapes become visible. For example, a study of green roofs taken to the scale of the whole of Long Island City showed that a green surface the size of Prospect Park could be created without the city or homeowners having to acquire land. At that scale you understand the real potential of green roofs.

Undoubtedly, work on this scale has become increasingly prevalent partly because of the transformation of our view of the city. Many writers attest to this, but Ann Spirn, in *The Granite Garden: Urban Nature and Human Design,* made the best case for it.[12] We have ceased to see the city as an industrial entity existing outside of nature; we need to reverse our strategy of nature in the city and instead pursue a strategy of the city in nature.[13] While in the past we simply inserted a park here and there, now we will work to make the city as porous as possible, gathering the waters that fall on it and the waters from rivers and reservoirs into a recoverable asset. The new strategy will also involve reducing the urban heat island through fifth façades; cleaning water before it enters rivers by making it journey through green systems; making many streets into green corridors; making public transportation the most desirable way for people to travel, a pleasure rather than a punishment; having air not fouled by gasoline; and creating a place to experience other parts of nature.

The shift of the world's population to cities, along with the deleterious state of most nineteenth-century industrial water, sewage, and energy infrastructure, has made the city an urgent—indeed, the most urgent—place to address the fundamental change in outlook and systems that we need to undertake.

Of course, the leap to a citywide perspective brings with it a much more complicated clientele and a dramatic entry into political and real-estate interests. At this scale, landscape has to enter, for the first time, a conflict-ridden arena of competing interests; for such projects, a single client in reality consists of several different agencies. The greatest initial difficulty is deducing the real agenda of each of these entities. The second task is learning which will prevail. For example, in our present work in Shanghai's French Concession, the client is both the Shanghai City Planning Office (for a park) and the Shanghai Media Ministry (for a theater to be sited in the park). As a result, the proportion of parkland to theater site has been changed many times. Though the competition brief stated that 70 percent of the surface should be park and 30 percent theater, once we won the competition the allotment for the park area shrank steadily.

Thus the city, as the object of landscape, changes the way landscape designers work, requiring complex alliances and crowdsourcing.

As part of the transformations being sought, landscape work at city scale also requires the engagement of a diverse public, which will in turn make possible a new relationship between human beings and nature. This engagement is already under way, and it will gather speed through urban experiences that trigger the collective imagination. Those affective experiences need to be expressed through aesthetics, the subject of Part 3.

Landscapes from our immediate industrial past and landscapes from our more distant past were all human cultural interactions with nature. They represented the particular understanding of nature of their respective eras. The transformation of landscapes we have seen in this section are similarly a response to our own time's view of nature.[14]

The concept of constructing nature opens the door to a new cultural interface with it. This is the interface that questions the lawn and demands that we transform our cultural interaction with it. We may not want to call this change progress. We continually insert our culture in different ways into the world to achieve new understandings.

Through machines, the work of the Industrial Era released and harnessed forms of energy with powers that exceeded the physical capabilities of animals or people and revealed principles of nature that had not been readily evident before. Our excesses in the use of that energy were also revealed, as some of our actions impoverished and damaged the life of the entire earth. Our culture in the late twentieth century redefined nature, and the "natural" was modified accordingly.

This modification has brought about transformations to our physical space and has pushed landscape to the fore as the discipline of our time. Landscape is no longer merely a visually pleasing background. It is not a picture. It is a living, changing enterprise, with us as active agents deeply woven into it. This constantly evolving nature now confronts Kant's concept of beauty as a fixed state. That confrontation is the subject of Part 3. **19**

19. Landscape renders the city as constantly evolving in response to climate, geography, and history.

Interweaving Architecture, Landscape, and City

3

Interface

Interface is the area between landscape and architecture, and by extension between nature and culture. The concept was created to make connections between them.

Slashing apart architecture and landscape is the modern movement's twentieth-century invention. Looking back from our 2008 perch, we see it more clearly than in its own time. The modern movement's invention is basically an object (architecture) standing on a flat plain (landscape). A five-foot DMZ separates the two. Nothing may interfere with the object, the architecture.

The early twentieth century was a heroic moment in which architecture tore itself away from everything. Sculpture, painting, landscape—all were cut off from architecture's tectonic shelf.

An abstracted, cleaner, objectified architecture emerged. Of the other arts, only painting entered the fray for the modern—sculpture did so much later, veering away from representation. Landscape went into a long sleep, with occasional attempts to become "modern," aping architecture's tectonic model.

This reinvention of architecture was a colossal, brute effort of disconnection. Our effort now goes in the opposite direction, seeking reconnection.

The aesthetic concentration on the juncture—the interface—is new. The concept of interface was jointly developed by me and architect Joel Sanders in a Yale School of Architecture Advanced Studio over the last few years. The idea was then taken into our individual practices in landscape and architecture, respectively, and also to some joint projects.

A known architecture-and-landscape historical example can help to explain the way interface can work. Though the interface metaphor is new to our time, there are good historical examples of interface. I will describe a passage in a historical example, the Shugaku-in Imperial Villa in Kyoto, to make the idea concrete. Buildings in the villa are sited to view the landscape: the upper teahouse is placed to get a *Shakkei* view of mountains. Shakkei means layered. Nine layers of mountain can be seen from the front veranda of the upper teahouse. These are passages between the architecture and the landscape. Beyond these there is a wide and layered passage from the exterior to the interior of this teahouse. You approach the teahouse from a graveled courtyard, over stepping-stones that increase in frequency as you near the stone where you step up to take off your shoes and which is under the eaves of the building. After this stone, you step up to a lower wooden veranda, completely open (no screens), followed by a second veranda, this one with sliding screens. Five steps of passage. This example stands in contrast to the abrupt cut of the modern movement between the sealed building and the surrounding landscape.

The concept of interface extends to the juncture between nature and culture. Sustainability has brought us face to face with the reality of having followed a cultural path, since the eighteenth century, that ignores its effects on nature. A connection between them that sustains both is urgently needed. A dramatic change in their relationship needs to be fostered by the connection, a connection that needs to make that new relationship visible. This means developing an aesthetic language that deals with this juncture.

Aesthetics

Above all, interface brings us to a place in which we need to deal with aesthetics. The transformation that our new relation with nature brings about affects form directly.

Aesthetics is not about w of pollution, or about the creation of another fixed landscape picture, or about new technology. Aesthetics is not a frill but a necessity: a form of engagement for the people who use the spaces described here. It can connect people to nature in a new way, changing their experience of it. It can be a response to the new content.

Wrapping new landscape designs in old forms is a failure. Doing so hides the story and the demands of a present in which a paradigm shift has occurred. The two different designs for the stormwater park in Minnesota, presented in Part 2, are pertinent. The first design shows that because of its naturelike form, the true meaning of the project—the creation of a new form for draining and cleaning water—has been ignored and forgotten. The park is enjoyed as a pleasurable landscape—a bonus for the inhabitants—but its true nature is not understood. On the other hand, the second design's mechanical system, adapted from cranberry bogs, was valuable in giving evident expression to this transformed landscape. It made the workings of the water management system visible, important at this moment of transition.

Having shed both a teleological view of nature (that is, that nature is moving toward a fixed end) and a fixed notion of beauty, we find ourselves in new territory.

New form is a way of engaging people in imagining a transformed space, landscape, or city. Without the visibility of these new forms, neither a transformation nor a new engagement with nature can occur. With new forms we are able to engender a new relation with nature.

An example of this issue of form is the Farmington Canal, in New Haven, Connecticut, discussed in Part 2, which reaches from the suburbs to the center of the city. We were the authors of the master plan, but it was ultimately built, contrary to our intention, as a suburban country trail. Though linear parks are now visible as new landscapes, most people see them mainly as a piece of suburban country trail. They do not understand that the linear park's power lies in connecting the central city with its suburbs.

In the same vein, in the case of green roofs, it is important that the fifth façade be visible. Indeed, the name *fifth façade* itself—as opposed to green roof—stresses the element of visibility. The green roofs of Silvercup Studios and Gratz Industries, both in New York, are fifth façades, seen from the Queensboro Bridge. Sixty thousand cars and many subway trains cross the bridge every day. Those drivers and passengers constitute a sizable population that may view those fifth façades as they become increasingly visible over time, filling in and becoming a large mass of patterned color, revealing a new relationship with nature and opening the door to reimagining the city.

But a new landscape aesthetic is a separate process that needs its own treatment. The cultural shifts in our understanding of nature, of which ecology is the latest, have at times led to the mistaken assumption that the landscape aesthetic results from working to achieve ecological outcomes. Part 1 dealt with the issues in art and nature that show the problems with such an assumption.

This is not to say that the new understanding of the natural does not require particular ways of doing things and expressing them. But there is still a difference between that and the creation of aesthetic forms. So where is the starting point? The form is what reaches and moves people.

Aesthetics is a topic as yet untouched in the design of new landscapes. We are defining anew the aim in the design of present-day landscapes. We are building them. But how and where and in what way aesthetics enters into them is not evident. The designs in this chapter make a beginning. They make a beginning in our case by deciding that one starts by placing an aesthetic language *over* the functional substrata. A historical example may make this clear. John Summerson has succinctly described how a Roman architecture of arches and vaults—applied on its exterior the five classical orders as the aesthetic message. The Colosseum is his illustration. The iconic order of the columns on the exterior of the Colosseum obeys nothing but its own traditional aesthetic rules. The shape and size of the piers behind the columns and of the arch have come through the exigencies of convenience and construction. Over time the orders (Tuscan, Doric, Ionic, Corinthian, composite) took on very nuanced ways of integrating into the fabric of the building from the Roman beginnings through the Renaissance and Baroque, and quite different from the modern movement in architecture with its machine aesthetic of uncluttered surfaces applied to a concrete or steel frame tectonic, which is part and parcel of a machine aesthetic.

If we were to take an example from landscape history, the seventeenth-century French landscape would be appropriate in its extending a geometry over a terrain irrespective of the terrain's form.

For my office, for today's landscape design, the starting point of the application of an aesthetic lies in shaping spaces and not objects within the landscape. Secondly, it lies in connecting *visibly* with many elements of the rest of nature as feasible. Thirdly, the tectonics can be used to reinforce the visibility of the other two shaped spaces and the connectivity. Where we are now is on the application of aesthetics on tectonics.

From Thin to Thick Edge

The concepts of Thin Edge and Thick Edge are introduced as formal devices which, like the crumbs on Hansel and Gretel's trail, serve as markers of the path one has traveled but disappear as one moves along. In the end, they serve primarily to lead to an area worth focusing on: the interface. In a nutshell, the aesthetic path traveled in this section moves beyond concentrating on edges to a new area *between* water and land, or the seam *between* architecture and landscape, or any line that separates territories. In the end, such lines become thick bands, and exploring them produces work that seems to be truly of the present, in a new area in which ideas can be tried. It is as if by drawing a thin line you pulled up a new territory hidden under it. The resulting Thick Edge is an area where a new relationship between humans and nature, between architecture and landscape, or between landscape and city can be worked on and made visible. It creates new territory but doesn't dictate meaning.

Once the line thickened, the aesthetic path taken was the band itself as an indistinctly edged, porous element in which the materials from one side could seep into the other, what Joel Sanders and I would call eventually call *interface*—concentrating there on the passage between architecture to landscape. But interface came out of earlier thinking about edges and what I called at first the Thin Edge and later the Thick Edge.

The work of J. M. W. Turner, Mark Rothko, and Edouard Vuillard, which said something, it seemed to me, about edges, helped me develop my thinking about porosity in the Thick Edge. (Admittedly, I could have been overlaying my own reading on their work, which they may have rejected outright.)

In Turner's watercolors and in what he called his "beginnings" (studies for later paintings), there is an erasure of objects which seem to become immanent. The object becomes a mass of color, melting into the rest of the composition.

Rothko got rid of objects altogether but could keep one color present while giving you another, glowing from inside, around, or below it. Each color seems to have run over the edge of another, and this overlaying appears to provide a way to move away from clear-cut edges.

Vuillard weakens edges by patterning all surfaces forcefully so that none is dominant. The juxtaposition of each object with a strongly patterned surface of similar weight and complexity diminishes the outline of the separate objects in a painting, and creates a space that overruns the individual items in it.

When I started to look for a language with which to represent landscape in our office, it was at first for my own benefit, and for that of my colleagues. The drawings we made to represent what we were doing seemed to be out of sync with the intentions we had about the landscape. And it wasn't just dissatisfaction with the superrealism of the current 3D Max and Photoshop computer program renditions. Apart from the present adoption of superrealism as the dominant visual mode, computer rendering per se is not the issue. Computer renderings can take many different paths. Before choosing one of them, we needed first to clarify just what our aim was in rendering the image of the landscape we were designing.

Whatever system we used, we were not achieving the real aim of our design: to create space. The renderings yielded objects—trees, people, grass, shrubs, fountains, benches—but not space. Could we find a way to depict the space we wanted to create? It was not undifferentiated space, but space between objects, with the objects serving to give it rhythm, to create the spaces in between. Do you put trees twenty feet or forty feet apart? Consider the spaces in between, not the trees. This is the kind of shaped space we're after. If you look at Capability Brown's drawing of clusters of trees dotted over the landscape, you have space between the trees in the bosk and you have space in between the bosks; both have a rhythm. Although we tried, it seemed that we couldn't make those spaces visible. There needed to be a fluidity between the objects, not a sealed line around them; we needed to convey a porosity which overcame the different objects, flowing into the space we were trying to create. Thinking about the work of Turner, Rothko, and Vuillard was helpful for this task.

But our predicament in finding an appropriate form of representation in a time of change is not new. Landscape artists at the start of the English Picturesque experienced similar difficulties. If one looks at the graphics they produced in the late eighteenth century, one sees a struggle to move out of the geometric layouts and patterns of the preceding period. I do not mean the attempts by such draftsmen of the period as Knipf, Kit, Rigaud, and Rocque. Like renderers today, they took the designs created by others and put them in a familiar, accepted format. They were not interested in trying to produce a new one, since they were not the creators of the shift. Some clear changes do appear in the work of Charles Bridgeman, who makes the passage to the Picturesque. His plans follow the classical practice of rendering a bird's-eye view of a landscape. But over time, the geometric layouts become lighter and looser. The site as a whole is no longer a series of Euclidian geometric figures. What distinguish the drawings attributed to Bridgeman are the enormous spaces empty of design, in contrast to the classical layouts, in which the entire surface is patterned (figs. 158, 159). Similarly, the somewhat unrefined drawings of William Kent come as a shock. The relatively crude eye-level perspectives that Kent drew by hand succeed very well in showing the character of the landscape he was creating. The clumsy human figures and dogs in his landscapes, compared to the polished geometries of the earlier classical aesthetic, give the impression that he does not draw very well. They have the rawness of the new. He is perhaps taking his cues from sketches for theater sets rather than from classical landscape renderings (figs. 160, 161).

Experiments in representation during the Picturesque era (which we have touched on only briefly here) departed from the established practices of their immediate past. Those who were both shaping and intuiting a new reality needed to find another way of representing it. Like them, we face such a challenge today (figs. 162–172).

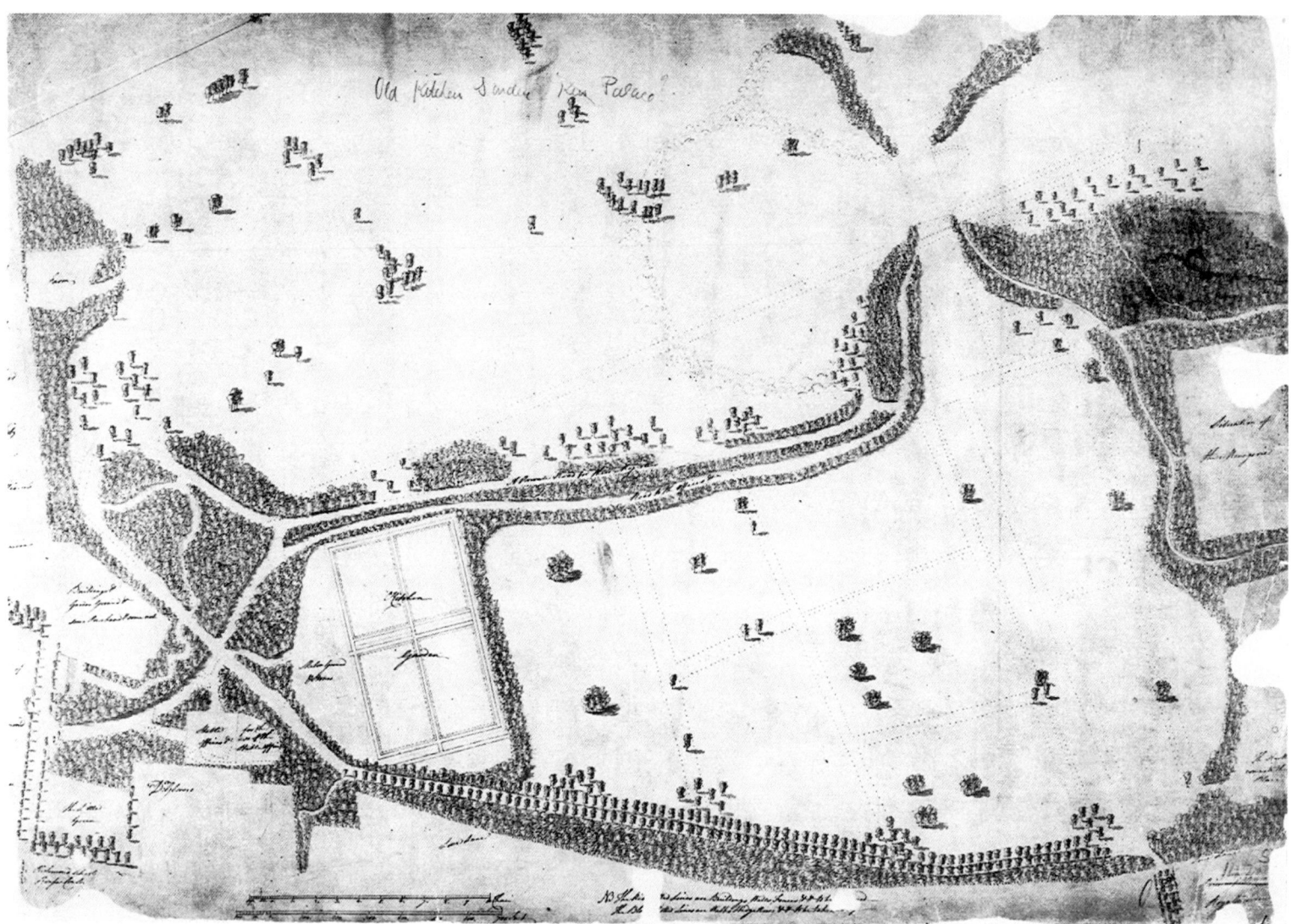

Fig. 158. Plan for Richmond Gardens, attributed to Charles Bridgeman.

Fig. 159. Plan for the Duke of Queensberry's house at Ambresbury, Wiltshire, by Charles Bridgeman, 1738.

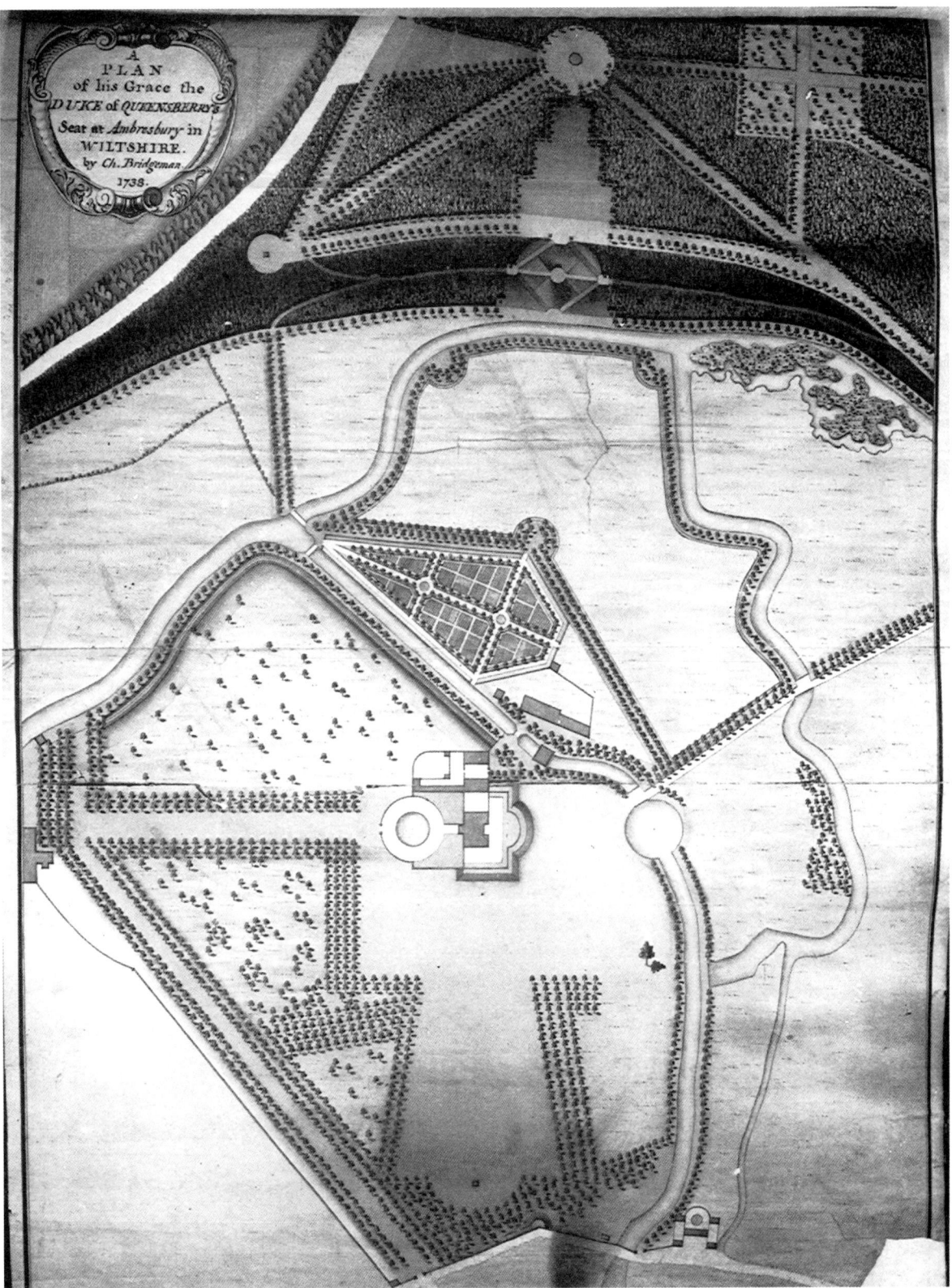

160

161

Fig. 160. The grounds of Euston with a view of temple, signed by J. Vardy and dated 1755, but attributed to William Kent.

Fig. 161. Interior of Merlin's Cave, by William Kent.

Fig. 162. Mathematics Building Courtyard, Institute for Advanced Study, Princeton University, Princeton, New Jersey, 1996.

163

164

Fig. 163. Kent Falls Trail, Kent Falls State Park, Connecticut, 2006.

Fig. 164. Arverne, New York, 2001. Design charette.

Fig. 165. Representation experiment I, Housatonic Fields, New Milford, Connecticut, 2006.

Part 3 153

165

166

167

Fig. 166. Representation experiment II, Housatonic Fields.

Fig. 167. Representation experiment III.

Fig. 168. Representation experiment IV.

Fig. 169. Representation experiment V.

168

169

170

171

Fig. 170. Representation experiment VI.

Fig. 171. Representation experiment VII.

Fig. 172. Representation experiment VIII.

The Thin Edge

The works of Turner, Rothko, and Vuillard were paths for me toward a way to work on edges, all kinds of edges. In some early projects, the design concentrated on an intense narrow line, conceived as a Thin Edge. It was an artistic preoccupation that started with resistance to the excessive attention focused on objects. Landscape in the twentieth century had become a collection of objects, but my interest lies in creating space. The shift in attention from object to space in landscape design led me to try to find ways to diffuse the outline of such objects as trees, walls, trellises, and fountains, favoring instead the space between them.

Edges became more and more important to my work. At first they were literally a line, a thin line—the fence at NTT, for example (discussed below)—that divided a public space from a semipublic one. Its importance in the project became primary, and my first impulse was to vary the fence along its length so it would not be homogeneous. My next impulse was to interrupt it, to bring about breaks that you could pass through. Another line, or Thin Edge, was that of linear parks. Our design emphasized the expansion sideways which linear parks could develop over time; one image I used for this was the legs of a centipede.

Whether it was the circumstances particular to one project or another, or a specific event that pushed me to concentrate on an edge, is not as important as the fact that such moments opened the door to a set of ideas which addressed many longstanding issues: passage, ecotone (change of systems) and interface.

Nippon Telegraph and Telephone Headquarters, Tokyo

The open space of NTT headquarters was a rarity in that densely built-up city. The space was generated by two prerequisites: a pedestrian right-of-way along the site and the need to accommodate technology fairs on the plaza designed for its new building. These spaces could flow into each other on most days, but because the technology fairs were limited to the trade, the two areas needed to become totally separate once a month, when the gates on the fence dividing them would close. I therefore decided to focus the design on

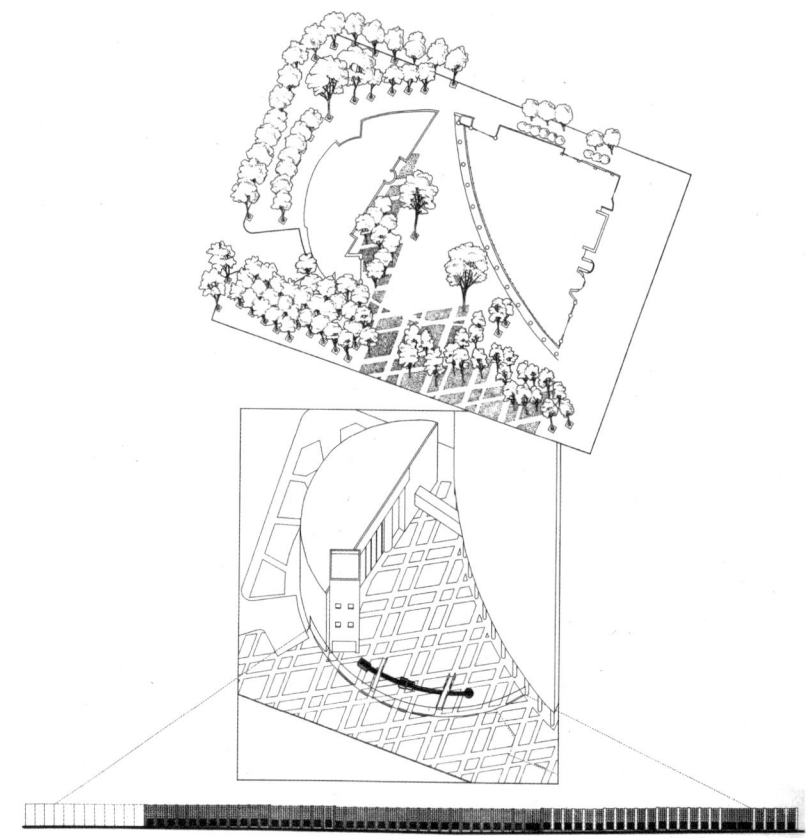

173

Part 3

Fig. 173. Nippon Telephone and Telegraph Headquarters, Tokyo, 1995. Axonometric drawings separating planting from hardscape.

Fig. 174. Nippon Telephone and Telegraph Headquarters.

this dual-character line, sometimes impassable and sometimes porous. I made it into a landscape calling attention to itself rather than to its function as a divider or a security structure. Because the project was for a high-tech company, the fence became a language that explored the relation between the natural and the artificial in the project. Closest to the building, the fence posts were all wood; in the middle they were made of stainless steel and wood; and finally, as the fence ended, at the Museum of Telephone Technology (a small building included in the site), they were all stainless steel. The sequence was a transformation from the use of a found natural material (wood) to a found but then added-to and strengthened material (iron ore + carbon + high heat). The fence was paralleled by a linear fountain in the NTT plaza that developed similarly, one end concrete, the other steel. Its streambed was modified artificially to create two hydrological patterns, contrasting surfaces of water flow. These resulted from studies of fluidity—patterns of nature—but were built in stainless steel and concrete. This Thin Edge challenged visitors to make sense of the play between nature and artifice presented by the fence and the fountain. Their forms borrowed freely from minimalism and conceptual art. Thus the artistic intention was unmistakable, but it remained open to multiple interpretations.

The plaza itself was made porous and alternated the yellow stone of the building with gravel and a few large trees. The public walkway, on the other side of the fence, away from the NTT building, was made as green as possible: vines on the walls, trees, grass. The two openings in the fence (closed only for technology fairs) lined up with small bridges over the fountain, one in wood, the other in stainless steel.

The Thin Edge, the fence, carried the weight of the project; the rest of the space was kept as empty as possible. After the fence was built, as I traveled throughout Japan, the sight of mountain after mountain covered by a single species (the "hinoki," or cypress) for the building industry made me doubt the validity of the wood-versus-steel premise. Was the wood really less artificial than the stainless steel because less direct intervention was needed to transform it into building material? Wasn't the story of whole mountains stripped of their native forest for a single-species plantation an even more dramatic intervention? These thoughts led me to bring three wild trees from the mountain and plant them in the inner court, thus extending the interplay of nature and artifice to the whole space.

The significance of the project lies, however, in the discovery of the Thin Edge—the edge between a public and a semipublic place. The design energy was placed on the line itself—the fence—and on parallel lines on each side (public walkway outside, linear fountain inside). But the overlaying, passages, and crossings, marked by gates and intensified by bridges (stainless steel and concrete), were not the focus. It would be much later that the value of a fluidity between the two sides was understood. There was a lesson too in the narrative of the Thin Edge. It may have been useful as springboard, but it was subsequently scrapped; the interpretation of what is done should be left to others (figs. 173–180). **20**

20. Landscape can show artistic intention without imposing a pre-determined meaning.

Fig. 175. Nippon Telephone and Telegraph Headquarters. Selection of "monument trees."

176

Figs. 176, 177. Nippon Telephone and Telegraph Headquarters.

177

178

179

Figs. 178, 179. Nippon Telephone and Telegraph Headquarters. Detail of stainless-steel fountain.

Fig. 180. Nippon Telephone and Telegraph Headquarters. Rendering (as part of an initiative to reinvent ways of representing landscape).

180

Abandoibarra Master Plan and Plaza Euskadi, Bilbao

In 1998, the city of Bilbao engaged in the reclamation of a derelict industrial harbor and, through an international competition, commissioned a master plan to transform it into a vital center of activity. While we were in charge of the street and open-space master plan, the buildings' layout was masterplanned by Cesar Pelli and Associates and a Bilbao architect, Eugenio Aguinaga. The individual buildings were designed by an international roster of architects: Robert Krier, Ricardo Legorreta, Rafael Moneo, Alvaro Siza, Robert A. M. Stern, and Pelli himself. Both the master plan's open-space designs and the building layout have been followed; most of the master plan has been built and is in use.

I conceptualized the master plan as a series of parallel lines, or thin bands, each representing a different zone or flood level, each of a different material. Its most critical space, the line between the water and the land, had already been determined; the master plan reinforced it with parallel spaces (walkway by the water, walkway three feet above the shore, boulevard with sidewalks, and green center median for a light rail).

This series of parallel Thin Edges in the master plan governed the design, starting at the ecotone and moving outward. Each of these lines was treated as a Thin Edge and charged with a function. But the additive potential of the parallel edges was understood and expressed clearly by connecting them. One main straight road, Ramon Rubial, cuts across these parallel lines and moves from city level to water level—a forty-two-foot drop—and then, via a new bridge, to the University of Deusto on the other side of the river.

The fulcrum of the plan, where the second and third levels end up and connect with existing city streets, became the central plaza—Plaza Euskadi—which we would later be commissioned to design.

The master plan became a legal document that could be changed only in minor ways. (The biggest change that occurred was to allow the Moneo library to be built one floor higher than originally planned; figs. 181–186).

The Plaza Euskadi, under construction, is one of Bilbao's new public spaces. It serves as the node that facilitates passage from El Ensanche ("addition to the older city"), the nineteenth-century section of the city, to the new Bilbao, by the river. As intermediary, it also continues the green of the nineteenth-century Doña Casilda Park.

It is potentially a linear park from the old city to the university across the river, and its linear quality was stressed as its major civic focus. Winning the competition to design the Campa, the space between the Plaza Euskadi and the Nervión River, made the project move from Thin to Thick Edge. This master plan is an example of the sections of cities as new projects in our time (figs. 187–192).[1]

The Thick Edge

The Thick Edge became a way to approach the interface of two disciplines, landscape and architecture or landscape and city; of two materials (water and land).

Several projects illustrate a transition from the Thin to the Thick Edge. Pivotal in the development of the latter is the public space we designed in St. Louis. The Thin Edge concentrated on the passage from one space to another: from a private to a public space, as in NTT, or in the ecotone of water and land, as in the Abandoibarra master plan. But in St. Louis, the Thin Edge became the Thick Edge, and it meant starting from the passage between water and land and going much further. The transition from Thin to Thick created an indistinct zone in which new phenomena could be experienced that were neither architecture nor landscape, neither water nor land.

The example of Shugaku-in, the imperial villa in Kyoto mentioned earlier, illustrates well the abstract idea of the Thick Edge. The thickening of the juncture between building and landscape is what the Thick Edge is about. It is not a matter of one aspect taking over the other. It is perhaps becoming alternating sheaves of landscape and building, not only horizontally, but also vertically.

The aim is neither burial nor blur, but rather a complex interface with different elements to make for a fluid passage. The thicker this edge, the better the interface. It makes for a multitude of subtle

Fig. 181. Abandoibarra Master Plan, Bilbao, Spain, in progress. Existing site and site after installation of river-edge park.

181

conditions for both architecture and landscape and creates an in-between spatial entity, unknown as yet, where new growth can occur.

At first this idea developed as a Thin Edge because we saw it as a slender border. But then we realized that our focus was too narrow, and we considered what could happen if that zone was expanded. Finally, though concentrated on the edges of railroad rights-of-way or waterfronts where water and earth meet, these bands seemed to contain vast possibilities. This wider perspective could be applied to many situations, one of which is the interface between landscape and architecture.

The point where architecture and landscape meet is where new approaches are most needed. The sealed box of the modern movement's architecture has been opened to allow work with the exterior. Instead of concentrating heating and cooling systems in mechanical artifacts buried inside buildings, the exterior landscape is using a variety of new means—from geothermal ground-source heating and cooling to green roofs to air extractors to earth-duct cooling through floor grills—to link architecture to its exterior in unexpected ways. Functionally, then, the search for sustainability has interwoven the building with its exterior through its underground, through its roof, and through freestanding exterior devices, from photovoltaic panels to windmills and other energy collectors.

The actual physical interface of architecture and landscape in visual terms is only in its beginnings. So far, it is neither readable nor acknowledged. Its forms don't yet make it explicit. The concept of the Thick Edge, where landscape and architecture merge, creates a *zone* of density and concentration of resources; it creates a new arena for design.

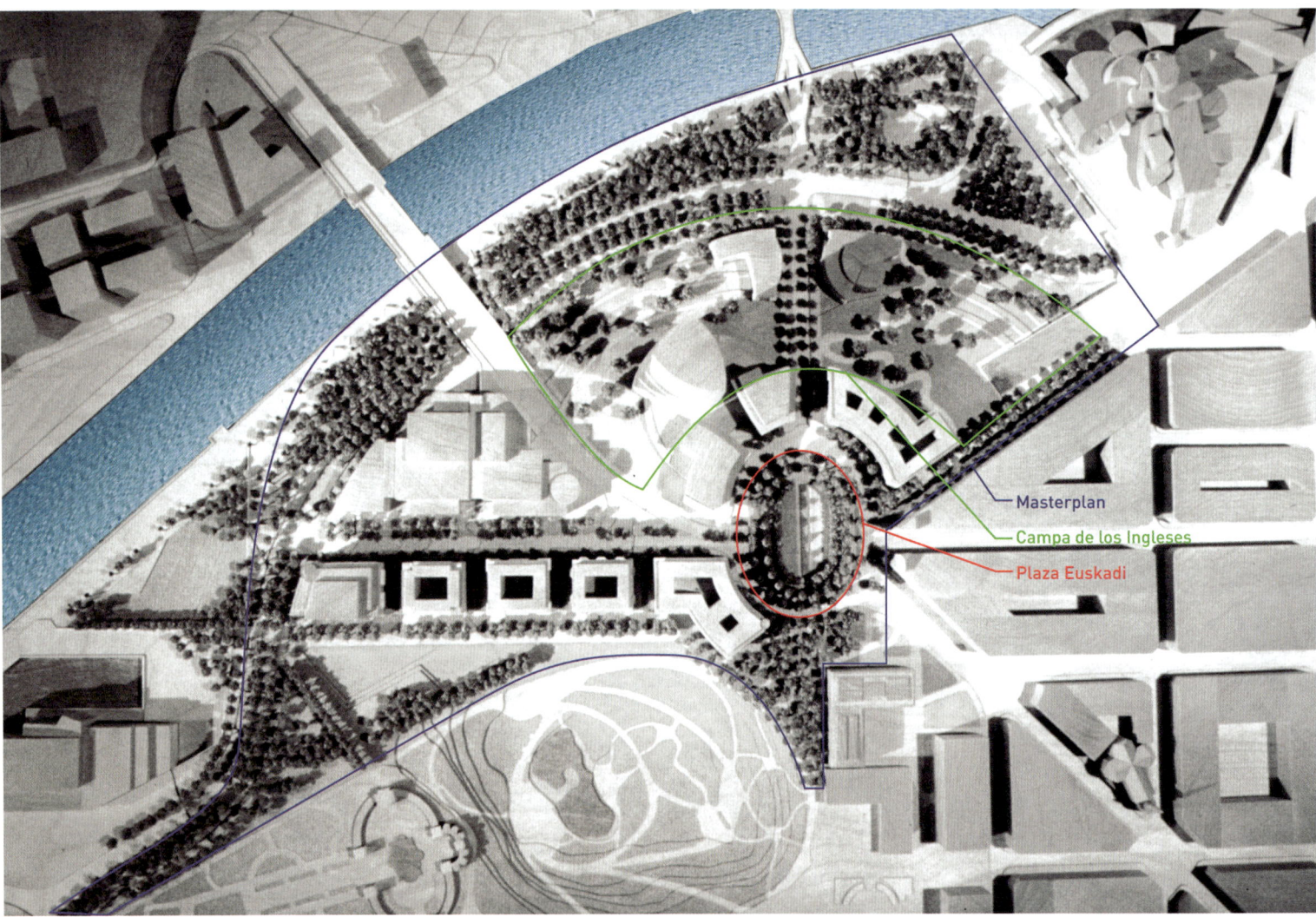

Fig. 182. Abandoibarra Master Plan. Model.

Fig. 183. Abandoibarra Master Plan. Diagram showing relationship between master plan and the Campa de los Ingleses Park and Euskadi Plaza.

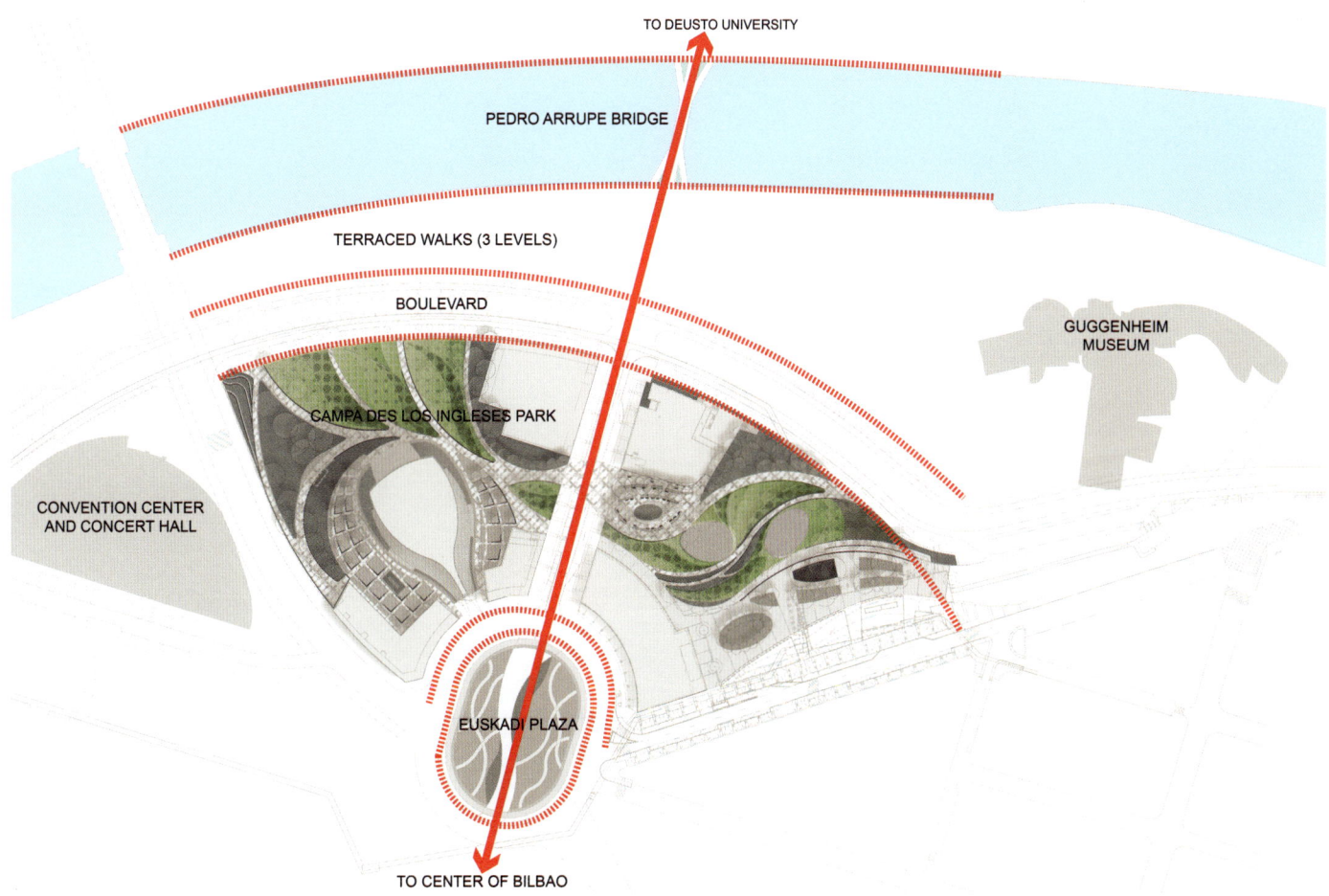

184

Figs. 184–185. Abandoibarra Master Plan.

185

186

Fig. 186. Abandoibarra Master Plan.

Fig. 187. Plaza Euskadi, Bilbao, Spain, in progress. Plan.

Fig. 188. Plaza Euskadi. Rendering of proposed fountain.

Figs. 189–190. Plaza Euskadi. Early study model for fountain.

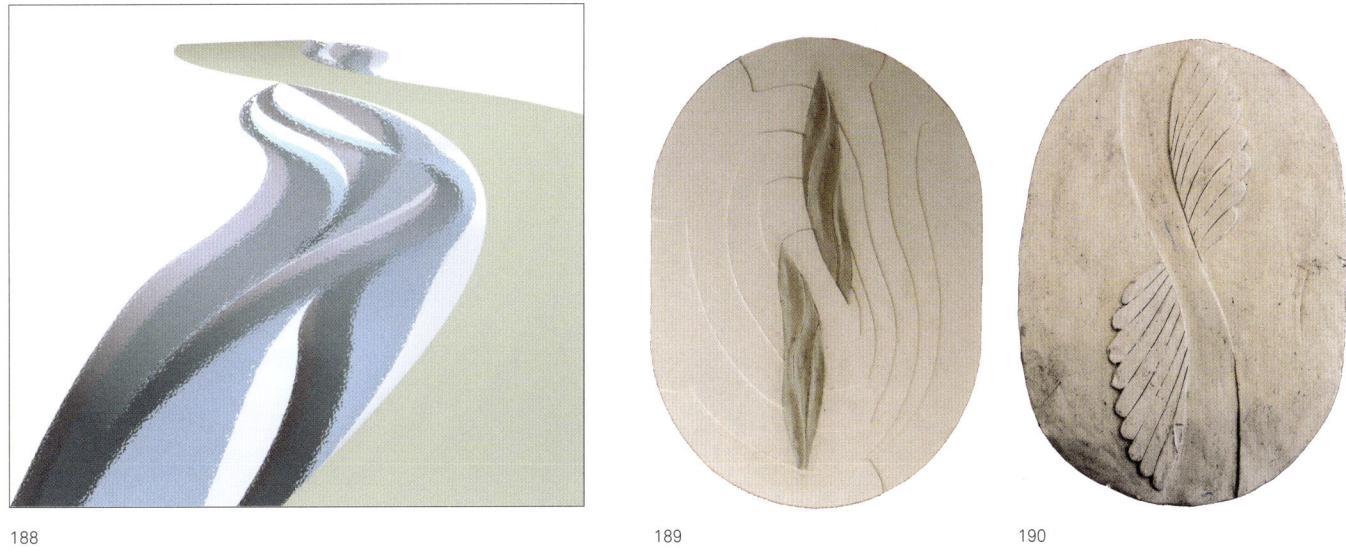

187

188

189

190

191

Fig. 191. Plaza Euskadi. Early rendering of fountain.

Fig. 192. Plaza Euskadi. Rendering (as part of an initiative to reinvent ways of representing landscape).

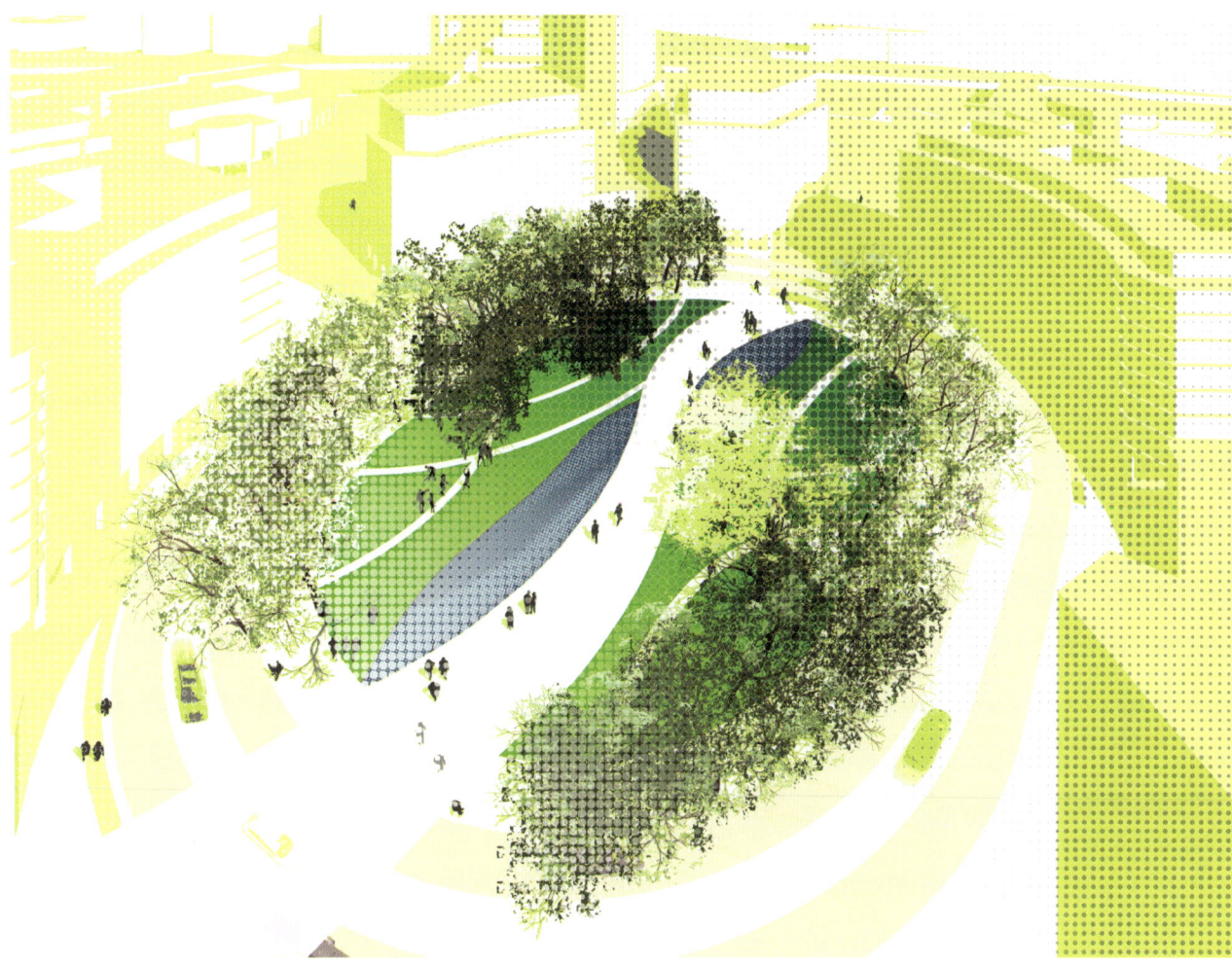

192

St. Louis

The brief for the master plan was to reconnect the city to the Mississippi and to the Great River Greenway (GRG), a new greenway and bikeway encircling greater St. Louis. The narrow site we worked on is a desolate, isolated piece of land. The master-plan surveyor found a dead body there; it had lain undiscovered for several days.

Saarinen's Gateway Arch, the magical stainless steel catenary curve that identifies St. Louis worldwide, is also the marker of our site: a narrow band of land, sitting forty feet below the arch, with steps leading down from it to the great Mississippi River. Nothing could be better than working next to this mysteriously beautiful monument.

The strip of land was part of the old St. Louis port, which was on the land now occupied by the arch and its park, built forty feet up with torn-up port fill. It was a busy port until the early twentieth century. The handsome 1874 Eads Bridge, to the north, and the Poplar Bridge, to the south, bookend the first phase of the project.

For each project discussed in this section, there was a moment of entry that gave me a deeply physical sense of it. For St. Louis, it was a late-afternoon ride on one of the city-line boats anchored at the foot of the arch by the narrow strip below the site of our project. In the late afternoon heat, close to sunset, twenty or twenty-five of us boarded a boat resembling an old Mississippi steamship.[2] The arch looked ethereal against the sky. Drinks in our hands, as the sun went down, we set out north, up the brown Mississippi. The captain said, "We're going up to the conFLUence [pronouncing it like a true St. Louisian] with the Missouri. It's the Missouri that gets the river all brown—river should have been called the Missouri. The Mississippi coming down from Minnesota simply empties into it. You can see the two colors of the water there, and it is the Missouri that brings down all the branches and debris." Upriver, both shores are surprisingly free of buildings. On the Missouri side, only an abandoned power station—possibly of use to the project? Low vegetation on both sides until the earth rises above the river's flood level. The river smells of mud. I asked about the St. Louis steamship company that had had dancing on its decks, where Louis Armstrong and so many other jazzmen got their start and made their way out of New Orleans. Yes, they knew of it, long out of business—famous, though. Any dancing left? No, dinner cruises now. We returned after sunset, the arch looming in the last stretch, its one side dark, but because of the triangular section of its profile, still picking up light. We were deposited at its feet. Not a bad arrival.

But in St. Louis there were three other meaningful connections to the Mississippi besides traveling on it. I have already mentioned the Eads Bridge, located at one end of our site's first phase. James B. Eads, its designer, became for me a symbol of the best of St. Louis, a man who went down to the bottom of the river in a forty-gallon whiskey barrel that had been converted into a diving bell of his own design in order to study the conditions of the riverbed. He wrote, "I had occasion to descend to the bottom in a current so swift as to require extraordinary means to sink the bell. . . . The sand was drifting like a dense snowstorm at the bottom. . . . At sixty-five feet below the surface I found the bed of the river, for at least three feet in depth, a moving mass and so unstable that, in endeavoring to find a footing on it beneath my bell, my feet penetrated through it until I could feel, although standing erect, the sand rushing past my hands, driven by a current apparently as rapid as that on the surface."[3]

Eads fought the Army Corps of Engineers over Mississippi River policy, proposing a different way of managing the river. After Katrina, his research deserves a rereading.

The second additional connection to the Mississippi was the story of the jazz boats, and the third was the Saarinen arch, an extraordinary monument.

We developed four schemes: Promenade, Serrated Edge, Banks and Islands, and Terraces and Islands. All four made the point that, whatever the scheme, the site itself needed to be reconnected to the city, and not just by stairs to the level of the arch and park. Connected to the Eads Bridge. Connected to the Poplar Bridge. Connected to the underground garage on the arch's site. Connected to Washington Avenue and, finally, connected through the Eads and Poplar

Fig. 193. St. Louis Waterfront, in progress.
River debris.

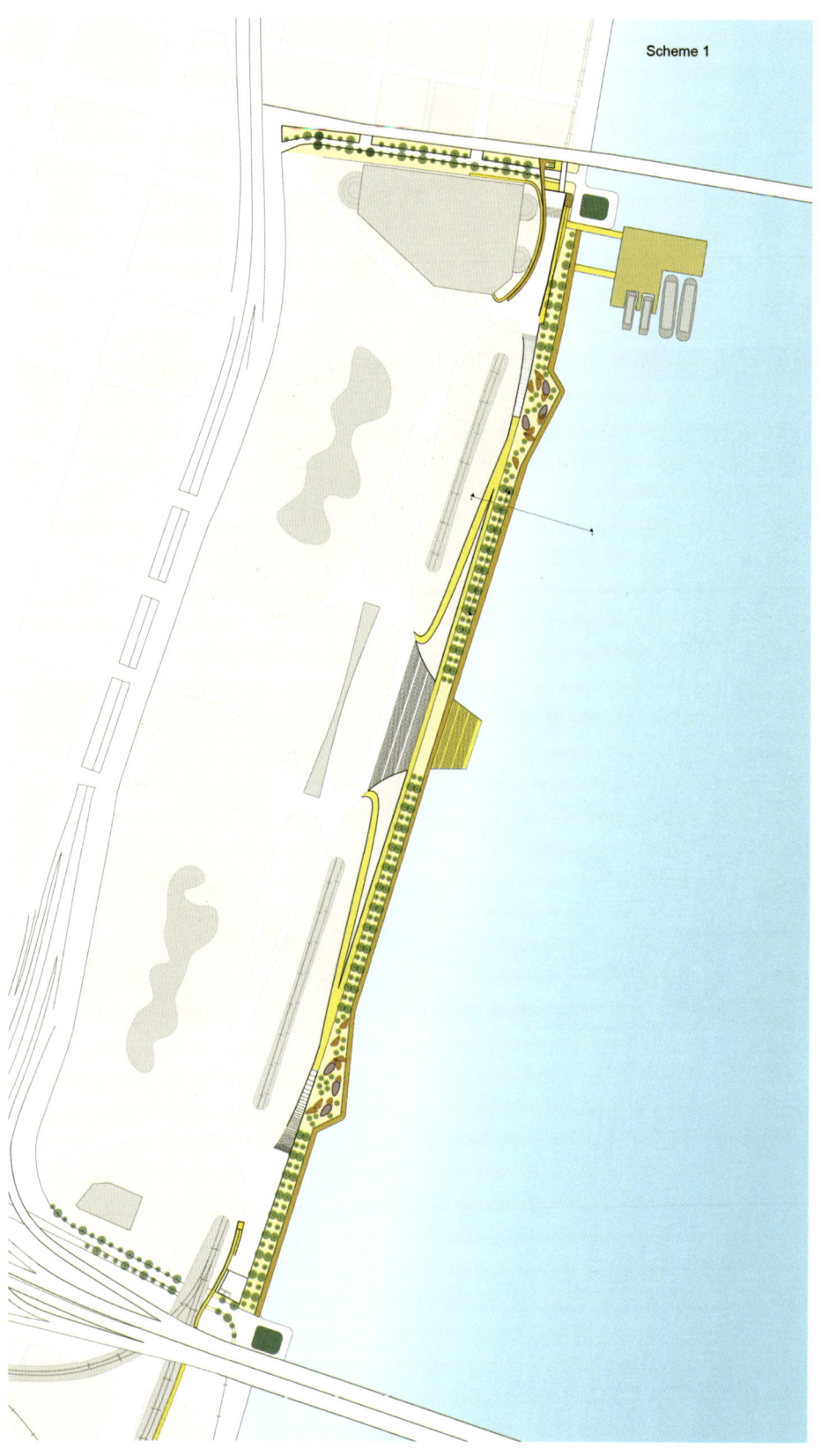

Scheme 1

Fig. 194. St. Louis Waterfront. Scheme 1.
Fig. 195. St. Louis Waterfront. Scheme 2.

Part 3 179

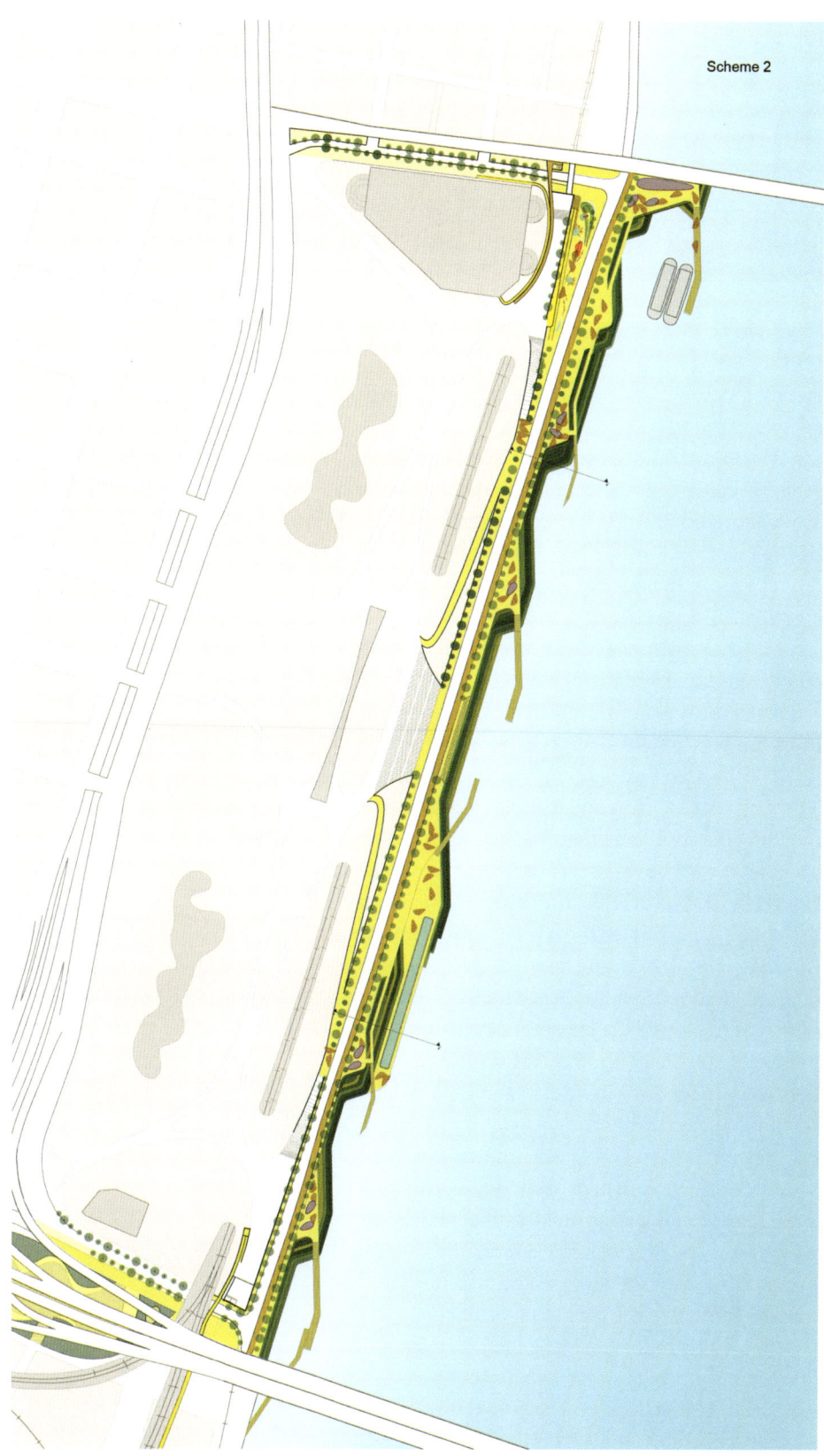

Scheme 2

195

Bridges, and by water taxi, perhaps, to East St. Louis, across the river. In fact, the Great River Greenway was to connect to this frontage. We incorporated the GRG's bike path into the plan by making a pontoon over the water as a celebratory arrival to St. Louis and the arch. This broader connectivity also suggested that the GRG serve as collector of both the biomass from the greater St. Louis park system and the organic flotsam from the Mississippi on our site at certain times of the year, all of which could be converted into energy by a biomass facility to be installed in the abandoned power plant just north of our site (fig. 193).

The first of our four schemes worked within the limitations of the site and with the narrow band available, removing traffic from it to expand the usable public space (fig. 194).

The second scheme extended piers into the water, creating a serrated edge (fig. 195).

The third included both terraces and piers, the piers more akin to islands (fig. 196).

The fourth plunged fully into the river and made the main public space a water experience (fig. 197).

The ideas behind this fourth scheme embraced working with the river and its fluctuations as a modern opportunity. Rather than treat parts of the space as lost to the threat of flooding at various levels, we created a system of floating spaces that allows the public to encounter the river in a different way at each water level. With the help of Consulmar, a firm of naval architects, we developed a system of islands which went beyond the old decorated-barge concept, making instead modular floating units that were light, easy to repair (with quick removal of a damaged section), adjustable to changing water heights, and anchored in ways that allowed limited motion.

Two forums were held to show the public the development of the ideas and the final four schemes. A vote rating all four was called for in the second forum. The fourth scheme was the favorite. This marked the end of the master plan effort.

In passing to the next stage, which meant presenting our scheme to a long list of agencies, we were teamed with HOK and CDG Engineers, as well as our naval architect from Consulmar. The Army

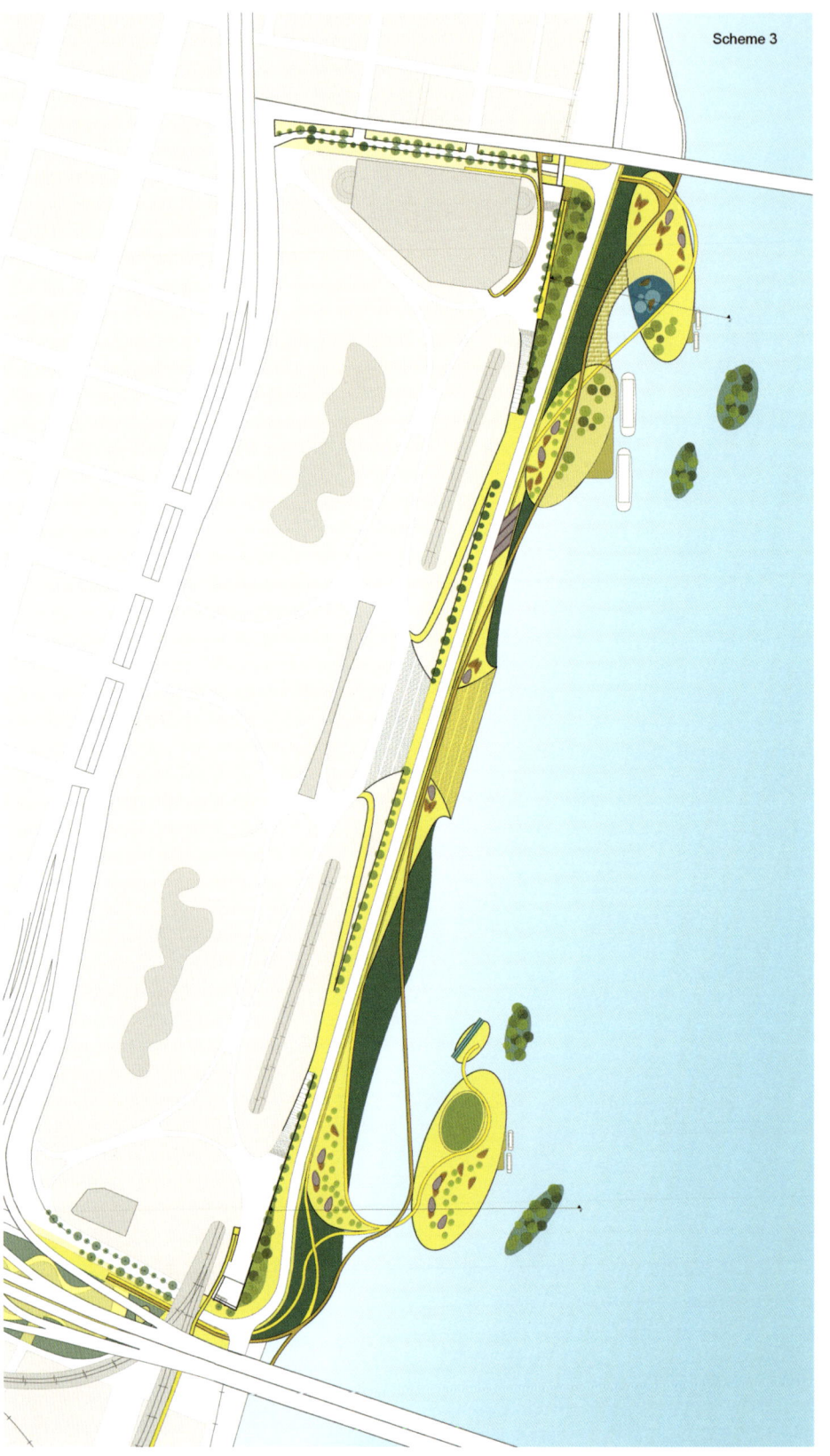

196

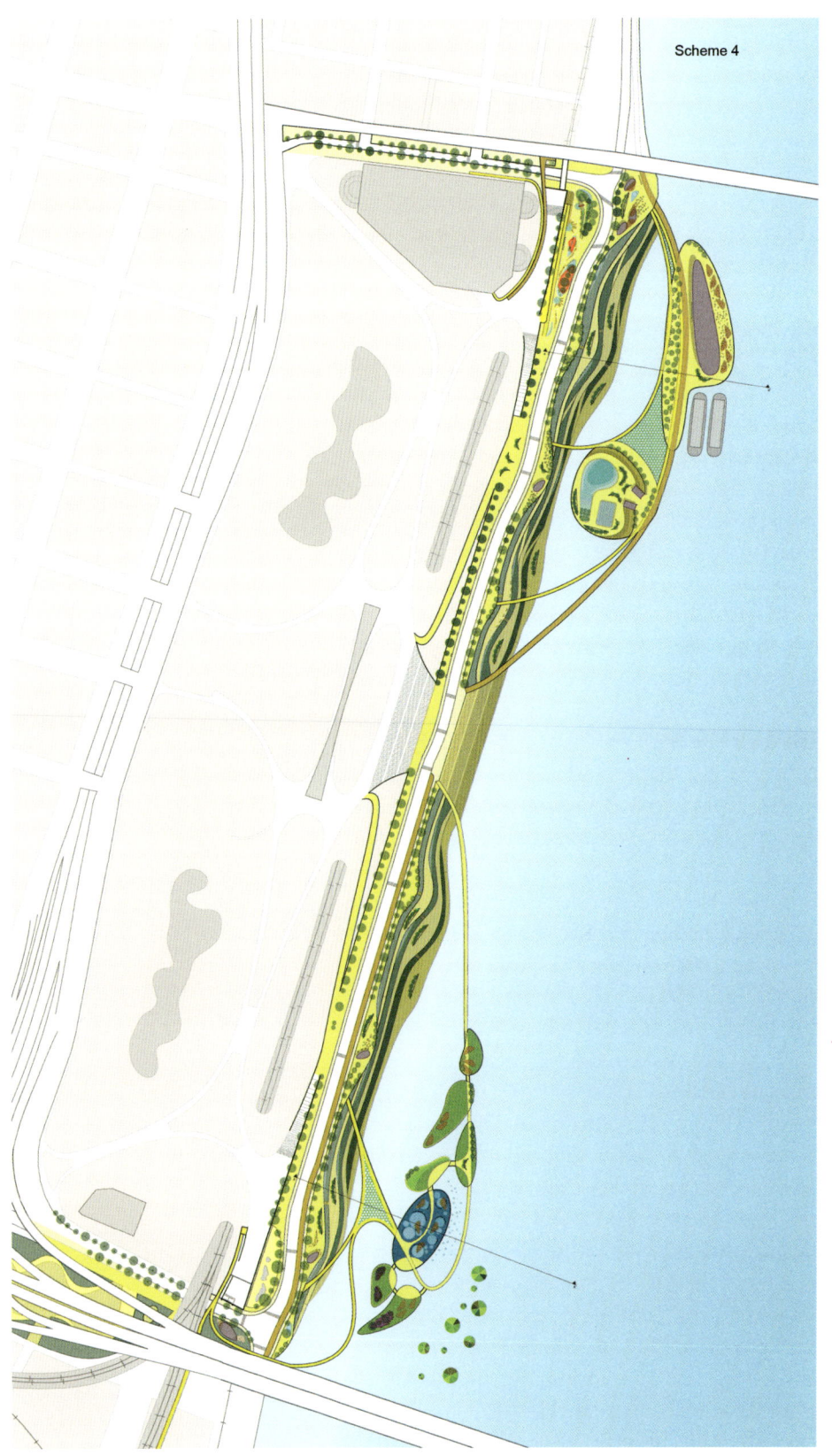

Fig. 196. St. Louis Waterfront. Scheme 3.
Fig. 197. St. Louis Waterfront. Scheme 4.

Corps of Engineers was the first of these agencies, and it had the most comprehensive set of criteria; other agency approvals depended on their preliminary go-ahead. As the Corps proposed, the scheme was tried out at a test site. This revealed some difficulties with the scheme; by making small modifications, we dealt with each issue and moved on to the next set of questions.

In the St. Louis scheme it is not the islands—the specific objects—that matter the most. It is the extension outward of the line of the shore, a line that varies according to the water level—close or far, up or down—that is key. Here the Thick Edge emerged. Because of its location, on a site made emblematic by its connection to the arch, this edge is significant to all the inhabitants and visitors of the metropolitan area. For that reason, we insisted on having the project forge and emphasize the connections between this area and the whole city. This undertaking needs to include the largest possible constituency in its urban metropolis. The aesthetic of the Thick Edge introduces a new experience of nature for everyone. The experience is one of establishing a better human relation with the rest of nature, and with the river above all, moving with the level of the water. Of including ways of introducing plant and bird life. Of using the water to produce the energy to light up the whole project. The more people who experience it, the more diverse they are, and the more activities they engage in, the broader the dissemination of this new sense of nature will be.

Present urban and suburban lives are deeply alienated from nature. Landscape projects such as this one can introduce an intimate relationship between human and other natural life (for example, the river) and make this connection as accessible as possible to as many people as possible.

What is critical to the story of St. Louis is not the floating islands or their technology, or any specific program for any of the other uses of the islands. Rather, it is the focus on what mattered most about that site: the mighty Mississippi River and our giving all our attention to establishing a new human connection with it—a way of being on the river that created the opportunity to enjoy a truly fluid (rather than static) experience of its many moods and levels. Which is why, of all the experiences of visiting the site, the one of actually being on the river was the one that mattered most. If you wished to reconnect to the river, going out onto it would be the transformative experience. You could then give that experience new form (figs. 198–205). **21**

21. Landscape can bridge the line between ourselves and other parts of nature—between ourselves and a river.

198

199

Fig. 198. St. Louis Waterfront. Rendering of Scheme 4 in summer.

Fig. 199. St. Louis Waterfront. Rendering of Scheme 4 in winter.

200

201

Fig. 200. St. Louis Waterfront. Ferry station as an interface between landscape and architecture, developed with architect Joel Sanders.

Fig. 201. St. Louis Waterfront. Rendering of Scheme 4.

Part 3 186

202

Fig. 202. St. Louis Waterfront. Rendering of ramp from bridge to site.

Fig. 203. St. Louis Waterfront. Rendering of ramp from Gateway Arch to water's edge.

Fig. 204. St. Louis Waterfront. Rendering of project from opposite bank of the Mississippi River.

Overleaf:
Fig. 205. St. Louis Waterfront. Rendering (as part of an initiative to reinvent ways of representing landscape).

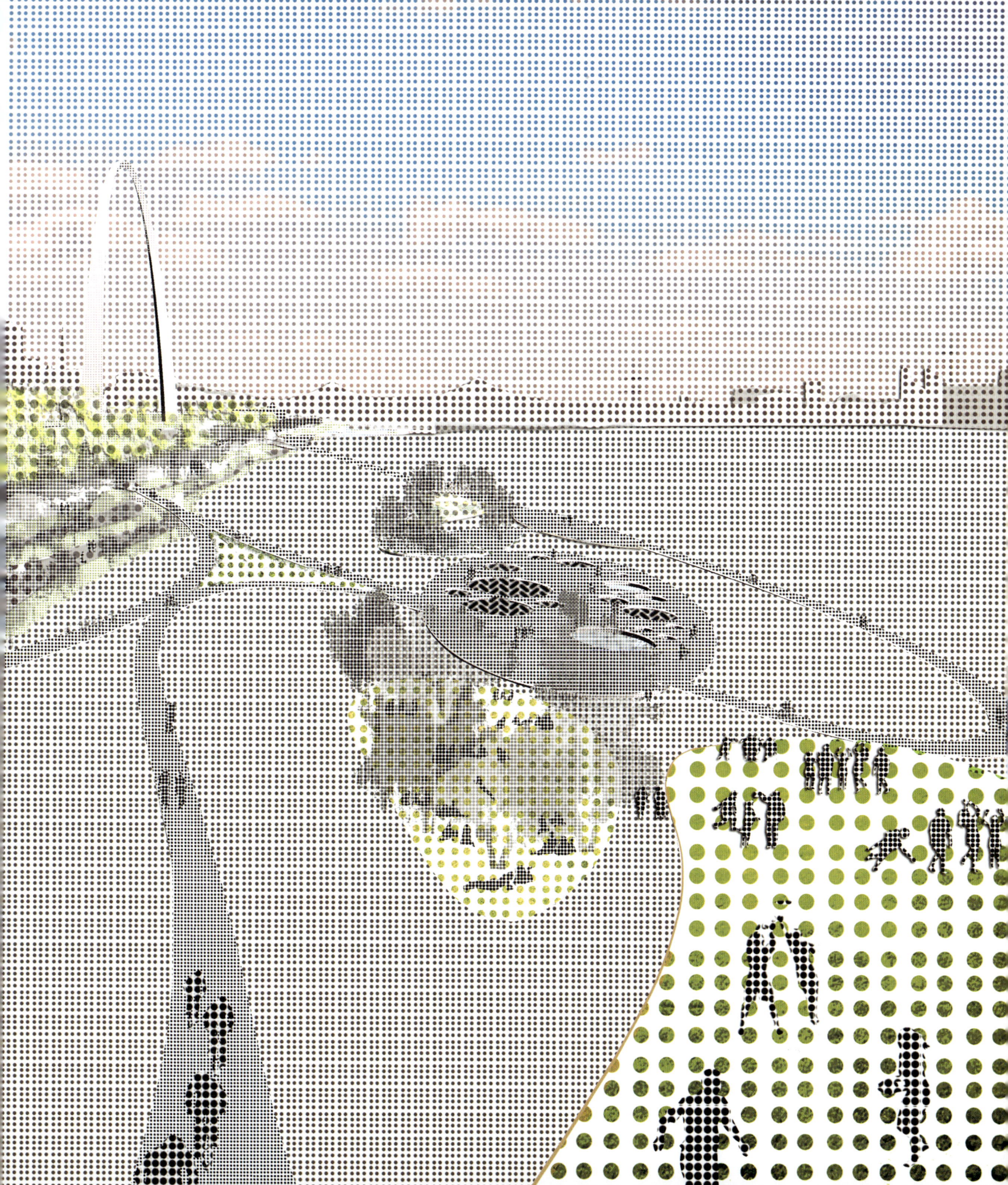

The Thick Edge

And so the conceptual tool of the Thick Edge created an indistinct area open to new possibilities along edges. Edge at first meant an actual divisionary line. Its possibilities then grew, as the many ways of crossing it were explored. Finally, in what began as a look at expanding the line of an ecotone of water and land by creating intrusions or passing from one area to the other, it grew into a Thick Edge. Once the Thick Edge was in place in the St. Louis master plan, it was clear that it was a concept particularly useful for crossing numerous disciplinary lines. In fact, the Thick Edge encompassed many ways of creating an interface between a wide range of dissimilar elements, including disciplines, materials, and spaces. Interweaving was one of those ways.

Interfacing

The final projects presented here—Shenzhen, China; NYC 2012 Olympics; Bilbao Campa; and the master plan for Sejong Public Administrative Town (PAT), Korea—are all instances of applying the Thick Edge to the passage between two disciplines, or two dissimilar elements. In Shenzhen, the passage flows from park to bridge to mall; in NYC 2012 Olympics, from marsh to earthform and earthform to temporary stadium. In Bilbao Campa, the crossings become a three-dimensional band in which dissimilar buildings are inserted; and in Sejong's PAT, they create the interweaving of public space and building at different elevations where ground seems to change into building and building into ground.

Shenzhen, China

Ours was one of five entries in a competition for a large cultural park in the center of Shenzhen, a new Chinese city growing at a frightening rate. Two ideas govern our design.

The first recognizes the forces at work in modern cities and accordingly does not interpret the park as an isolated and passive urban precinct. Rather, the park is treated as an active shaper of the city—a conveyor of pedestrians, bikers, and skaters through it; a cultural space akin to a museum (a function which, up to now, has generally been allotted only to buildings); a fluid connector of green systems (as opposed to an island), with arms extending to unite as many living pockets in the city as possible, enhancing the sustainability of all. The park is conceived as a set of strands weaving through the city, enlarging at times into ribbons of intensified activity and overlapping cultural functions.

The second idea governing the design of this park sets all its forms in the intersection of landscape and architecture. The landscape is treated as a continuous surface that sculpts the land three-dimensionally according to the city's particular dynamic. In it, layers cross and weave; surfaces change into volumes. We therefore do not attach the forms of this park to a symbolic order, but instead seek a three-dimensional topography that results from the junctions of landscape with the roads, buildings, and programs at work in this new city. The intersection of landscape with architecture gives rise to a new entity we call parkitecture. Though we were finalists in this competition, we did not win it. Nevertheless, it remains a project that we consider the most successful in the interweaving of landscape, architecture, and city (figs. 206–208). **22**

22. Landscape is becoming the main actor of the urban stage, not just a destination.

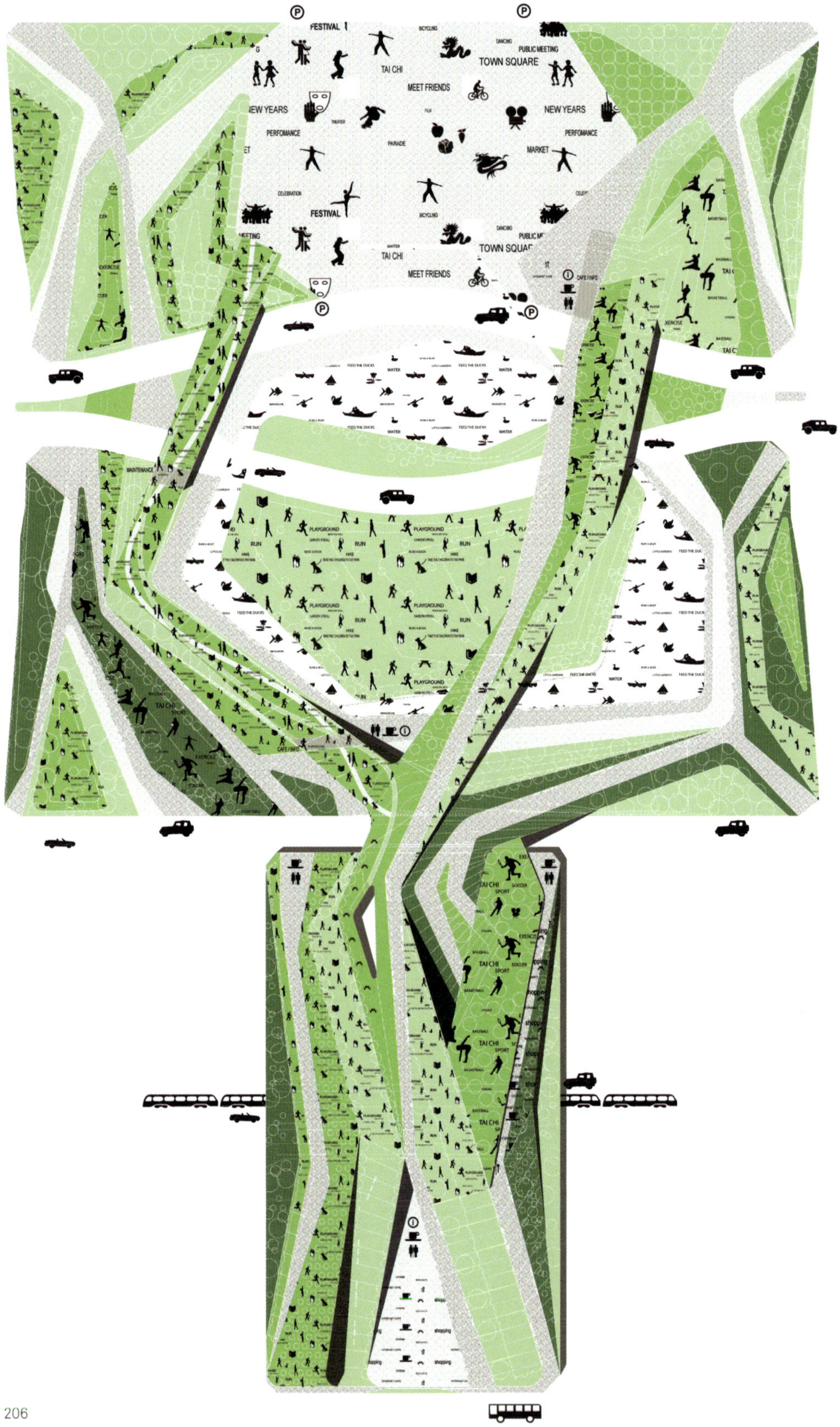

206

207

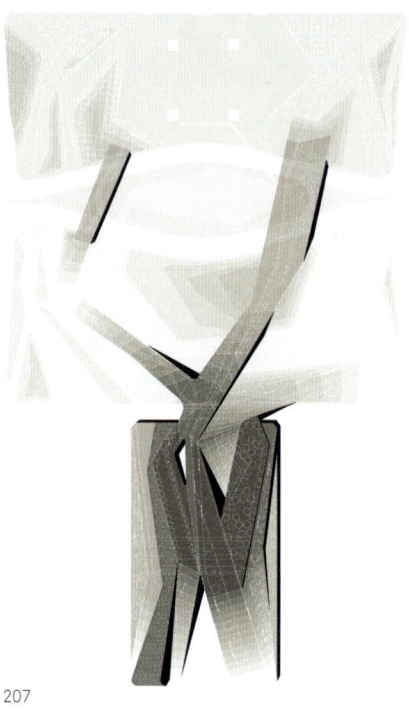

Fig. 206. Shenzhen Cultural Park, Shenzhen, China, 2003. Diagrammatic presentation showing crossings of major highways.

Fig. 207. Shenzhen Cultural Park. Abstract three-dimensional diagram.

Fig. 208. Shenzhen Cultural Park. Model.

Earthworks: NYC 2012 Olympics

We made visits by ferry and car to the site, on Staten Island, in late summer (figs. 209–215). We walked along trails that were part of a park created by Robert Moses and in bad condition. A golf course abuts it and slopes down to a vast landscape of beautiful marshes, the Kill snaking slowly through them. The site for the equestrian venue is on the marshes at the crossing of two roads, heavily traveled and elevated above flood level. We walked through the site, passing many areas for kids' sports and a field for model-airplane flying, watching a miniature craft soaring above. Vegetation profuse and high, difficult to penetrate. A sweet mentholated smell from leaves. We decided we needed to return in late fall, after the plants had lost their foliage. The lay of the land read differently then, as the vegetation had died back. The marshes were even more beautiful. It would be good to be elevated over the marshes and have that as the main, all-encompassing view. The marsh's water mirrors the clouds and sky. The sedges, spartina grasses, phragmites, all brown, give the marshes a smoky effect, a blurred brown surface.

Designed in 2003 and sited on Staten Island, this project is the interface of a temporary equestrian facility—a demountable stadium for thirty-five thousand spectators—and an S-shaped mound that provides an elevated pathway over the floodplain and marsh. The sculptural mound defines two spaces for spectators, the amphitheater and an overlook for behind-the-scenes observation of the equestrian warm-up fields. Besides facilitating viewing, the earthwork creates a secure boundary between fields, stables, and the general public.

Reversing the traditional relationship of landscape to graphics, a dot pattern, taken from dot-matrix printing, organizes the planting as well as the building's graphics, thus unifying the design. A pattern of Ben-day dots printed on the vertical scrimlike stadium façade merges visually with an identical pattern of planted dots scattered horizontally across the landscape. This graphic pattern blurs the boundary between built elements and earthwork. As it threads its way through the mound, a large landscape ribbon with the dot-matrix pattern defines a public circulation route that links the stadium and the private practice area for horses. At the same time, the graphic pattern unites the principal programmatic elements. A stadium façade, a covered canopy for VIP and press seating, and a pedestrian bridge that terminates at a green roof covering the stables are all clad in it.

In addition to the main venue, a network of equestrian tracks and trails, including a cross-country course, weaves its way through LaTourette Park, in the center of Staten Island, and along the edges of the neighborhood golf course. It is designed to travel sustainably through existing ecosystems without cutting down forest or large masses of vegetation.

This project would have left New Yorkers with a fully sustainable public park equipped with an amphitheater once the demountable stadium was removed and the bowl-like earth mound remained after the Olympics. It would have left a facility for sports and concerts, state-of-the-art stables, and a network of pedestrian, horse, and bike trails. After the Olympic Games, facilities such as the grand dressage arena would have remained to be incorporated into the park as permanent elements, supporting further equestrian activity. Other structures would have been removed or reprogrammed to fit the community's needs. Visitors to the park could have continued to use the earthwork as a vantage point for watching baseball and soccer games on the fields that were used for training horses. Over time, the planted dots would have continued to grow outward, merging into a more subtle pattern over the site.

Because London was awarded the 2012 Olympics, the project did not go ahead. But it was honored as one of the five best unbuilt projects of 2005 by the New York chapter of the American Institute of Architects. **23**

23. The edge between architecture and landscape can be porous.

Part 3   196

209

210

Fig. 209. Earthworks: NYC 2012 Olympics, Equestrian Venue. Staten Island, New York, 2004.

Fig. 210. Earthworks: NYC 2012 Olympics, Equestrian Venue. Diagram of earth mound.

Fig. 211. Earthworks: NYC 2012 Olympics, Equestrian Venue.

Fig. 212. Earthworks: NYC 2012 Olympics, Equestrian Venue. Detail of planting scheme derived from dot matrix pattern developed for exterior skin of stadium.

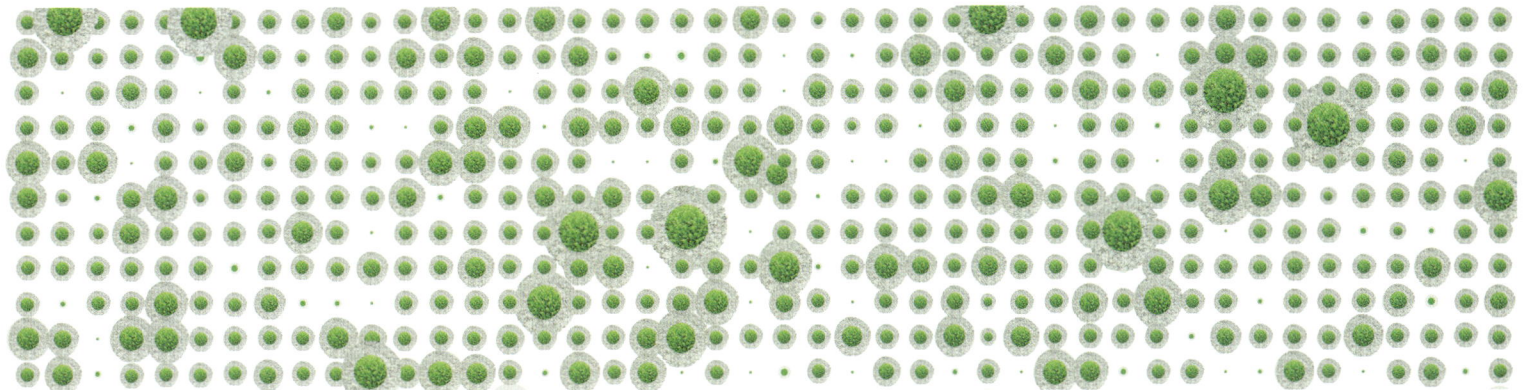

211

212

213

Fig. 213. Earthworks: NYC 2012 Olympics, Equestrian Venue. Boardwalk separating training areas from pedestrians.

Fig. 214. Earthworks: NYC 2012 Olympics, Equestrian Venue. Detail of event area.

Fig. 215. Earthworks: NYC 2012 Olympics, Equestrian Venue. Entrance.

214

215

Campa de los Ingleses, Bilbao

Winning the open international competition for the Campa de los Ingleses, the only undesigned space left in the Abandoibarra master plan, was most gratifying, considering how deeply we had thought about the site and how much time we had spent on it (fig. 216). Here the connection between the designed plaza and the thin, arced lines of different ecotones below seemed to move into the realm of the Thick Edge. It is therefore the most satisfying of all the work we are doing in Bilbao; it is where all the thinking and cumulative experience from earlier projects truly jelled.

The entry into a project is rarely what one expects. Usually it is a site visit, where the physicality of the site leaves a signature impression. But it is not always visual; it can be a scent, or a sensation—feeling cold or hot, for example. In Bilbao what most strongly marked the work was the continuous, very thin rain. It resembles a vapor and is given a special name: *chirimiri.* It is accompanied by steel gray skies and an absence of warm light. It is a condition so frequent that in the first two years of going to Bilbao I never saw a dry pavement. The reaction to this is to want light and things that are warm in color or white, or that reflect light, which is why the titanium chosen by Frank Gehry for the Guggenheim is right. The rain also yields a greenness, since water is so plentiful; accordingly, we proposed setting the light rail on a grass median. Second to chirimiri in making an impression was the thirteen-meter drop from the level of the city to the waterfront. Much of the work in the master plan and the Campa was devoted to making the thirty-five acres of the old port site not feel like a hole, and trying to gracefully stitch together the city and river levels.

The Campa is an expansion of the set of parallel ribbons of landscape designed for the master plan, and it rises immediately behind them up to the city level, thirteen meters higher. The project entailed bending the ecotones into three-dimensional forms, even tucking pavilions within them, making a thick line that joins the arcs parallel to the water's edge to the slope and the slope to the plaza above. The ribbons of paths ascending to the city level curve and turn to ramp up the walk, allowing us to deform the slope in three dimensions.

We are entering the construction document phase. The design phase has been finalized, based on the scheme with which we won the international competition. Construction was to begin in 2010 (figs. 217–223). **24**

24. Landscape can be like poetry, highly suggestive and open to multiple interpretations.

216

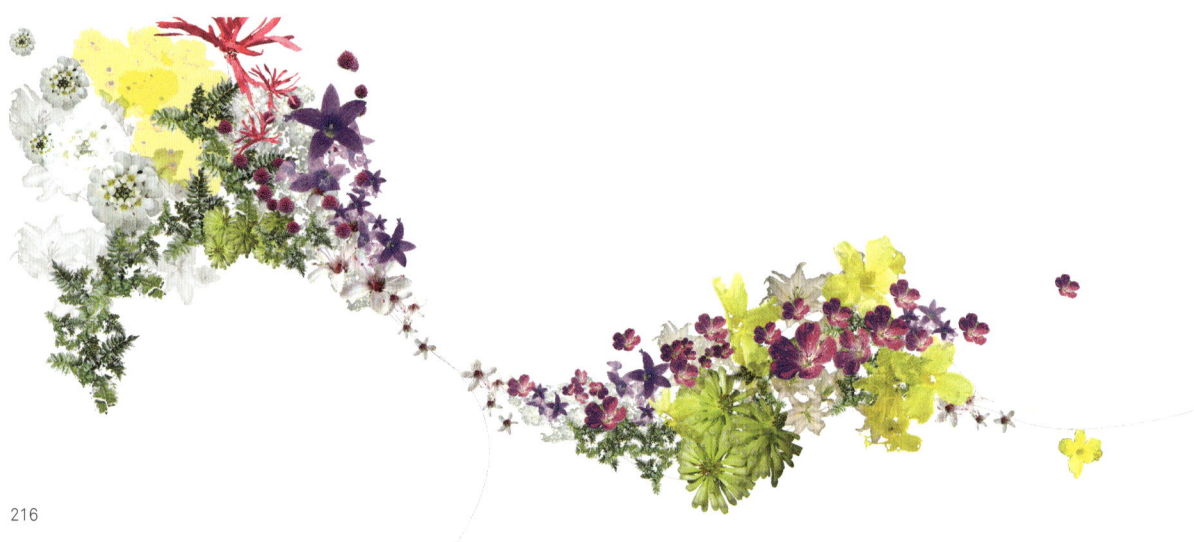

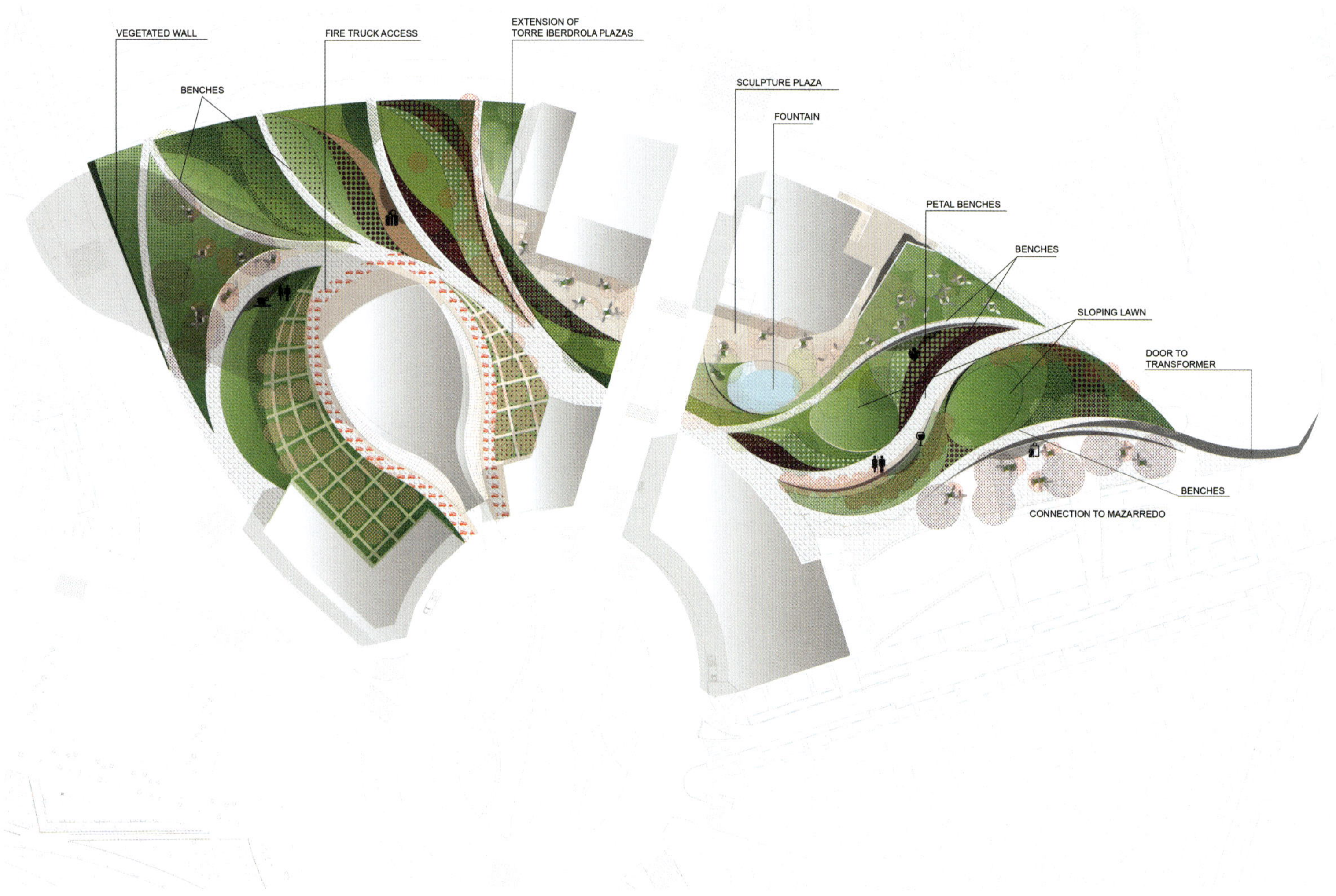
VEGETATED WALL
FIRE TRUCK ACCESS
EXTENSION OF
TORRE IBERDROLA PLAZAS
BENCHES
SCULPTURE PLAZA
FOUNTAIN
PETAL BENCHES
BENCHES
SLOPING LAWN
DOOR TO
TRANSFORMER
BENCHES
CONNECTION TO MAZARREDO

217

Part 3 203

218

Fig. 216. Campa de los Ingleses, Bilbao, Spain, 2007. Abstract diagram of site.

Fig. 217. Campa de los Ingleses. Plan.

Fig. 218. Campa de los Ingleses.

219

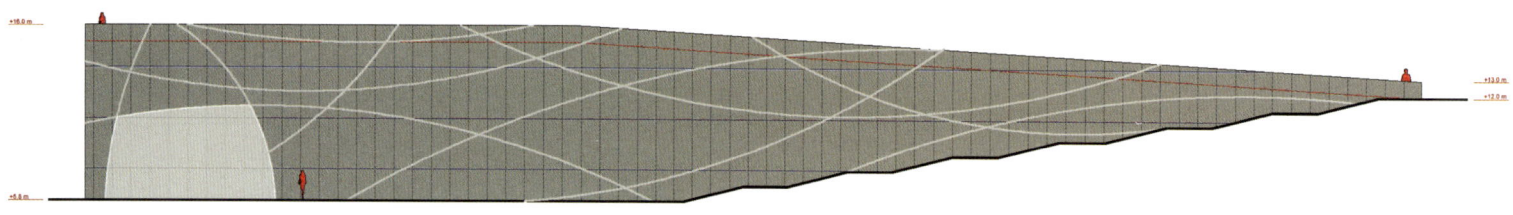

220

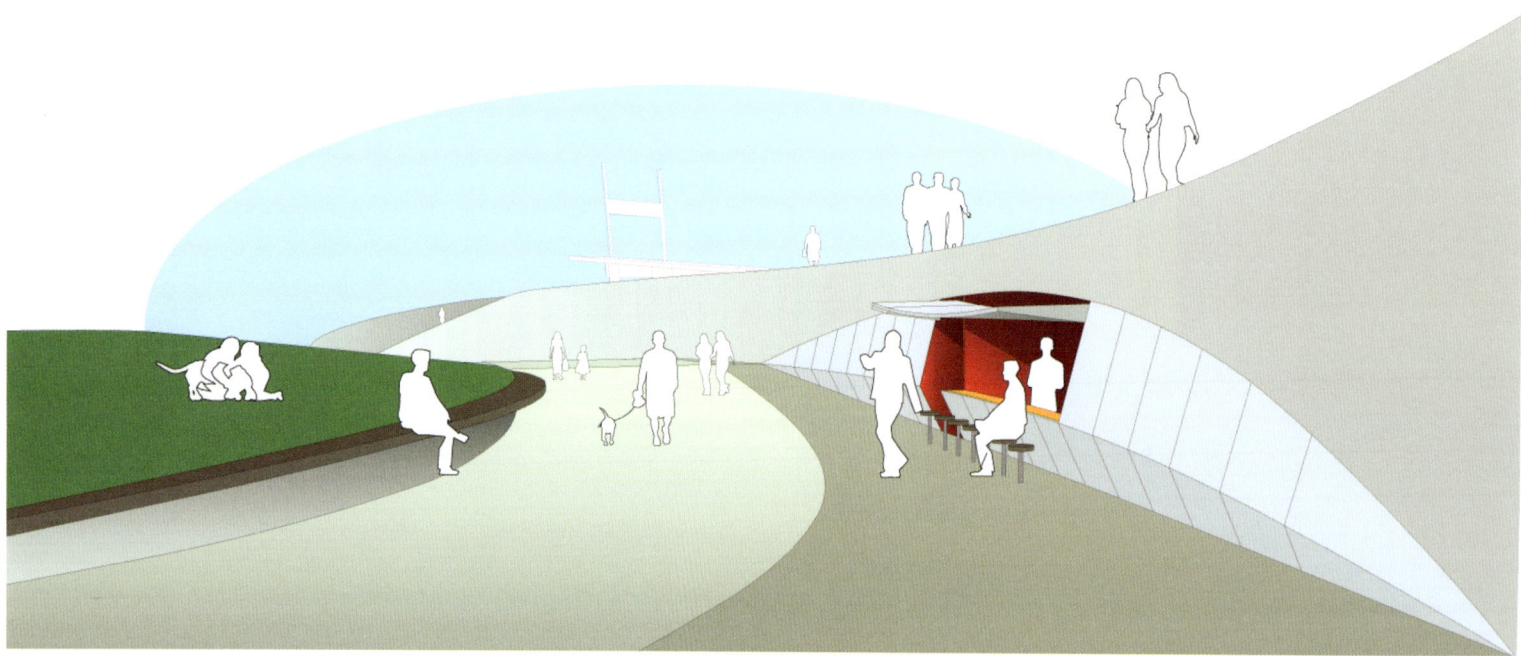

221

Fig. 219. Campa de los Ingleses. Section.

Fig. 220. Campa de los Ingleses. Elevations of stainless-steel walls.

Fig. 221. Campa de los Ingleses. Rendering of café tucked into contours.

Fig. 222. Campa de los Ingleses. Skating rink.

Fig. 223. Campa de los Ingleses. Paving pattern.

Public Administrative Master Plan, South Korea

Travel from Seoul to Sejong via the fast train, and during the hour-long journey, as you look out the window, you will see valley after valley, usually surrounded by blue mountains, all of a similar height. Mountains are everywhere. Seventy percent of Korea is mountainous. The site for PAT is more bowl-like, but, as with the landscape viewed from the train, blue mountains surround it. In the flat part of the bowl the rice fields are now at their intense, maximum greenness, although the aqueous reflectivity of their terraces is not visible. The mountains and the rice fields are the Korean landscape. The city will sit in the flat part of the bowl. But it is not entirely flat—a lower mountain juts out from the most level part. Although such mountains are usually removed to create more level space, we kept this one. Rice fields usually go too, to make more room for cities. We proposed keeping some of them, placing them by the pond that serves as a water storage system. It is hot, August. The ditches by the sides of the rice fields contain a mixture of vegetables and flowers, looking accidental. The demolition of a few small houses has begun. In the same area, a house is being built. The person showing us around says that such construction is typical, as speculators hope to get more money out of the government. Later, back at the government offices, demonstrators with a loudspeaker fill the afternoon with chanting. I am told that they are protesting the amount that the government is paying them for their property. The then president of Korea, Rho Mu Hyun, backed the construction of the Public Administrative Town in Sejong, as well as the transfer of half of the government ministries there, as a way to draw population away from Seoul. Work on the infrastructure has already started. Two competitions have been run. Together with Haeahn, a Korean architecture firm, and its New York branch, H Associates, we won the first one, for the master plan. We are also designing Phase 1, which includes the building and site for the first ministry. A Korean architect won the competition for Phase 2, the next ministry building and site. The rest is in the lap of the fates.

Winning the competition for the Public Administrative Town (PAT) gave us the opportunity to put landscape to work at the ultimate task of its new twenty-first-century role: creating a city. The PAT site is in the inner part of a ring-shaped, structured city. Together with the mountainous northern area, the eastern Jangnam Plain, and a thirty-year reserved zone, PAT will become its heart.

Several small residential ring towns surround PAT in the form of clusters of high-rise apartment buildings. The construction has already begun. These towns of towers, all built according to the model preferred throughout Korea, will be set off by our flat, open design at the city center. The contrast with the low-rise Government Complex at its core will be all the more dramatic.

The scheme is based on achieving an interweaving of architecture and landscape (fig. 224). The framework for PAT, on which the interface hangs, consists in:

> *A flat city.* Horizontal displacement at ground and roof level makes for a pedestrian-oriented, public-spaced city.

> *A connected city.* The government ministries are all linked by means of two public levels, unifying public services without placing them all in one massive building.

> *A wasteless city.* Reuse of garbage, biomass, sunlight, and water eliminates all waste. Sustainability is achieved with a new system of veins and arteries that serve building and landscape as one. The new connectivity of interior to exterior and the interface between architecture and landscape facilitate sustainability by creating rain gardens, reusing gray water, and instituting wind and solar energy systems.

The Aesthetic

The form of the project, the intended aesthetic, lies in the vertical dimension. The most important element along this vertical axis—what we call the Iconic Plane—is that of the surrounding mountains, which, viewed from the sixth-floor rooftops, create a dark blue horizon line around the whole perimeter.

Fig. 224. Public Administrative Town Master Plan, Sejong, South Korea, 2007. Plan showing government buildings in orange.

Fig. 225. Public Administrative Town Master Plan, Sejong, South Korea. Rendering (as part of an initiative to reinvent ways of representing landscape).

Fig. 226. Public Administrative Town Master Plan. Rendering of lakeside cultural facilities.

The second important dimension vertically is the Ground Plane (fig. 225). We have worked assiduously at confusing the lobby level of the buildings with that of the landscape, making it move upward and downward through ramps that connect to the other main public level, from which one can see the blue line of mountains. Both of these levels are public, open, and continuous. At the top level, green roofs create an uninterrupted public park that functions as a fifth façade and allows people to move from one government building to another.

The third plane, Landscape, connects both Iconic and Ground and is part of each. It was conceived as a piece in motion: as trees grow in it, they will change the relations among the parts. Landscape seems to be everywhere; sometimes it is the Ground Plane, the topography; sometimes the Iconic Plane, which frees you to feel as if you were in a bowl surrounded by the blue line of the mountains. Thus it seems to be both vertical and horizontal. It goes from the basement, where there are some green spaces, to the sky.

The park on the roofs is intended as a fifth façade. Each of the six towns surrounding the Public Administrative Town is a collection of towers looking down on this park and the government buildings below it, which declare their publicness and accessibility. The edges of the buildings have been treated as Thick Edges, where an interface between architecture, landscape, and city occurs. You are never quite sure which is which.

Horizontal Organization

PAT has an inner and an outer zone, separated by the undulating, ring-shaped Government Complex. Commercial businesses penetrate the Government Complex, linking the two zones. Residential areas are located in the outer ring, connecting them to residential areas outside of PAT. Mixed-use districts between the commercial and residential areas provide smooth transitions between the two. Cultural facilities are sited adjacent to the reservoir and other water sources to emphasize their role as public amenities and recreational centers. Situated near parks and creeks, government facilities act as mediators and linkages among all of the town's programs, and unify them into a whole (fig. 226).

Street Life

Every street in PAT has two dimensions: horizontal and vertical. In the plan, streets lead people to the places they need to go and up to the elevated park on the Iconic Plane in sections. Streets are divided into several functional categories, such as automobile/fast road, pedestrian/slow street, scenic drive, and commercial thoroughfare. In the pedestrian street, in the inner commercial district, is a retail-friendly environment with maximum store frontage along the landscape surfaces leading to the Iconic Plane, the highest destination.

Ground Floor Plan: Pavilions on the Park

Laid near open space, water, and park, the Government Complex garden is designed to draw open-space connections inside its territory; there are no fences, hedges, or other distinctive separating elements. The entrance hall is the only portion of the complex under the piloti. The transparent lobbies stand like pavilions in the park and have public and government functions. People can easily access and use them for information, exhibition, and civic services at any time—when they're taking a walk in the park for, example.

Typical Government Office Floor

The office area on a typical floor is composed of three bands along the main circulation route. The exterior double skin is for the building's environmental control and provides a shortcut for circulation to other levels. Work space is designed with optimal depth for natural lighting, using a basic unit composition. A supporting facility band provides a buffer from noise and congestion from the main corridor.

Parking Below the Iconic Plane

Public parking for the Government Complex is right under the green roof and reached by a dedicated circulation route: the government express line. Natural contours create direct, rampless access from the major automobile road to the parking area. Once

Fig. 227. Public Administrative Town Master Plan. Rendering of canal and government building.

on the government express road, people can drive straight to the parking lot above their destination. This entryway to the Government Complex will be a new experience, providing convenience and a view, unlike conventional underground parking.

Elevation as Indicator

Because of its lengthy and winding shape, the Government Complex can be seen from almost every street in PAT. The exterior of the complex is composed of a double skin. The inner skin is color-coded with various materials and patterns that correspond to each ministry group and institution. Through this readily observable connection, the Government Complex will act as a visual indicator for each district in PAT, providing a citywide visual code (fig. 227).

Toward a Wasteless City

In nature, waste from one system becomes the food for another. PAT emulates nature's efficiency, boasting four infrastructure systems that reuse waste and reduce pollution while performing essential functions for the city. Green roofs and street-side swales clean both air and water. The sewage plant turns waste into fertilizer and energy. A new titanium dioxide paving technology creates building and street surfaces that actually neutralize NOx, dangerous air pollutants. What is good for the environment does not need to be bad to look at. Nor do city processes need to occur behind the scenes. By making the systems that support it both visible and beautiful, the wasteless city celebrates them.

Interface

Sustainability in architecture and landscape interweaves inner and outer spaces on an urban scale. Both the Iconic Plane and the Ground Plane parallel the building layouts and create motion vertically and horizontally across the site. They integrate city functions into daily life and connect citizens to their government.

PAT will be a novel experience for the public. People who have seen this winning entry to the competition are surprised by the boldness of the jury in selecting it. Its intention was to interweave the city with its surroundings. The essence of the project was the creation of unexpected ways to move between levels vertically. This included the desire to make the mountains part of the project, embracing the topography (fig. 228).

In Korea, because of the high ratio of mountains to flatland, the first impulse in working on any site is to flatten it out; as a norm, mountains and hills are removed from building sites. In the case of PAT, however, the majority of the topography is left intact, incorporated into the project. In the very first ministry to be built, nearly a fifth of the site is a major hill, used to ease the climb up to the sixth level. This first parcel is under our control, so we will achieve our aim with it. The international competitions for the rest of the buildings and sites will follow the master plan, and so we hope they will as well, but that will depend very much on their juries.

This overriding vertical dimension is like a tree with roots feeding on the water plane underground and rising through layers of floors to a canopy at the level of the mountains, reaching for the sky. It serves as an image of what we were planting here with this group of buildings.

A Walk Through Sejong's Public Administrative Town

One hour by fast train will take you to Daejeon Station. Transfer to the rapid-transit bus to go to Sejong City. The bus goes around the ring road, dropping passengers at each specialized town. Densely packed apartment towers on megablocks, the standard urban scene in Korea, flank the ring road. As we approach PAT, the scene opens to a flat plane, which gives an unobstructed view of what at first appears to be sixteen hundred acres of parkland space. A closer examination reveals that this open plane is actually composed of green roofs and treetops (fig. 229).

The ring road slopes down, and the bus drops us off at the ground level, linked vertically with the Government Complex, below. We decide to walk onto the green park atop the buildings to get to our destination, a ministry office. Here the blue line on

Fig. 228. Public Administrative Town Master Plan.

229

the horizon, drawn by the mountains encircling the site, is keenly felt. It reads as if it were at roof level, though in fact the mountains are at a much higher elevation. You feel contained in a bowl of blue. This line, under the open sky, dominates the feeling of the roof space. Big trees are planted only far below, leaving the view on this level completely open. Strolling here on the roof feels like being in the air with the treetops at our feet. Maples, dogwood, and shrubs in fall colors contrast with the evergreens in the rest of the town.

The end of the rooftop merges with a hill near the waterfront. There is public access from the hill through the rooftop to the ministry office we seek.

You can enter the building at either the top or the bottom. The verticality of the buildings contrasts with the dominant horizontality of the roof plane and the ground plane, the two public access and circulation areas. The government buildings are not separate, closed structures; they form a continuum at the ground and roof levels. Each building is woven into the space. It seems as if each has been put there just as a way to get you to the open air, the sky, and the view of the surrounding mountains (fig. 230).

The work on the master plan has ended; we have completed schematic design for **Phase 1**, which involves the building for the first ministry (figs. 231, 232). **25**

Fig. 229. Public Administrative Town Master Plan. Rendering showing government buildings in red with existing residential towers in white.

Overleaf:
Fig. 230. Public Administrative Town Master Plan. Second phase showing context.

Fig. 231. Public Administrative Town Master Plan. Second phase.

25. We must put the twenty-first-century city in nature rather than put nature in the city. To put a city in nature will mean using engineered systems that function as those in nature and deriving form from them.

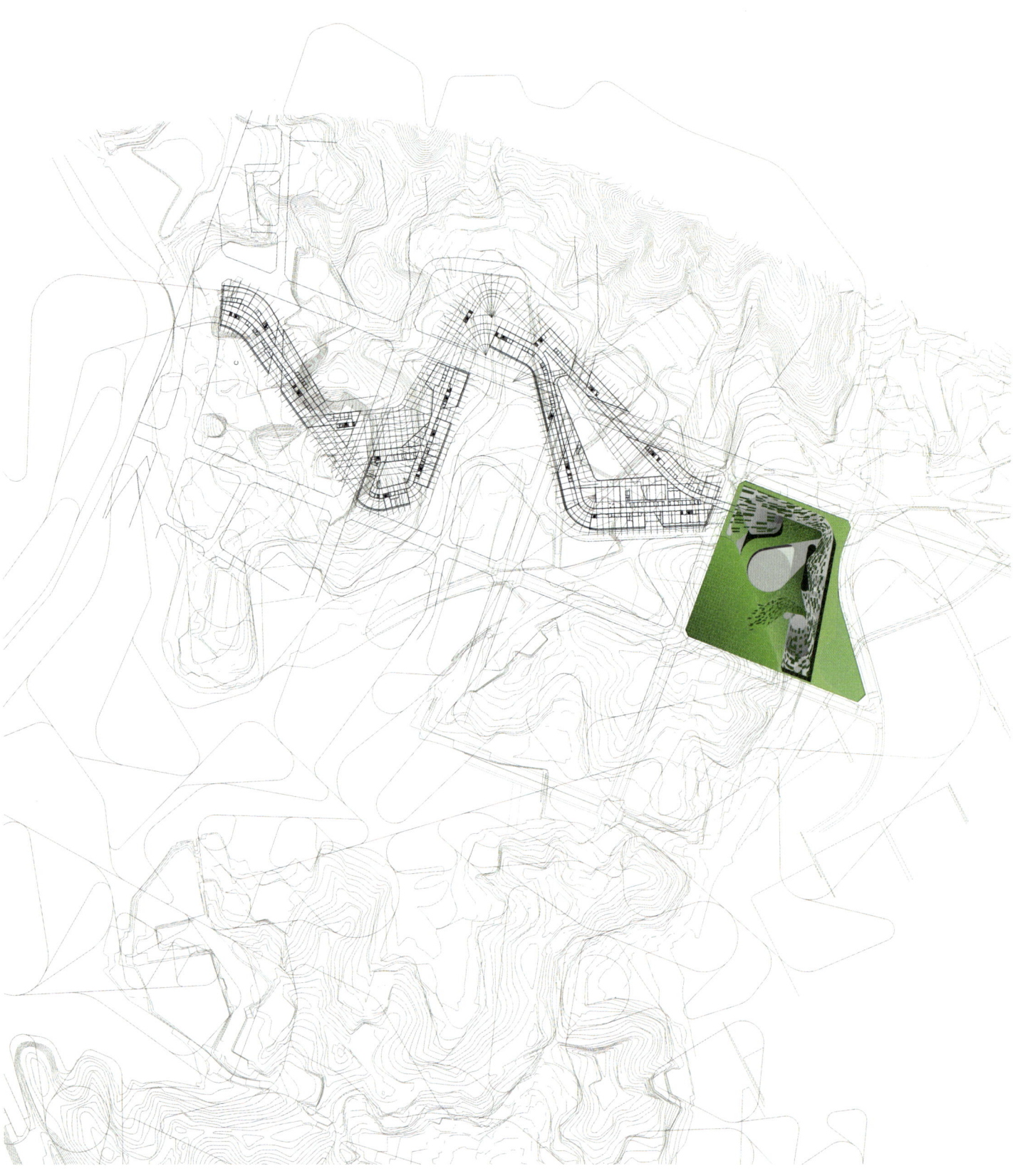

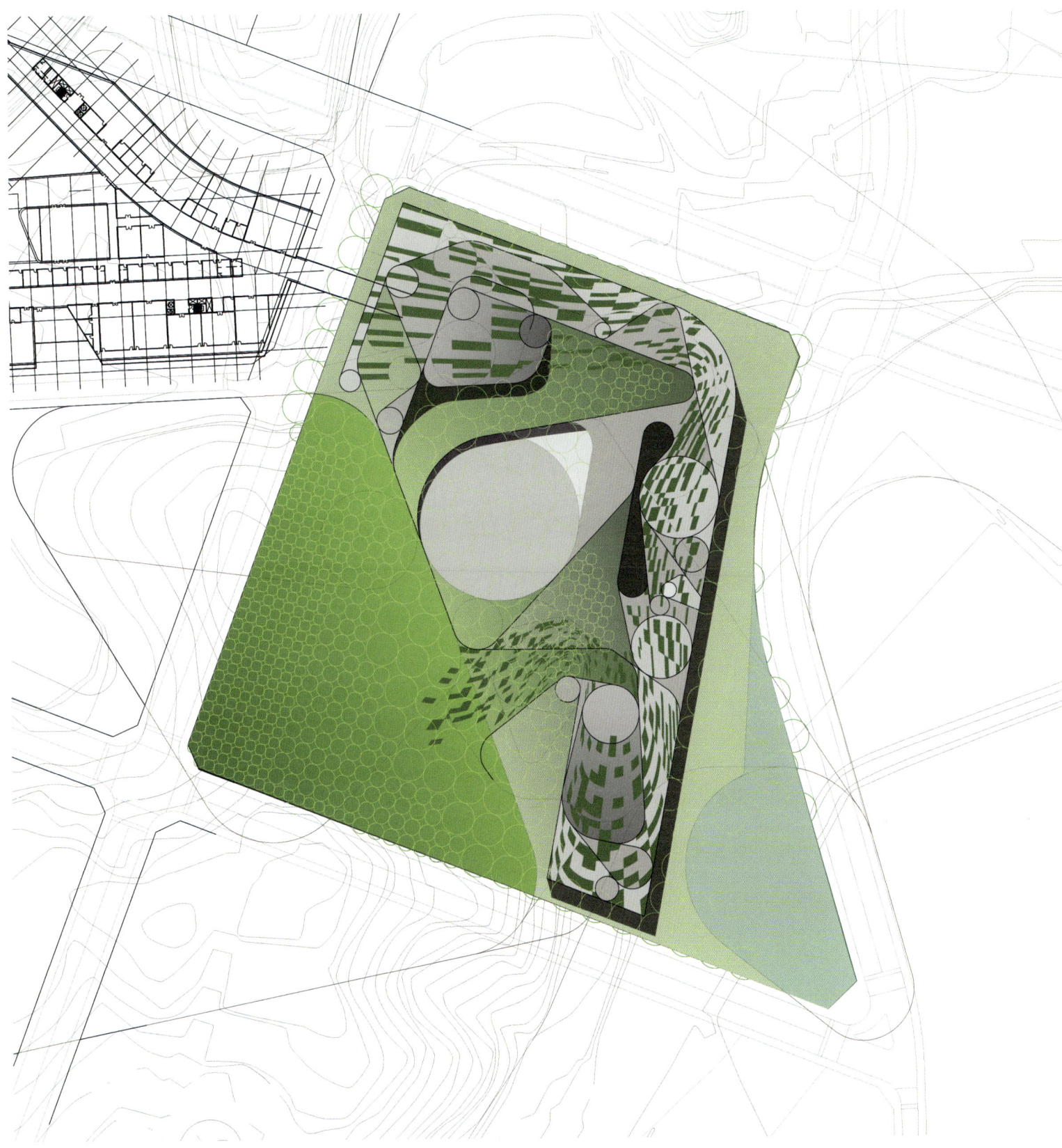

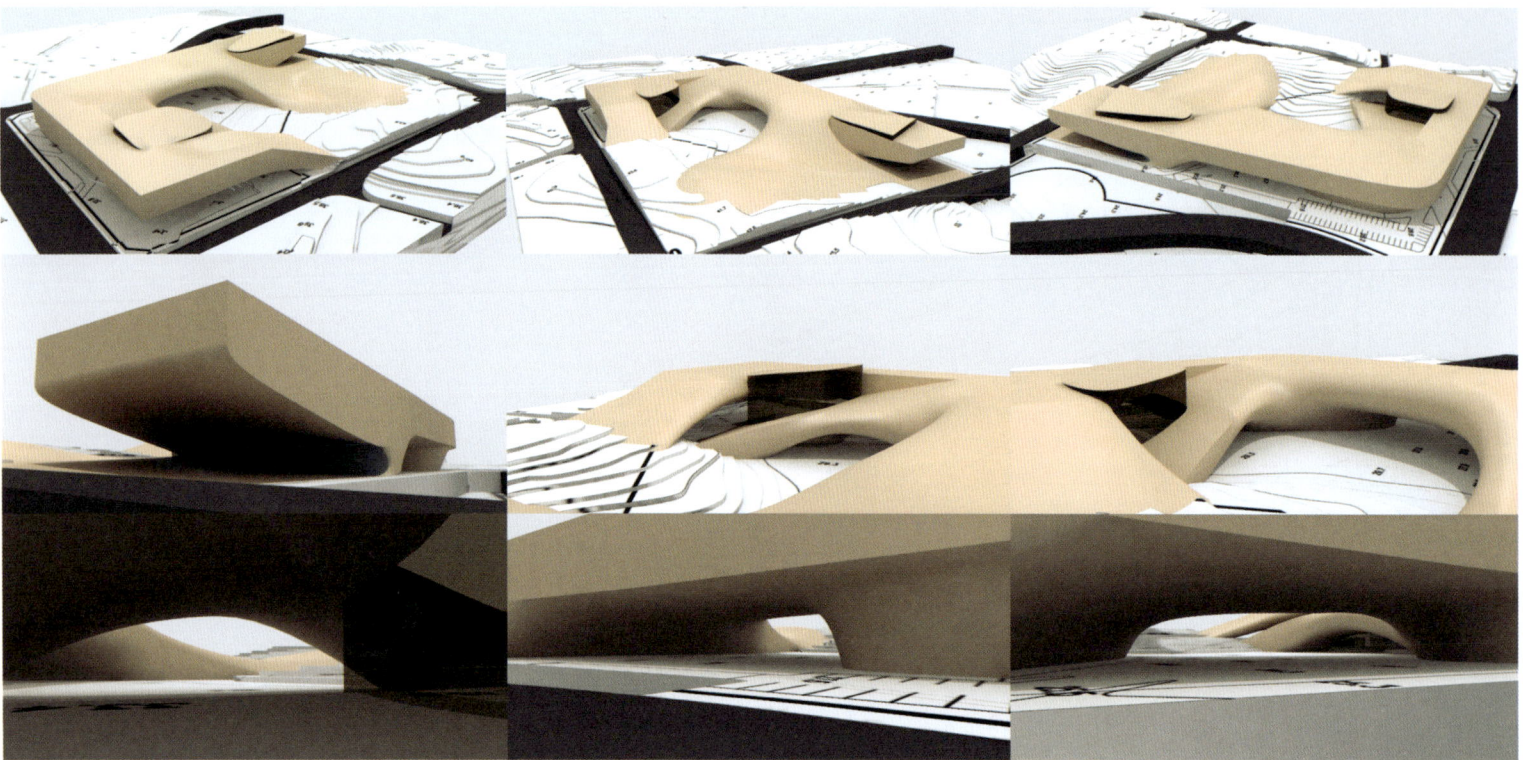

Fig. 232. Public Administrative Town Master Plan. Second phase, model.

Embedding the City in Nature

The crowded, dirty, dangerous cities of the nineteenth century were given parks as palliatives. Though they were the jewels of their cities, these parks sent an anti-urban message: this landscape is here to help you survive the city.

Landscape's task in cities today is markedly different, though the city is still its focus. It is not about creating parks. Nor is it about greening cities. Instead of embedding nature in the city, it is about embedding the city in nature. It is not about planting trees, but about creating a different relationship between landscape and its elements (water, earth, air) and the city. And between landscape and architecture, what I have called *interface*. This effort entails viewing cities in a very different way. It is not addressed by the typical master plan, or an urban design of street layouts and building massing, or a program mix that maximizes the return per square foot. Those can all be included, but they must be part of a balancing of our human needs with the city's geology, its water, its air, its flora and fauna. To embed the city in nature means paying attention to these parts for the design of a city and using engineered systems that work like systems from nature.

The emerging picture gives landscape the leading voice. Architecture, painting, and sculpture have each, at different times, fit their moment best and taken on the role of the mother art that speaks for all. Perhaps because it was better positioned than the others, or because it read into the present more deeply.

Landscape is in that position now. Architects, painters, and sculptors all acknowledge this through their interest in landscape.[4] Right now it seems that you can see further and deeper from a landscape-design platform. As painting in the early twentieth century became what we meant by Art, landscape is the Art for this era. But landscape allied with architecture and its spatial skills makes the best of this moment.

This changes landscape's subject. It changes its aim, it changes its arena, it changes its way of working. Its subject is the city, its aim to put the city in nature by creating a new relationship between them. Its arena is now political. It must enter the fray if it is to affect cities. Joined with architecture, it is the discipline best prepared to transform the city into a life-giving environment. The need for this is urgent.

Landscape artists joined with architects in a new role can help people develop a new compact with nature that emerges from their own localities. This new landscape and architecture must endeavor to educate people to move from passivity to active engagement with their transformed space—a major political act.

As we step gingerly over the shards of the past, overwhelmed at times by walking through ruins, impatiently eager to encounter something fresh, every now and then we may perceive something pushing through that speaks of a new beginning. Barely visible unless we look hard, hardly distinguishable in the ruins, in danger of being trampled, small protrusions emerge here and there. This text is an attempt to uncover them and to decipher their message about our time.

Coda

In this book I propose a new definition of landscape, bringing together ideas from biology, evolutionary theory, and ecology.

All three have recently altered our view of nature. Biology shows that even at the level of our cells, we are a historical structure that adapts old pieces to new uses—but that history does not move toward an end we plan. Evolutionary theory shows us a nature constantly changing, and us changing with it. Ecology puts us inside nature and shows our interdependence with its many parts.

Two tasks emerge from this redefinition: landscape must create a new kind of city, and it must broker a new type of relationship between humans and the rest of nature. For the first, we need to put the city into nature. For the second, we must undo the harmful model of industrialization.

New landscapes (for example, linear parks) are emerging from the effects of these changes in our understanding of nature. These new landscapes give us our first look at these transformations at work. But to understand these things at the specific level, concrete examples of each, as actually designed, are needed. I have attempted to reach this level of concreteness, moving from general statements to specific projects, with examples of designs by my office.

The new city comes out of putting all these specific entities to work in it. Next we need their design to broker a new relationship between us and the rest of nature. While the new landscapes are now visible, the new relationship with nature is dependent on new forms. Design expertise is essential to bring about this change. Aesthetics are still at odds with ecology, but some design paths connect between them. One path is that of concentrating the design on the interface, the boundary—for example, the boundary between land and water, between landscape and architecture, between landscape and city. Interface is the metaphor used for this aesthetic exploration. The Thick Edge was the earlier name for the aesthetic path developed for our office's work as we crossed from ecology to form. Later, with the academic work with Joel Sanders, we developed jointly this idea into the interface of porous entity.

The redefinition of landscape and by extension of architecture has begun. But it is not yet understood. It will be fully carried out when we apply ourselves to represent it in all its newness.

A Landscape Manifesto

1. Nostalgia for the past and utopian dreams for the future prevent us from looking at our present.

2. Nature is the flow of change within which humans exist. Evolution is its history. Ecology is our understanding of its present phase.

3. All things in nature are constantly changing. Landscape artists need to design to allow for change, while seeking a new course that enhances the coexistence of humans and the rest of nature.

4. Landscape forms encapsulate unseen assumptions. To expose them is to enter the economic and aesthetic struggles of our times.

5. Historical precedents do not support the common prejudice that human intervention is always harmful to the rest of nature.

6. Shifts are taking place before our eyes. Landscape artists and architects need to give them a name and make them visible. Aesthetic expertise is needed to enable the transforming relations between humans and the rest of nature to break through into public spaces.

7. High visibility, multiple alliances, and public support are critical to new landscape genres that portray our present.

8. Landscape—through new landscape elements—enters the city and modifies our way of being in it.

9. New landscape elements can become niches for species forced out of their original environment.

10. The new view of plants as groups of interrelated species modifying each other, rather than as separate and fixed, exemplifies fluidity—a main motif of landscape form.

11. Nostalgic images of nature are readily accepted, but they are like stage scenery for the wrong play.

12. In his *History of the Modern Taste in Gardening* (1780), Horace Walpole writes that William Kent "was the first to leap the fence and show that the whole of nature was a garden." Today landscape has leapt the fence in the opposite direction, to the city, making it part of nature.

13. Existing urban spaces can be rescued from their current damaging interaction with nature.

14. Landscape artists can reveal the forces of nature underlying cities, creating a new urban identity from them.

15. Landscape can create meeting places where people can delight in unexpected forms and spaces, inventing why and how they are to be appreciated.

16. A landscape, like a moment, never happens twice. This lack of fixity is landscape's asset.

17. We can heighten the desire for new interactions between humans and nature where it is least expected: in derelict spaces.

18. Emerging landscapes are becoming brand-new actors on the political stage.

19. Landscape renders the city as constantly evolving in response to climate, geography, and history.

20. Landscape can show artistic intention without imposing a predetermined meaning.

21. Landscape can bridge the line between ourselves and other parts of nature—between ourselves and a river.

22. Landscape is becoming the main actor of the urban stage, not just a destination.

23. The edge between architecture and landscape can be porous.

24. Landscape can be like poetry, highly suggestive and open to multiple interpretations.

25. We must put the twenty-first-century city in nature rather than put nature in the city. To put a city in nature will mean using engineered systems that function as those in nature and deriving form from them.

Notes

Introduction

1. See Diana Balmori, "Landscapes That Renew," in *Sustainable Architecture,* White Papers (New York: Earth Pledge Foundation, 2001), 19–23.

2. This perspective, which has matured over the years, was from the beginning informed by Balmori's awareness of the uneasy relationship between contemporary art and beauty. Yet, in spite of her continuous interest in contemporary art in New York, Balmori has argued that the art of landscape demanded a different attitude: "Since the 1980s, aesthetic approaches have been questioned in landscape. Ecological concerns have led to the view that aesthetic issues are an elitist conceptual structure, capriciously laid upon a site without any attention to its natural characteristics. Further, the obvious difficulty in explaining aesthetics has made the questions of delight and appeal in art arcane themes, although these, in fact, are the main forms of communication with its public." Diana Balmori, "Cranbrook: The Invisible Landscape," *JSAH* 53 (March 1994): 31.

3. There is nothing metaphysical, however, in Balmori's methods. See Diana Balmori, "A Productive Stormwater Park (Farmington, Minnesota)," in *Handbook of Water Sensitive Planning and Design,* ed. Robert L. France (Boca Raton, Fla.: Lewis, 2002), 175–91.

4. Balmori quotes the following definition of sustainability: "ability of an ecosystem to maintain a defined/desired state of ecological integrity over time." Diana Balmori and Gaboury Benoit, *Land and Natural Development (LAND) Code: Guidelines for Sustainable Land Development* (Hoboken, N.J.: Wiley, 2007), 2.

5. "Perhaps designers should not ever intend to produce a fixed finished model, but rather understand that a landscape is something that is going to continue to change so that there is not a specific form that should be legislated and fixed." See Diana Balmori, "A Path in the City, a Path in the Woods," *PLACES,* no. 4 (Berkeley: University of California, 1990), 65.

6. In her tentative outline for future parks, Balmori wrote: "It will not be Eden . . . and it will not be the Peaceable Kingdom, for which we yearn. It will however be the place where we sense life, its brevity, fragility, mutability, and intensity, and its connectedness among all living forms." Diana Balmori, "Park Redefinitions," in *The Once and Future Park,* ed. Deborah Karasov and Steve Waryan (New York: Princeton Architectural Press, 1993), 44.

7. This is a theme that she has often expressed in writing. For instance: "A park is a human framing of nature's essential powers: its capacity for constant change, its ability to transform, and finally its generative and life-sustaining force that functions independent of human ordering or intervention." Diana Balmori, "Landscape vs. Architecture," *Landscape Architecture* (1989): 36–37.

8. In a retrospective of her work for *Process: Architecture,* published in 1998, Balmori writes: "In certain ways all work after the NTT project became affected by what I learnt of Japan through Masahiro Soma, and though it does not cover or express the precise influence, I would say that since the NTT project there has been a much greater emphasis on the temporal, on aspects of change in a landscape." Diana Balmori, "Introduction: Built Work, Thought Work," in *Process Architecture: Diana Balmori, Landscape Works* (Process Architecture, 1997), 15–16.

9. Donald A. Schön, *The Reflective Practitioner: How Professionals Think in Action* (London: Temple Smith, 1983).

10. F. Herbert Bormann, Diana Balmori, and Gordon T. Geballe, *Redesigning the American Lawn: A Search for Environmental Harmony* (New Haven, Conn.: Yale University Press, 2001).

11. See Diana Balmori, "Re-framing the Work of City-Making," *Korean Landscape Architecture* (September 1995): 162–71.

12. Works by each of these landscape architects are mentioned in Balmori and Benoit, *Land and Natural Development (LAND) Code.*

13. Balmori and Benoit, *Land and Natural Development (LAND) Code.*

14. For a presentation of the history and content of classical art theory, see Rensselaer Wright Lee, *Ut Pictura Poesis: The Humanistic Theory of Painting* (New York: Norton, 1967).

15. See Balmori, "A Productive Stormwater Park," 175–91 (esp. 177 and 179).

16. Balmori said, in a private conversation in July 2007: "The relationship to art and history is a hidden trend in all the works. It is not voiced, but constantly important, and yet sometimes antagonistic. Historical material is a provider of questions. I have traveled from being an historian to being anti-history. The relationship [of art to history] has to be transformed. The past should not be repeated." Notes by the author.

17. Diana Balmori, "Live Fences: Hedges," in *Between Fences,* ed. Gregory K. Dreicer (Princeton: Princeton Architectural Press, 1996), 49–55.

18. See Diana Balmori, "A New Kind of Park," in *Landscape Transformed,* ed. Michael Spens (London: Academy Editions, 1996), 44–47.

19. This is a recurrent question in Balmori's work. See Balmori, "Cranbrook: The Invisible Landscape," 31.

20. Balmori, "Landscape vs. Architecture."

21. See Diana Balmori, "Redefining the Boundary, Defining the Modern," *Progressive Architecture* (August 1991).

22. "The problem of defining the boundaries between architecture and landscape is one of the most important issues confronting both art forms today. It is not sufficient to have one art form define and prevail over the other. At La Villette, the problem of frame has not been addressed." Balmori, "Landscape vs. Architecture," 36–37.

23. F. Hamilton Hazlehurst, "Jules Hardouin Mansart and André Le Nôtre at Dampierre," in *Tradition and Innovation in French Garden Art: Chapters of a New History,* ed. John Dixon Hunt and Michel Conan, with the assistance of Claire Goldstein (Philadelphia: Pennsylvania University Press, 2002), 44–67.

24. German sociologist Georg Simmel (1858–1918), in a penetrating analysis that contrasts the experience of a painting and the experience of a landscape, proposed that the background created by a landscape was a kind of mood that he called *stimmung*. The word defies translation, but the idea is very general. The same thing can be said about the perception of a landscape in non-Western cultures. See Michel Conan, ed., *Middle East Garden Traditions: Unity and Diversity* (Washington, D.C.: Dumbarton Oaks, 2007).

25. Setting a place may involve all sorts of topological strategies. This is clearly illustrated by a short critical piece by Diana Balmori on the Irish Hunger Memorial, by the sculptor Brian Tolle in collaboration with Juergen Riehm and David Piscuskas of 1100 Architect, of New York, and Gail Wittwer-Laird, a landscape architect. See Diana Balmori, "Review: Irish Hunger Memorial," *e-Oculus* (August 15, 2002).

26. The relationships Balmori achieves between architecture and landscape are neither hierarchical (architecture commanding landscape—as in Baroque palaces, or landscape ruling architecture—as in twentieth-century environmentalism) nor dialectical (the contradictions between landscape and architecture leading to a superior form of art or design), but mutually inclusive as in a yin-yang relationship. This is most clearly expressed in recent projects for Bilbao, Trenton, and PAT.

27. See Fernand Léger, *Fonctions de la peinture* (Paris: Gallimard, 1997), 48.

28. In a journal article about the amphitheater for the equestrian games in New York, Balmori wrote: "A pattern of Ben-day dots that is printed on the vertical scrim-like stadium façade visually merges with an identical pattern of planted dots now scattered horizontally across the landscape, blurring the boundary between the built elements and the earthwork." Diana Balmori, "Earthworks 2012," *ELA* 205 (2005): 54–57.

29. See, for instance, John Beardsley, "Article on Diana Balmori's Work," in Balmori, *Process Architecture,* 5–10 (esp. 6).

30. There is, however, a direct relationship between Rothko's strategies and Balmori's blurring of forms by dot matrices in the representation of her projects. See Diana Balmori, "Representation and Presentation," in "Features: Balmori Associates," *Environment and Landscape Architecture of Korea* 205 (2005): 50–51.

31. Balmori was much engaged in the creation of Robert Smithson's Floating Island, by Minetta Brook and the Whitney Museum of American Art, in October 2005. This collage of a picturesque landscape, in homage to Frederick Law Olmsted's design of Central Park, was placed on a barge that traveled around Manhattan from September 17 to 25, 2005.

32. "With its values of utility and access, the model of the street offers an alternative to public spaces conceived as monumental plazas, massive city centers or Olmstedian park." Diana Balmori, "Public Space and Public Life: Designing a Public Life," *Modulus* 21 (1991): 84–95 (see esp. 84).

33. See Diana Balmori, "Shenzhen Cultural Park," *ELA* 205 (2005): 90–93.

34. See Balmori Associates' project Plaza Euskadi, Bilbao, Spain, 2007.

35. In Balmori's view, ethical judgment bears on the will of the creators, not on the practical functions of the landscape, and the idea of perfection is irrelevant to her projects.

36. See the Analytic of the Beautiful, first moment, al. 45, "Beautiful Art Is an Art in So Far as It Seems Like Nature," in "Critique of Aesthetic Judgment," in Kant's *Critique of Judgment*. Quoted after the translation in Albert Hofstadter and Richard Kuhns, eds., *Philosophies of Art and Beauty: Selected Readings in Aesthetics from Plato to Heidegger* (Chicago: University of Chicago Press, 1976), 313.

37. We may think of the experience of a public city park that was introduced by Central Park, in New York, for instance. Alain Corbin has provided many examples of a history of desires, including his *Lure of the Sea: The Discovery of the Seaside in the Western World, 1750–1840*, trans. Jocelyn Phelps (Cambridge, Mass.: Polity Press, 1994), and *Time, Desire and Horror: Towards a History of the Senses*, trans. Jean Birrell (Cambridge, Mass.: Polity, 1995).

38. See Balmori, "Path in the City," 50–67.

39. This accounts in particular for the large and varied cooperation she has engaged in, and also for her call for many forms of cooperation between the public and private sectors. See Balmori, "Park Redefinitions."

40. Clement Greenberg, *Art and Culture: Critical Essays* (Boston: Beacon, 1971).

41. Jane Amidon, ed., *Peter Walker and Partners: Nasher Sculpture Center Garden* (New York: Princeton Architectural Press, 2006), 41.

42. She would agree with many contemporary authors that the discourses about nature in myth, literature, the arts, or science are all obviously cultural constructions. Yet she means something much more radical: nature itself is coproduced by humans and nonhumans. This implies a moral demand upon humans to reflect upon the transformation of the course of human and nonhuman life that they can bring about.

43. Personal communication with the author, July 2007.

44. In a discussion of the trends toward social segregation and privatization of public space, Balmori calls for a concerted effort toward change in landscape architecture, without engaging in the naive belief that such change would solve all social problems: "We must recognize that to allow these new towns—the galactic cities, urban villages and edge cities—to function as fortresses, separating one group from the 'other' (the poor, the homeless, those of another race) makes any kind of public life within them a fraud. It is an abdication of our responsibility to build a viable public life." Balmori, "Public Space and Public Life," 84–95. See also Balmori, "Re-framing the Work of City-Making," 169.

45. Following seminal works by Alain Corbin, landscape historians have focused on the invention of new forms of desire for landscape, which have been reflected in large changes in the practical uses of nature for leisure throughout the world. See, for instance, Corbin's discussion of the invention of the desire for the seaside in *The Lure of the Sea*.

46. Fernando Chacel, *Paisagismo e Ecogênese = Landscaping and Ecogenesis* (Rio de Janeiro: Fraiha, 2001).

47. Scania (Skåne in Swedish) is the name of the plains region around Malmö.

48. In 1994, 126 fully grown pine trees were brought from the Bord forest, in Normandy, and transplanted in the large plaza created by Dominique Perrault. The whirlwinds resulting from the presence of the library towers have uprooted a number of trees and led the library management to bind the remaining ones with metallic cables. The result is neither idyllic nor ecological; moreover, this landscape is inaccessible to library patrons.

49. She sees landscape as a reflective structure. It results from movements of opinion and praxis, and embodies this changing culture and diffuses it back to its visitors: "The linear park offers an inner frontier . . . : The trails return control of the land to us as individuals and as people. This has far-reaching consequences: the linear park represents a movement toward an envisioning of our own communities." Balmori, "New Kind of Park," 45.

Part 1. History and Nature/Nature and Art: A New Departure

1. Anthony Ashley Cooper, third Earl of Shaftesbury, "The Moralists, a Philosophical Rhapsody," in *Characteristicks of Men, Manners, Opinions, Times*, ed. Douglas den Uyl (Indianapolis: Liberty Fund, 2001), vol. 2, part 3, sect. ii.

2. Kant, "On the Division of the Fine Arts," in *Critique of Judgment*, para. 51.

3. Lawrence Weschler, *Seeing Is Forgetting the Name of the Thing One Sees: A Life of Contemporary Artist Robert Irwin* (Berkeley: University of California Press, 1982), 59.

4. Robert Smithson, "Conversation in Salt Lake City," in *Robert Smithson: The Collected Writings* (Berkeley: University of California Press, 1996), 298.

5. Robert Smithson, "Discussions with Heizer, Oppenheim, Smithson," in *Collected Writings*, 250.

6. Though the relationship of landscape and art has been intermittently explored by different artists and landscape architects in the past twenty years, Peter Walker and Martha Schwarz have specifically been pressing landscape to enter the language of the art of its time.

Martha Schwartz's Dublin Grand Canal Square is an example of this, carried to the scale of a large urban site. See Tim Richardson, *Avant Gardeners* (London: Thames and Hudson, 2008), 259.

In art, Ian Hamilton Finlay and Derek Jarman have put forth landscapes which reinterpreted the relation of art with landscape: Finlay's garden "Little Sparta" makes landscape a place of confrontation with society. Jarman makes it a revelation of past damage and promotes a less interventionist new landscape. See Yves Abrioux, *Ian Hamilton Finlay: A Visual Primer* (Cambridge, Mass.: MIT Press, 1992); Derek Jarman, *Modern Nature: The Journals of Derek Jarman* (London: Century, 1991); and Derek Jarman, *Derek Jarman's Garden* (London: Thames and Hudson, 1995).

Sculptors, for their part, in moving out into the landscape and away from museums, began to face some of the issues encountered by landscape architects. This topic is well covered in John Beardsley, *Earthworks and Beyond: Contemporary Art in the Landscape* (New York: Abbeville, 1984).

Stephen Bann has recently written about the work of the Musée Gassendi, in France, which aims toward a fusion of art and nature; it is a geology museum that is engaging artists to make the geology of this part of the Alps visible. See Stephen Bann, "A 'Garden of the Hesperides': The Landscape Initiative of the Musée Gassendi, Digne, and the National Park of Alpes de Haute-Provence," in *Contemporary Garden Aesthetics, Creations and Interpretations*, ed. Michel Conan, (Washington, D.C.: Dumbarton Oaks Research Library and Collection, and Spacemaker, 2007), 235–49.

7. François Jacob, "Le Bricolage de l'Evolution," in *Le Jeu des Possibles* (Paris: Fayard, 1981), 70 and 86:

"L'évolution . . . travaille sur ce qui existe déjà, soit qu'elle transforme un système ancien pour lui donner une fonction nouvelle. . . . Les êtres vivants sont en fait des structures historiques. Ce sont littéralement des créations de l'histoire."

I thank Michel Conan for introducing me (partly, I think, to stop my complaints about the dead weight of history) to the work of François Jacob.

8. The new conditions in landscape work have produced a considerable expansion of topics to be considered. Some are addressed in James Corner and Alex S. McLean, *Taking Measures Across the American Landscape* (New Haven: Yale University Press, 1996); Kenneth Helphand, *Defiant Gardens: Making Gardens in Wartime* (San Antonio, Texas: Trinity University Press, 2008); Nial Kirkwood, ed., *Manufactured Sites: Rethinking the Post-Industrial Landscape* (London: Spon, 2001); and John Beardsley, *Gardens of Revelation: Environments by Visionary Artists* (New York: Abbeville, 1995).

9. Much of this section is loosely adapted from Bormann, Balmori, and Geballe, *Redesigning the American Lawn,* 7–27 and 66–89.

10. Yves Abrioux, *Ian Hamilton Finlay: A Visual Primer* (Edinburgh: Reaktion, 1985), 38.

11. M. Talbot, "Ecological Lawn Care," *Mother Earth News* 123 (1990): 60–73.

12. Warren Schultz, *The Chemical-Free Lawn* (Emmaus, Pa.: Rodale, 1989).

13. O. P. Engelstad, ed., *Fertilizer Technology and Use,* 3d ed. (Madison, Wis.: Soil Science Society of America, 1985); Francesca Lyman with Irving Mintzer, Kathleen Courrier, and James Mackenzie, *The Greenhouse Trap: What We Are Doing to the Atmosphere and How We Can Slow Global Warming,* World Resources Institute Guide to the Environment (Boston: Beacon, 1990), ix.

14. Sandra Postel, "Managing Freshwater Supplies," in *State of the World,* ed. Lester R. Brown (New York: Norton, 1985).

15. William J. Flipse et al., "Sources of Nitrate in Groundwater in a Sewered Housing Development, Central Long Island, New York," *Ground Water* 22, no. 4 (1984): 418–26.

16. Arthur J. Gold et al., "Nitrate-Nitrogen Losses to Groundwater from Rural and Suburban Land Uses," *Journal of Soil and Water Conservation* 45, no. 2 (1990): 305–10; World Resources Institute, in collaboration with the U.N. Environment Programme and the U.N. Development Programme, "Freshwater," in *World Resources, 1992–93,* ed. Allen L. Hammond (New York: Oxford University Press, 1992).

17. J. M. Halstead, W. R. Kearns, and P. D. Relf, "Lawn and Garden Chemicals and the Potential for Groundwater Contamination," in *Proceedings of Ground Water: Issues and Solutions in the Potomac River Basin/Chesapeake Bay Region* (Washington, D.C.: National Water Well Association, 1989), 355–69.

18. U.S. Congress, Office of Technology Assessment, *Facing America's Trash: What Next for Municipal Solid Waste?* OTA-O-424 (Washington, D.C.: U.S. Government Printing Office, 1989); B. Gavitt, "Recycling Clippings Eases Pressure on Landfills," *Turf* 4, no. 2 (1991): 20–22.

19. D. N. Jones, "Temporal Changes in the Suburban Avifauna of an Inland City," *Australian Wildlife Research* 8 (1981): 109–19; P. Mason, "The Impact of Urban Development on Bird Communities of Three Victorian Towns—Lilydale, Coldstream, and Mt. Evelyn," *Corella* 9, no. 1 (1985): 14–21.

20. This treasured role for the lawn still holds for certain places in cities where a green fulcrum in a congested area can serve an urban population. The recent renovation of Bryant Park, by Laurie Olin, is a good example of this, in which the lawn is framed nearly as in a picture and set as a treasured landscape. See J. William Thompson, *The Rebirth of New York's Bryant Park* (Washington, D.C.: Spacemaker, 2006)

21. Walt Whitman, "Leaves of Grass, 1855," in *Complete Poetry and Collected Prose* (New York: Viking, 1982), 31.

22. *Valley Farmer* 8 (St. Louis, 1856).

23. Laws of Nebraska Territory, Third Session, 1857, enacted April 13, 1857, cited in Leslie Hewes, "Early Fencing on the Western Margin of the Prairie," *Nebraska History* 69 (1982): 342, n. 12.

24. Bradley H. Baltenstensperger, "Hedgerow Distribution and Removal in Nonforested Regions of the Midwest," *Journal of Soil and Water Conservation* 42 (1987): 60–64.

Part 2. Transformations: Overcoming the Past

1. Antecedents to linear parks exist—for example, Olmsted's superb "Emerald Necklace" in Boston. But I am referring here to the reinvention and transformation of a corridor used for another purpose, usually industrial.

2. Contemporary work—not directly a linear park—that carries the agenda of a related type, the highway, further, is that of Bernard Lassus, in two of his projects. See Michel Conan, *The Crazannes Quarries by Bernard Lassus: An Essay Analyzing the Creation of Landscape* (Washington, D.C.: Dumbarton Oaks Research Library and Collection, and Spacemaker, 2004) and Bernard Lassus, "A Landscape Slope—The Rest Area of Nîmes-Caissargues/1992," in *The Landscape Approach* (Philadelphia: University of Pennsylvania Press, 1998), 164–67. In both, there is imaginative development in areas connected with highways.

See also Patricia Johanson's "Gardens for Highways" in Xin Wu, *Patricia Johanson's House and Garden Commission: Reconstruction of Modernity* (Washington, D.C.: Dumbarton Oaks Research Library and Collection, and Spacemaker, 2007), 2: 106–29.

The appearance of highway-related work in landscape can also be seen in Kathryn Gustafson's projects: Cuirasse (a tunnel entry to a Paris banlieue) and Les Pennes (a highway entry to Marseille). See Jane Amidon, *Moving Horizons: The Landscape Architecture of Kathryn Gustafson and Partners* (Basel: Birkhäuser, 2004), 38 and 44.

3. The analysis of the performance of the green roof on top of Silvercup Studios is based on data collected from the green roof research station from December 2005 through December 2006. Report by Dr. Robert D. Berghage of Pennsylvania State University and Christopher Wark of Green Roof Innovations/SHADE Consulting LLC.

Temperature Reductions: The Silvercup Studios' green roof significantly lowered the daily roof membrane temperature fluctuation and considerably eliminated the heat load through the roof during summer months.

- The maximum temperature observed on the conventional roof membrane was 141.8 degrees F, compared to 96.8 degrees F on the green roof membrane.
- The minimum temperature observed on the conventional roof membrane was 14 degrees, compared to 24.8 degrees on the green roof membrane.
- The maximum difference in temperatures between the conventional and the green roof membranes was 86 degrees.

Additionally, ambient air temperatures were reduced on the green roof because of the process of evapotranspiration.

- The maximum ambient air temperature observed at six inches above the conventional roof membrane was 111.2 degrees, compared to 105.8 degrees at six inches above the vegetation of the green roof.
- The maximum difference in ambient temperatures observed above the conventional and the green roof surfaces was 41 degrees.
- The differences between the ambient air temperatures above the conventional and the green roofs were statistically significant throughout the year.

The report concluded that heat gain through the roof in the summer can be lowered by 90 to 100 percent by the green roof, leading to reductions in energy consumption for air conditioning by 30 to 50 percent in summer and nearly 50 to 100 percent in spring and autumn.

Roof Protection: The green roof reduced daily temperature fluctuations, and, combined with the shade protection from the sun's UV rays, should minimize the wear and tear of the roof surface and extend the membrane's life.

- The maximum daily fluctuation in the roof membrane temperature was 98.6 degrees at the conventional roof membrane and 41 degrees at the green roof membrane.

Stormwater Management: The green roof was able to retain and detain stormwater with significant reductions in peak runoff flow. This effect was most pronounced in low-intensity rainfall events, during events with dry antecedent conditions, and during shorter-duration rainfalls.

Water Quality: The green roof improved water quality of the runoff water: the runoff from the green roof had lower concentrations of heavy metals, such as zinc (Zn) by 73 percent and iron (Fe) by 68 percent, compared to the conventional roof.

4. An example from contemporary practice of the design of a site and its parking lot for good water management is Michael Van Valkenburgh's Herman Miller factory, in Canton, Georgia. The 550-car parking lot, constructed wetland meadows, and absorptive pond have been integrated into one landscape design. See Deborah Snoonian, "Drain It Right: Wetlands for Managing Runoff," in *Architectural Record* (August 2001), 129.

5. Peter Latz's Landscape Park Duisburg-Nord has transformed a wastewater ditch into a clear water canal (the New Emscher). This part of the excellent park project is a valuable example of the attention given to water in the transformation of this industrial site into a public park. Water pumped from this canal drops at several points after traveling through the gardens. See Peter Latz, "Landscape Park Duisburg-Nord: Metamorphosis of an Industrial Site," in *Manufactured Sites: Rethinking the Post-Industrial Landscape,* ed. Nial Kirkwood (London: Spon, 2001), 150–51.

6. Loosely adapted from my chapter "Productive Stormwater Park," in *Handbook of Water Sensitive Planning and Design,* ed. Robert L. France (Boca Raton, Fla.: Lewis, 2002), 175–92. Robert L. France, B.Sc., M.Sc., Ph.D., is associate professor of landscape ecology and science director of the Center for Technology and Environment (CTE), Graduate School of Design, Harvard University. This handbook listed the best water projects in the United States of the past ten years.

7. A contemporary example of work on this transformation of a port into new urban space is that of Adriaan Geuze; West 8's Toronto waterfront project won a competition in 2006. See also Stig L. Andersson's project "Bjørvika: 7 New Urban Spaces in the Oslo Harbor," which creates a unifying space through a continuous floor of black basalt surrounding the edges of the town on the water. Bjørvika is discussed in Michel Conan, "An Urban Awakening to the Sense of Life," *Wunderstadt* (Berlin: Aedes, 2005), 4–9.

8. Urban Meadow, Brooklyn
   Scientific Data
   - New York City = 4,200 acres of roof and 11,533 acres of vacant land, the equivalent of 13 Central Parks.
   - 1 New York City resident = 8 tons of CO_2 emitted each year (43.8 pounds per day).
   - Brooklyn = 19.8 million tons of CO_2 annually = 30.8 percent of New York City's CO_2 emissions.
   Air Filter
   - NYC trees remove an estimated 42,300 tons of carbon per year.
   - 1 tree = 30 pounds of carbon capture = 110 pounds of CO_2 per year.
   - Urban Meadow, Brooklyn = 9 trees = 270 pounds of carbon capture = 990 pounds of CO_2 per year.
   Water Filter
   - New York City sewer system excess = 40 billion gallons of untreated sewage that flows into the local waterways and harbor per year.
   - Urban Meadow, Brooklyn = 240,000 gallons of water saved from entering the sewer system.
   Natural Air-Conditioner
   - Paved surfaces = 50 degrees F hotter than landscape.
   - Air temperatures = 1 to 2 degrees cooler in newly vegetated landscape.
   Urban Meadow, Brooklyn = cleaner air, reduced runoff, and cooler temperatures.

9. West Park, across the borders of Burkina Faso, Benin, and Nigeria; and Siachen Peace Park, across the India-Pakistan border, are examples.

10. Saleem H. Ali, ed., *Peace Parks: Conservation and Conflicts Resolution* (Cambridge, Mass.: MIT Press, 2007) is the first publication to acknowledge this emerging type of park.

11. Herbert Bormann and Gene Likens, "Acid Rain: A Serious Environmental Problem," *Science* 184, no. 4142 (June 1974): 1176–79.

12. See Ann Spirn, *The Granite Garden: Urban Nature and Human Design* (New York: Basic, 1984).

13. Of the most recent books connecting landscape to city, Charles Waldheim, ed., *The Landscape Urbanism Reader* (New York: Princeton Architectural Press, 2006) is the most comprehensive and timely.

14. George Hargreaves' Crissy Field/San Mill Creek Salt Marsh Restoration project in San Francisco is an apt example of the creation of a landscape for healing industrial damage (a 1990 oil spill).

Part 3: Interweaving Architecture, Landscape, and City

1. On work at city scale, see Peter Walker's Circular Park in Nishi Harima, Japan, and Nishi Harima Science Garden City, both part of Arata Isozaki and Peter Walker and Partners' master plan for a new town: Peter Walker and Partners, *Landscape Architecture: Defining the Craft* (San Francisco: Oro, 2005), 120–23 and 180–87.

2. Among those on the boat tour were Todd Antoine, senior planner, Great Rivers Greenway; Rollin Stanley, executive director, City of St. Louis Planning and Urban Design Agency; Peggy O'Dell, superintendent, National Park Service; Bob Moore, historian, National Park Service; Frank Mares, deputy superintendent, National Park Service; Jenny Nixon, vice president, Metro; James Cloar, president, Downtown St. Louis Partnership; Rob Davinroy, chief, river engineering, U.S. Army Corps of Engineers.

3. James B. Eads in *Addresses and Papers of James B. Eads,* ed. Estill McHenry (Slawson, 1884), 153.

4. Eisenman/Olin have collaborated on the Holocaust Memorial in Berlin, a landscape-driven project. See Julia Czerniak, Cynthia Davidson, and Laurie Olin, *Fertilizer: Olin/Eisenman* (Philadelphia: ICA Philadelphia, 2007). Other examples of architects' work in landscape are Diller/Scofidio's Blur Building, Swiss Expo 2002, Yverdon-les-Bains; Miralles/Pinós' Igualada Cemetery Park, Spain; FOA's Southeast Coastal Park, Barcelona; Weiss/Manfredi's Olympic Sculpture Park, Seattle.

Selected Project Credits

Newport Garden
Newport, Rhode Island
2006
1,460 square feet
Client: Nicholas Scheetz
Design Team: Diana Balmori, Mark Thomann, Karen Tamir, Sangmok Kim, Kira Appelhans, Emily Abruzzo, Martha Desbiens, Kristi Stromberg Wright
Architect: Outerbridge Horsey Architects

Frances Daly Fergusson Courtyard, Vassar College
Poughkeepsie, New York
2003
5,000 square feet
Client: Vassar College
Design Team: Diana Balmori, Paul Butkus

Farmington Canal Greenway Master Plan
New Haven, Connecticut
1995
9 miles long
Client: Farmington Canal Rail-to-Trail Association, Nancy Alderman, director
Design Team: Diana Balmori, Ana Maria Torres, Robin Cash, Mariko Masuoka, Christopher Siefert
Design Consultant: Alan Plattus
Architect: Pelli Clarke Pelli Architects

Farmington Canal, Yale University
Malone Engineering Center
New Haven, Connecticut
2006
200 yards long
Client: Yale University
Design Team: Diana Balmori, Javier González-Campaña, Mark Thomann, Paul Butkus, Kathleen Bakewell, Adrienne Cortez, Julie Farris, Cecilia B. Martinic, Karen Tamir

Gwynns Falls Trail Master Plan
Baltimore
1995
14 miles long
Client: Trust for Public Land, City of Baltimore, Department of Parks and Recreation
Design Team: Diana Balmori, Ana Maria Torres, William Coyne, Fran Leadon, Kirsten MacDougall
Project Coordinator: Feth Strommen
Environmental Sculptor: Meg Webster
Architect: Jonathan Fishman
Urban Historian: Edward Orser
Hydrologist: Paul Barten

The High Line
New York, New York
2004 (competition finalist)
1.5 miles
Client: Friends of the High Line
Design Team: Diana Balmori, Mark Thomann, Emily Abruzzo, Martha Desbiens
Architects: Zaha Hadid Architects; Studio MDA; SOM
Historic Preservation: BCA
Civil Engineer: Langan Engineering & Enviro. Svc.
Structural Engineer: Arup
Cultural Advisers: Creative Time; The Kitchen; Public Art Fund
Lighting Consultants: Halie Light; L'Observatoire International
Graphic Design: Pentagram

Silvercup Studios
Long Island City, Queens, New York
2005
35,000 square feet
Client: Silvercup Studios, Inc.
Funder: Clean Air Communities
Design Team: Diana Balmori, Mark Thomann, Sarah Wayland-Smith, Martha Desbiens, Abby Feldman, Sangmok Kim
Architect: Shalat Architects, P.C.
Landscape Contractor: Greener by Design

Gratz Industries
Long Island City, Queens, New York
2007
11,000 square feet
Client: Gratz Industries
Design Team: Diana Balmori, Mark Thomann, Sarah Wayland-Smith, Martha Desbiens
Design Consultants: Pratt Institute Center for Community and Environmental Development (PICCED); Pratt Planning and Architectural Collaborative (PPAC)
Landscape Contractor: Greener by Design

The Solaire
New York, New York
2003
9,530 square feet
Client: Albanese Development Corporation for Hugh L. Carey; Battery Park City Authority
Design Team: Diana Balmori, Javier González-Campaña, Kathleen Bakewell, Paul Butkus, Sarah Wayland-Smith, Cecilia B. Martinic
Architect: Pelli Clarke Pelli Architects
Associate Architects: Schuman, Licktenstein, Claman, Efron
Landscape Contractor: Steven Dubner

Broadway Penthouse
New York, New York
2007
2,200 square feet
Client: Matthew Blesso, Blesso Properties
Design Team: Diana Balmori, Mark Thomann, Kira Appelhans
Architect: Joel Sanders Architect
Associate Architect: ANDarchitects
Consulting Landscape Architect: R2P Studio Landscape Architecture
Landscape Contractor: Steven Dubner

Loews Miami Beach Hotel
Miami
2006
34,000 square feet
Client: Loews Miami Beach Hotel
Design Team: Diana Balmori, Mark Thomann, Sarah Wayland-Smith, Martha Desbiens

240 Central Park South
New York, New York
2007
13,000 square feet
Client: Douglas Lister Architect
Design Team: Diana Balmori, Mark Thomann, Martha Desbiens
Architect: Douglas Lister Architect
Landscape Contractor: Greener by Design

Botanical Research Institute of Texas (BRIT)
Fort Worth, Texas
Expected completion 2011
5.2 acres
Client: Botanical Research Institute of Texas
Design Team: Diana Balmori, Javier González-Campaña, Marta Rabazo, Johanna Phelps, Alice Feng
Architect: H3 Hardy Collaboration Architecture

Prairie Waterway/Park Place
Farmington, Minnesota
1996
91 acres
Client: City of Farmington
Design Team: Diana Balmori, William Coyne, Patty Crow, William Yocom
Adviser: Design Center for American Urban Landscape, Minneapolis
Engineer/Architect: Bonestroo, Rosene, Anderlik & Associates
Consulting Engineer: J. M. Montgomery
Hydrologist: Paul Barten
Environmental Adviser: Department of Natural Resources, St. Paul

Humboldt Avenue Reinvestment Study
Minneapolis
1996
9 square miles
Client: Hennepin County Works

Selected Project Credits

Design Team: Diana Balmori, Ana Maria Torres, Tom Hammerberg
Architects: Chan Kreiger & Associates, Inc.; Meyer, Scherer & Rockcastle, Ltd.
Economic and Community Development: Ken Meter
Hydrologist: Paul Barten
Graphic Design: Acorn Design
Advisers: Design Center for American Urban Landscape

Arverne
Arverne, New York
2001 (design charrette)
100 acres
Client: Architectural League
Yale School of Architecture Faculty/Design Team: Diana Balmori, Deborah Berke, Peggy Deamer, Keller Easterling
Architecture Students: Ben Bischoff, Mike Tower, Theodore Whitten
Landscape Students: Takanori Fukuoka, Javier Gonzalez-Campaña, Nathan Howe, Karen Lau, Cecilia B. Martinic, Jeffrey M. Tucker

Qing Huang Dao Park
Qing Huang Dao, China
2005 (competition, winning entry)
98 acres
Client: City of Quing Huang Dao
Design Team: Diana Balmori, Mark Thomann, Sangmok Kim, Rachel Whiteside, Martha Desbiens
Architect: MAD Architects Office

Parque de La Luz
Las Palmas, Gran Canaria, Canary Islands, Spain
2005 (competition, winning entry)
4,000 acres
Client: Ayuntamiento de Las Palmas de Gran Canaria; Autoridad Portuaria de Las Palmas de Gran Canaria
Design Team: Diana Balmori, Mark Thomann, Sangmok Kim, Martha Desbiens, Javier González-Campaña, Cecilia B. Martinic
Architect: Pelli Clarke Pelli Architects

Memphis Riverfront: Beale Street Landing
Memphis, Tennessee
In progress (expected completion 2010)
5 acres
Client: City of Memphis; Riverfront Development Corporation
Design Team: Diana Balmori, Javier González-Campaña, Mark Thomann, Martha Desbiens
Architects: RTN Architects; Bounds & Gillepsie Architects
Marine Engineer: Consulmar

Robert Smithson's Floating Island to Travel Around Manhattan Island
New York, New York
2006
Client: Minetta Brook; Whitney Museum of American Art
Artist: Robert Smithson
Design Team: Diana Balmori, Mark Thomann, Martha Desbiens
Advisers: Diane Shamash, Minetta Brook, Nancy Holt, James Cohan Gallery, Estate of Robert Smithson, John Rubin, Floating Cinema
Landscape Contractor: Tim Cahalin, Official LLC

Skid Rows, Queens Museum of Art
Queens Botanical Garden, Queens, New York
2005
Client: Queens Museum of Art
Design Team: Diana Balmori, Mark Thomann, Javier Gonzalez-Campaña
Collaborator: Brian Tolle Studio

Skid Rows, Mildred's Lane
Beach Lake, Pennsylvania
2008
Client: Mildred's Lane, Mark Dion and J. Morgan Puett
Design Team: Diana Balmori, Mark Thomann, Javier Gonzalez-Campaña
Collaborator: Brian Tolle Studio

Urban Meadow
Brooklyn, New York
2008
7,222 square feet
Sponsors: Clean Air Communities; ConEdison; New York State Council on the Arts (NYSCA); Lily Auchincloss Foundation; American Stevedoring, Inc.; Independence Community Foundation; Architectural League
Design Team: Diana Balmori, Mark Thomann, Sarah Wayland Smith
Landscape Designer: Julie Farris, XS Space
Advisers: Greenthumb, New York City Department of Parks and Recreation; Office of the Brooklyn Borough, Marty Markowitz, president; Center for Climate Studies, Columbia University; Stuart Gaffin, Ph.D., and Greg O'Keefe
Graphic Design: Alan Dye
Landscape Contractor: Tim Cahalin, Official LLC

Jordan River Peace Park
Israel/Jordan/Palestine
2008 (design charrette)
750 acres
Design Team: Yale School of Architecture—Diana Balmori, Alan Joseph Plattus, Hilary Sample, Jim Axley, Andrei Harwell, Ben Smoot, Lasha Brown, Gabi Ho; Bezalel Academy, Israel—David Guggenheim, Shmuel Groag, Ruba Marjieh, Michael Walma van der Molen, Merav Battat, Noam Bitran, Hila Lothan, Anat Dror, Aviad Sar Shalom; Palestinian team—Ranad A. Shqeriat, Nader Khateeb; Jordanian participants—Munqeth Mehyar (FoEME, Jordanian Director), Abed Sultan (FoEME)
Host Organization: Friends of the Earth Middle East (FoEME): Gidon Bromberg (Israeli Director), Mira Edelstein, Elizabeth Koch, Nicole Hariri, Tania Gorskay

Mathematics Building Courtyard
Institute for Advanced Study, Princeton, New Jersey
1996
15,000 square feet
Design Team: Diana Balmori, Peter Viteretto, Robert Gilchrest
MEP Consultants: Van Zelm, Heywood & Shadford, Inc.
Structural Engineer: Spiegel & Zamecnik, Inc.
Civil Engineer: Geotech; Melick-Tully & Associates, Inc.

Kent Falls Trail
Kent Falls State Park, Kent, Connecticut
2006
One-quarter-mile trail
Design Team: Diana Balmori, Mary Virginia Rickel, Mark Thomann, Sangmok Kim
Civil Engineer: Vollmer Associates LLP

Nippon Telephone and Telegraph Headquarters
Tokyo
1995
78,899 square feet
Client: Nippon Telephone and Telegraph
Design Team: Diana Balmori, Peter Viteretto, David Houston, William Coyne
Landscape Architect: Masahiro Soma
Architect: Pelli Clarke Pelli Architects
Civil Engineer: Yamashita Sekkei
Environmental Consultant: Wind Tunnel Lab: Ares, Inc.
Lighting Consultant: H. M. Brandston & Partners, Inc.

Abandoibarra Master Plan
Bilbao, Spain
In progress (1993 competition, winning entry)
8 acres
Client: Sociedad Bilbao Ria 2000
Design Team: Diana Balmori, Ana Maria Torres
Architects: Cesar Pelli and Associates, Eugenio Aguinaga

Plaza Euskadi
Bilbao, Spain
In progress
10,000 square meters
Client: Sociedad Bilbao Ria 2000; City of Bilbao, Spain
Design Team: Diana Balmori, Javier González-Campaña, Mark Thomann, Kira Appelhans, Johanna Phelps, Sangmok Kim, Kathleen Bakewell, Cecilia Martinic
Sculptors: Cao | Perrot Studio

Selected Project Credits

St. Louis Waterfront
St. Louis, Missouri
In progress
44 acres
Client: Great Rivers Greenway District; Danforth Foundation
Design Team: Diana Balmori, Mark Thomann, Javier González-Campaña, Kira Appelhans, Sangmok Kim, Johanna Phelps, Killian O'Brien, Christopher Kitterman, Ilse Frank
Planning: HOK Planning Group
Architect: Joel Sanders Architect
Marine Engineer: Consulmar

St. Louis Riverfront Master Plan
St. Louis, Missouri
2005
80 acres
Client: Great Rivers Greenway District
Design Team: Diana Balmori, Mark Thomann, Javier González-Campaña, Kira Appelhans, Sangmok Kim, Johanna Phelps, Christopher Kitterman, Ilse Frank
Planning: HOK Planning Group
Urban Strategist: Greenberg Consultant
Civil Engineer: Moffat and Nichol
Engineer: CDG Engineers, ABNA Engineering
Marketing: Vector Communications

Cultural Park
Shenzhen, China
2003 (competition, finalist)
136 acres
Client: Shenzhen Municipal Planning and Land Information Center
Design Team: Diana Balmori, Mark Thomann, Sangmok Kim
Architect: MAD Architects Office

Earthworks: NYC 2012 Olympics
Greenbelt Park, Staten Island, New York
2004 (competition winner)
800 acres
Client: NYC 2012
Design Team: Diana Balmori, Mark Thomann, Karen Tamir, Sangmok Kim, Adrienne Cortez, Cecilia B. Martinic, Kathleen Bakewell, Jason Holtzman, Javier González-Campaña, Emily Abruzzo
Architect: Joel Sanders Architect

Campa de los Ingleses
Bilbao, Spain
2007 (competition, winning entry; in design development, projected completion 2010)
6.5 acres
Clients: Sociedad Bilbao Ria 2000; City of Bilbao
Design Team: Diana Balmori, Mark Thomann, Javier González-Campaña, Kira Appelhans, Sangmok Kim, Ilse Frank, Kristi Stromberg Wright
Architect: RTN Architects
Engineer: Lantec

Public Administrative Town Master Plan
Sejong, South Korea
2007 (competition, winning entry)
2.7 million square meters
Client: Multi-Functional Administrative City Construction Agency
Design Team: Diana Balmori, Mark Thomann, Sangmok Kim, Catherine Byun
Architects: H Associates, Inc.; Haeahn Architecture

The following projects are discussed in Michel Conan's introduction:

NationsBank Corporate Center Plaza
Charlotte, North Carolina
1991
18,000 square feet
Client: NationsBank Corporation; Charter Properties; Lincoln Property Company
Design Team: Diana Balmori, Frank DeSantis, Robert Gilchrest, J. Morgan Grove, Tim Kennedy, Chris Siefert, Peter Viteretto
Architect: Pelli Clarke Pelli Architects
Civil Engineer: DPR Associates
Surveyor: GEOTECH: S&ME
Structural Engineer: Walter P. Moore and Associates
MEP Consultants: BL&P Engineers, Inc.

PARK(ING) Trenton
Trenton, New Jersey
2006 (competition)
53 acres
Client: State of New Jersey, Department of the Treasury, Division of Property Management and Construction
Design Team: Diana Balmori, Mark Thomanns, Kira Appelhans, Martha Desbiens
Civil Engineer: ACT Engineers
Graphic Design: Alan Dye
Environmental Engineer: Bioengineering Group
Community Programming: City Smiles
Visual Artist and Sound Designer: Ear Studio
Structural Engineer: Guy Nordenson and Associates
Historic Preservation: Hunter Research
Lighting Design: L'Observatoire
Architect: Robert A. M. Stern Architects
Urban Forestry and Soils: Urban Trees + Soils

Stapleton Waterfront
Staten Island, New York
2004 (competition)
64 acres
Client: NYCEDC
Design Team: Diana Balmori, Mark Thomann, Sangmok Kim
Architect: Joel Sanders Architect
Environmental Engineer: Bio Engineering Group

University College Dublin
Dublin
2007 (competition, finalist)
34 acres
Client: University College Dublin
Design Team: Diana Balmori, Mark Thomann, Sangmok Kim, Kira Appelhans, Catherine Byun
Architect: Zaha Hadid Architects

Toronto Central Waterfront
Toronto
2006 (competition)
3.5 kilometers
Client: Toronto Waterfront Revitalization Corporation
Design Team: Diana Balmori, Mark Thomann, Kira Appelhans, Sangmok Kim
Architects: H3; Lobko Architect; NARCHITECTS; Weisz + Yoes
Planning, Design, and Management: Halcrow
Landscape Architect: Sasaki Associates
Lighting Design: Snøhetta

World Mammoth and Permafrost Museum
Yakutsk, Russian Federation
2007 (competition, winning entry)
1.3 acres
Client: LaPaz Group
Design Team: Diana Balmori, Mark Thomann, Sangmok Kim, Catherine Byun
Architect: Leeser Architecture
MEP/Structural Consultants: Arup
Environmental Consultants: Atelier 10
Wind and Microclimate Consultants: RWDI
Lighting Consultants: Tillett Lighting Design

Governors Island
New York, New York
Competition in progress
172 acres
Client: Governors Island Preservation and Education Corporation
Design Team: Diana Balmori, Mark Thomann, Abby Feldman
Architect: Studio MDA

Acknowledgments

The nine years since I opened my office in New York have been extraordinarily productive in terms of projects and ideas, which serve as the foundation of this book. I only regret not having come to New York sooner. New York City, so supportive of creative life, has also brought me very capable collaborators, and I acknowledge them first.

I wish to thank the Graham Foundation for its generous support for this project.

Michel Conan, who at the time this book was being written was director of Garden and Landscape Studies at Dumbarton Oaks, provided invaluable criticism and deeply satisfying dialogue. Landscape has very few substantive forums, and still fewer discussions about its practice. Conan's interest in contemporary practice built a bridge to its historical side, which—though I had entered the field as a historian—I had jettisoned as soon as design became my central activity. Landscape, I felt, was too mired in the past, which stood in the way of new design, since—unlike the other arts—it has resisted the leap into the modern age. Conan's straddling of both areas allowed for a dialogue across them.

The Yale School of Architecture and Dean Robert A. M. Stern provided a forum for rethinking basic issues about the relationship of architecture to landscape, for which I am deeply grateful. In particular, my colleague Joel Sanders and I were able to teach an advanced studio course, which we called Interface, for three consecutive years. The ideas and work I shared with Sanders in this studio provided concentrated attention on the intersection of the two disciplines. The rich dialogue with Sanders, which continues, is reflected in the last section of this book. My thanks also go to Cesar Pelli, in whose office I had the opportunity to make a start in a landscape and urban design practice, which was invaluable to the practice I started in New York in 2001.

Warm thanks to Margaret Morton and Elizabeth Howard, Morton for her support during the hardest parts of putting together this book and for her photograph of a work day at our studio; Howard for pushing me to get these ideas down on paper and making the initial contacts that brought this about.

My thanks go to Noémie Lafaurie-Debany, who was the master organizer of this book; to Ron Broadhurst, for his good management of the long manuscript process; and to Elizabeth Segal, whose editing kept my text pithy, my aim in all writing. I thank the book designers Alan Dye and Brian Scott, who brought out the visual side of the book so well.

Finally, a special thanks to my editor at Yale University Press, Michelle Komie.

Collaborators

Staff at Balmori Associates since its beginning in 1990:

Emily Abruzzo
Anna Acetta
Khalid Almo
Amanda Amato
Kira Appelhans
Emily Artinian
Sally Atkins
Kathleen Bakewell
Christine Belton
David Black
Marya Bradley
Martha Burgess
Pau Butkus
Joelle Byrer
Catherine Byun
Andrew Cao
Bette Carlson
Olivia Chen
Anna Ciresi
Kim Cooper
Adrienne Cortez
Traci Costanzo
William Coyne
Patricia Crow
Thalassa Curtis
Lauren Dapiaoen
Santiago del Hierro
Deena Del Zotto
Sarah Derico
Martha Desbiens
Jennifer Domask
Julia Doran
Cristian Enachescu
Julie Farris
Abby Feldman
Alice Feng
Andrea Flamenco
Ilse Frank
Takanori Fukuoka
Eileen Garred
Javier González-Campaña
Joanna Gordon
June Grant
Rachel Gruzen
Christopher Hall
Thomas Hammerberg
Iona Harkin
Andrew Heid
Monica Hernandez
Christian Hillebrand
Nathan Howe
Elizabeth Hunt
Joo Won Im
Sharon Joyce
Andrew Keal
Meredith Kelly
James Kennedy
Heather Kilmer
Sangmok Kim
Mason Kirby
Christopher Kitterman
Nancy Kong
Noémie Lafaurie-Debany
Francis Leadon
Richard Lee
Yi-Feng Lin
Andrea Mantin
Vanessa Mariacher
Cecilia Bettina Martinic
Genevieve Maselli
Mayur Mehta
Sonali Nagle
Marc Newman
Killian O'Brien
Jacqueline Obst-Bell
Maria Laura Pereira
Anchalee Phaosawasdi
Johanna Phelps
Aaron Pine
Marta Rabazo
Linda Reeder
Mary Pelletier
Lara Rose
Christina Ross
Elihu Rubin
Yuichi Sakuma
Eric Samuels
Donald Schillingburg
Kristina Smith
Angela C. Soong
Catherine Spector
Peter Stegner
Kristi Stromberg-Wright
Robert Svetz
Philip Tam
Karen Tamir
Andrew Thomann
Mark Thomann
Ana Maria Torres
Jeffrey Tucker
Tamara Vassilidze
Sarah Wayland-Smith
Rachel Whiteside
William Yocom

Index

Numbers in *italics* indicate figures.

Abandoibarra Master Plan Plaza Euskadi (Bilbao), 166, *167–172*
aesthetics, 144–45; language of, placed over the functional substrata, 145; unrelated to ecology and sustainability, 11
Aguinaga, Eugenio, 166
Alderman, Nancy, 34
Ambasz, Emilio, xlii
American Lawn, xiv, 11; industrialization of, 14–17; introduction of, 12–14; remaking of, 22; transformation of, 17–18
Amidon, Jane, xxxvii
Anchor Park (Andersson), *xli*
Anderson, Thorbjörn, xxxvii
Andersson, Stig L., xlii, 229n7; Anchor Park, *xli;* Urban Garden, *xliii*
Andre, Carl, xl
Andropogon, xv
Angelo's garden, *xii*
anthropic landscape, xxviii
anthropic nature, xi, xxiv
architecture: reinvention of, 144; torn away from other arts, 143. *See also* landscape architecture
art: egoless, x; moral dialogue with, xv; nature and, 8–11; role of history in, xxxviii–xl
Arverne (Long Island, N.Y.), 88, 94, *96–99,* 152

Balmori, Diana, *viii;* antihistorical stance of, 226n16; art of, implying mutual transformation of humans and nonhumans, x; on art of landscape demanding a different attitude, 226n2; Buddhist influence on, xii; considering historical precedents in human-nonhuman relationships, xv; contributing to renewal of landscape architecture, xxxvii–xliii; creating experiences, xxxvii; creating a new nature, xliii; creating a topographical art form, xvii–xviii; design methodology of, xxxviii; experiencing the topographical art of, xxxii–xxxvii; interest of, in making landscape accessible to visitors, xlii–xliii; landscapes inspired by art, xl; landscapes serving three functional levels, xxxii; proposing a distinctive experience of beauty, xliii; pursuing transformation of nature, viii; reinventing public space, xiv; shifting attention from objects to space, 158; shunning essentialism, xl; stressing site as process, xii; studying U.S. and British hedges, xv; working in central city projects of sites linked to major activity centers, xxxvi; writing on history of U.S. and European streets, xv
Baltimore Municipal Art Society, 42
Baltimore Percent-for-Art Program, 42
Bann, Stephen, 227n6
Barten, Paul, 82
Baudry, Jacques, 20
Beale Street Landing (Memphis), xv, *xvi,* xxiv–xxvii, *xxxiv,* xlii, 112, *114–116*
beauty: distinctive experience of, xliii; fixed notion of, shedding, 144; new experiences of, xxxv–xxxvi
Berke, Deborah, 94
Beyer, Herbert, xlii

biotope, 10
"Bjørvika: 7 New Urban Spaces in the Oslo Harbor" (Andersson), 229n7
borders, straddling, 136
Bormann, Herb, 139
Botanical Garden of Las Palmas, 105
Botanical Research Institute of Texas (Fort Worth), 68, 74–76, *78*
boundary, xviii, 222
Brandeis Gratz, Roberta, 54
Bridgeman, Charles, 147
Broadway Penthouse (New York), *70*
Bromberg, Gidon, 136
Brown, Capability, 6, 12, 17, 146
Bryant Park (New York City), 228n20
Budding, Edwin, 14
Burle Marx, Roberto, xlii

Campa de los Ingleses (Bilbao), xviii–xxi, *xxii, xxxvi,* 190, 200, *202–205*
Canary Islands. *See* Parque de la Luz
Chacel, Fernando, xxiv, xlii
chemicals, used for the Industrial Lawn, 15
chirimiri, 200
Christo, xl
Circular Park (Nishi Harima, Japan) (Walker), 229n1
cities: accommodating natural processes in, 104–116; embedding, in nature, 219; importance of, in contemporary landscape design, 139–140
Clementsian succession, 10
climax, in a biotopic community, 10
clover, use of, in Freedom Lawn, 17
collage, importance of, in Balmori's topographical art work, xxiv–xxvii
Colosseum, 145
computer renderings, 146
connecting, importance of, in Balmori's topographical art work, xxviii–xxxii
consumerism, as anti-nature, 18
contrast, importance of, in Balmori's topographical art work, xxi
Corbin, Alain, 227n37, 227n45
cranberry bogs, 83
crowdsourcing, 42, 48
Cuirasse (Gustafson), 228n3

Dampierre, xviii
David, Josh, 48
Davis, Alexander Jackson, 14
Deamer, Peggy, 94
Delacorte Theatre (Central Park, New York City), 117
Design with Nature (McHarg), 55
Downing, Andrew Jackson, 14
drainage, from sewer pipes, 79. *See also* stormwater
Dublin Grand Canal Square (Schwarz), 227n6

Eads, James B., 176
Eads Bridge (St. Louis), 176
Earth Pledge, 55
Earthworks: 2012 Olympics, Equestrian Venue (Staten Island, N.Y.), viii–xi, 190, 194, *196–199*
Easterling, Keller, 94

ecogenesis, xxiv, xlii
ecology, 8, 10, 221; battle of, with aesthetics, 11
ecosystems, re-creation of, xxiv
ecotone, 104, 158
elevation, as indicator, 212
"Emerald Necklace" (Olmsted), 228n1
English Landscape School, 5–6
English lawn, 12
ephemeral gardens, xii
espaliers, 12, *21,* 22
Euston, grounds of (attrib., Kent), *150*
evapotranspiration, 54, 66, 83
evolution, 8, 10, 221

Farmington Canal (New Haven, CT), xxviii, *xxix,* 32, 34–41, 145
Farmington Canal Citizens Association, 34
Farmington Canal Rail-to-Trail Association, 34
Farris, Julie, 132
fertilizers, 14, 15
fifth façade, 54, 68, 145, 210
Finlay, Ian Hamilton, xxxviii, xlii, 12, 227n6
Floating Island (Smithson), 117, 120, *121–127*
floating islands, xxii–xxiv, xlii, 105 islands, 180
formalism, xlii
Forman, Richard T., 20
fossil fuels, used for the Industrial Lawn, 15
Frances Daly Fergusson Courtyard, Vassar College (Poughkeepsie, N.Y.), *xx,* xxi–xxii, 22, *24, 25*
Freedom Lawn, xv, 11, 17–18, 54, 132
Friends of the Earth Middle East (FOEME), 136
Friends of the High Line, 48

"Gardens for Highways" (Johanson), 228n2
Gas Works Park (Haag), 28
Gateway Arch (Saarinen), 176
Gehry, Frank, 200
Geuze, Adrian, 229n7
Gleasonian succession view, 10
Gore, Al, 18
Governors Island (New York), *xxxix*
Granite Garden, The: Urban Nature and Human Design (Spirn), 139
grass, role of, in English agriculture, 12
Gratz, Donald, 54
Gratz Industries (Long Island City, Queens, NY), 58, 64–65, 145
gray water, 66, 106, 136, 206
Great River Greenway (St. Louis), 176, 180
green roofs, xv, 28, 54–55, 212; Broadway Penthouse (New York), *70;* in a city's context, 68; data collected on, from Silvercup Studios, 228–229n3; Gratz Industries (Long Island City, Queens, NY), 64–65; importance to, of fifth façade, 145; Loews Miami Beach Hotel, *71;* Long Island City (Queens), 55–57; modular system for, 58; monitoring of, 63; Silvercup Studios (Long Island City, Queens), 58–63, 228–229n3; Solaire (New York), 66–67; 240 Central Park South (New York), *72–73*
Greenberg, Clement, xxxviii, xl
greens, commons transformed into, 14
greenways, 54. *See also* linear parks
Ground Plane, 210, 212

Ground Zero, 117, *118*
Guidelines for Sustainable Land Development (Balmori), xv
Guineo's garden, *xiii*
Gustafson, Kathryn, xxxvii, 228n3
Gwynns Falls Trail (Baltimore), 42–47

Haag, Richard, 28
Haeckel, Ernst, 8
ha-ha, 12
Hammond, Robert, 48
Hardy, Hugh, 74
Hardy, Rod, 79
Hazlehurst, Hamilton, xviii
heat island effect, 54
hedgerows, 12, 18–22
hedges, xv
Heizer, Michael, xlii
herbicides, 14
High Line (New York City), 32, 48–53, 58
History of the Modern Taste in Gardening (Walpole), 91
Holocaust Memorial (Berlin), 229n4 (Part 3)
Holt, Jane, xlii
Holt, Nancy, 120
horsemanship, as metaphor for understanding Balmori's work, viii, x
Housatonic Fields (New Milford, CT), *153–157*
house abandonment, due to poor subsurface conditions, 88
Humboldt Avenue Reinvestment Study (Minneapolis), 88, *89*, 90, *92–93*
Hundertwasser, xlii
hydrologic cycle, imitation of, xv

Iconic Plane, 206, 210, 212
Inconvenient Truth, An (Gore), 18
individual initiatives, importance of, xv
industrialization, relation of, to modern art, 11
Industrial Lawn, 14–17; as industry, 18
interface (interfacing), 143, 146, 158, 190, 219, 222; aesthetic concentration on, 144; approaching, through Thick Edge, 166; Campa de los Ingleses (Bilbao), 190, 200, *202–205*; Earthworks: 2012 Olympics, Equestrian Venue (Staten Island, NY), 190, 194, *196–199*; juncture of landscape and architecture, 144; juncture of nature and culture, 144; Public Administrative Town (Sejong, South Korea), 190, 206–214, *216–218*; Shenzhen, China, 190, *192–193*
international landscape design, xlii–xliii
interweaving, 206
Irish Hunger Memorial, 226n25
Irwin, Robert, 8, 10
Isozaki, Arata, 229n1

Jackson, J. B., 14
Jacob, François, 10, 18
Jacobsen, Eric, xlii
Jarman, Derek, 227n6
Johanson, Patricia, 228n2
Jordan River Peace Park (Israel/Jordan/Palestine), 136, *137–138*

Kant, Immanuel, xxxv, 6

Kent, William, 6, 91, 147
Kent Falls Trail (Kent Falls State Park, CT), *152*
Key Words (Williams), 8
Kienast, Dieter, xlii
Kit-Kat Club, 6
Krier, Robert, 166

Landesman, Heidi, 117
landscape: allying with architecture, 219; attempting to become modern, 144; brokering coexistence of human beings with rest of nature, 1, 3; creating new kind of livable city, 1, 3; fragility of, 117; designed for ease of enjoyment, xxviii; having fourth dimension of time, 117, 129; as human tool, for constructing new form of nature, viii–xi; large-scale, 55; linked with city and architecture, 27–28; as living, changing enterprise, 140; mood of, xviii; motion as most critical dimension of, 129; new definition of, 221–223; as reflective structure, 227n49; redefining for our time, 1; as source of pleasurable activities, x; temporary, 117–135
landscape architecture: becoming topographical art, xl; renewing, xii; shifts in, xii
landscape creation, as art of movement, xii
landscape design: changing scale of, 28; countercurrent in, coming from ecology, 10; engaging with all aspects of a sustainable world, 11; history of, 5–6
landscape of desire, new, constructing, xxxvi–xxxvii
landscape history, rejection of, 6
Landscape Manifesto, A (Balmori), 224–225
Landscape Park Duisburg Nord (Latz), 28, 229n5
Landscape plane, 210
Lassus, Bernard, xlii, 228n2
Latz, Peter, 28, 229n5
lawn mower, invention of, 14
lawns: becoming landscape of choice, 14; practical merits of, 17
Legorreta, Ricardo, 166
Le Nôtre, André, xviii
Les Pennes (Gustafson), 228n3
linear park, xxviii, 28, 30–32, 221; Farmington Canal (New Haven, CT), 32, 34–41; Gwynns Falls Trail (Baltimore), 42–47; High Line (New York City), 32, 48–53; as opportunity for reinstating hedgerows, 22; Plaza Euskadi as, 166; power of, 145; replacing housing areas with wet soils, 90; as Thin Edge, 158
"Little Sparta" (Finlay), 227n6
Loews Miami Beach Hotel, *71*
Long Island City (Queens, NY), green roofs for, 55–57

Manifesto, significance of, 1–2
Mansart, Jules Hardouin, xviii
Maria, Walter de, xl
Mathematics Building Courtyard, Institute for Advanced Study, Princeton (Princeton, NJ), *151*
McHarg, Ian, xlii, 55, 88
merging, importance of, in Balmori's topographical art work, xxii–xxiv
Merlin's Cave, interior (Kent), *150*
middle scale, 28, 55
Mildred's Lane (PA), 128
Mile Long Drawing (Maria), xl
mimetism, 10

Minetta Brook, 120
Mitani, Toru, xxxvii
Moneo, Rafael, 166
Moorish, William, 82
Moralists, The (Shaftesbury), 6
Morris, Robert, xl
Moses, Robert, 194
motion, as most critical dimension of landscape, 129
Murase, Scott, xv
Musée Gassendi, 227n6

Nasher Sculpture Center Garden, xl
Nations Bank Corporate Center (Charlotte, NC), *xix*
natural processes, accommodating, in cities, 104–116
natural selection, 8
nature: absent from Walker's thinking about landscape design, xxxviii; achieving traits of a deity, 6; alienation from, 182; art and, 8–11; art contributing to dynamics of, xxxv; Balmori viewing, as process in flux, xxxviii; coproduced by humans and nonhumans, 227n42; embedding the city in, 219; including human species in, 8; as model to imitate, xv; new experiences of, xxxii–xxxv; as new ideal, in eighteenth century, 6; opposing artifice, rejection of, xxi; process for transforming, xv; supporting human activities and nonhuman beings, xxvii–xxviii; teleological view of, shedding, 144; transformation of, x; untamed and urbanized, changing relationships of, xxviii; variety of meanings for, 8; weaving together different kinds of, xxvii
Newport Garden (Newport, RI), *21*
New York City Parks Department, Community Garden "Green Thumb" program, 132
Nippon Telegraph and Telephone Headquarters (Tokyo), xxi, 158–160, *161–165*
Nishi Harima Science Garden City (Japan), 229n1
nonequilibrium, 10

Olmsted, Frederick Law, xxxviii, 6, 14, 228n1
Olmsted Report (Baltimore), 42
Osage-orange, 20

PARK(ING) Trenton (Trenton, NJ), *xxiii, xxxiii*
parkitecture, 190
Parque de la Luz (Las Palmas, Canary Islands), xv, *xxiv, xxviii, xxix, xxv*, 105–111
passage, 158; importance of, in Balmori's topographical art work, xxi–xxii
pasture, as landscape feature in colonial America, 14
Peace Parks, 136
Pelli, Cesar, 166
Perrault, Dominique, xlii, 227n48
pesticides, used for the Industrial Lawn, 15–16
Picturesque, 6, 8, 11, 28, 146–147
Piscuskas, David, 226n25
Plan for the Duke of Queensberry's house at Abmresbury, Wiltshire (Bridgeman), *149*
Plaza Euskadi (Bilbao), xxviii, 166, *173–175*
Pope, Alexander, 6
popular movements, importance of, xv
ports, abandonment of, allowing for large-scale change, 104

Prairie Waterway/Park Place (Farmington, MN), xv, xvii, 79–86, 144
Public Administration Town (PAT) (Sejong, South Korea), xviii, xix, xxvii, xxix, 190, 206–214, *216–218*
public spaces: changing, into city gardens, xii; demands on, xv; reinvention of, xiv
public structures, floating docks transformed into, 28
pulchritudo adhaerens, xxxii, xxxv

Qing Huang Dao Park (China), xvii–xviii, 88, 100, *101–103*
Queens Art Museum, 128

Rails-to-Trails, 30
railway lines, converting, to linear parks, 30–32
rain gardens, 28, 68, 79
rainwater disposal, 54
Redesigning the American Lawn (Balmori), xii–xiv
Reflective Practitioner, The (Schön), xii
Repton, Humphrey, 6
Rho Mu Hyun, 206
Richmond Gardens (attrib., Bridgeman), *148*
Riehm, Juergen, 226n25
rivers, nineteenth-century engineering approach to, 104
Robert Smithson's Floating Island to Travel Around Manhattan Island, 117, 120, *121–127*
roof cover, xv
roof gardens. *See* green roofs
Rothko, Mark, xxii, 146, 158
Ro Wilson garden, *xiv*
Running Fence (Christo), xl

sandbars, 94
sand dunes, importance of, 88
Sanders, Joel, 144, 146, 223
Sasaki, Yoji, xxxvii
Schön, Donald, xii
Schwartz, Martha, xlii, 227n6
Secant (Andre), xl
sedums, use of, in green roofs, 58, 64, 66
Serra, Richard, xl
setting, importance of, in Balmori's topographical art work, xviii–xxi
Shakkei, 144
Shenzhen, China, 190, *192–193*
shorelines, delicacy of, 88
Shugaku-in Imperial Villa (Kyoto), 144, 166–67
Silvercup Studios (Long Island City, Queens, NY), 58–63, 145; data collected from, 228–229n3
Simmel, Georg, 226n24
Siza, Alvaro, 166
Skid Rows, 128–129, *130–131*
Smick, Lee, 82
Smith, Elizabeth, 34
Smithson, Robert, viii, xl, 120; Balmori's homage to, xv; transitioning to new view of nature, 8–10. *See also Robert Smithson's Floating Island to Travel Around Manhattan Island*
Snodgrass, Ed, 58
Solaire (New York), 66–67
space: creation of, 146; importance of, as embodying shift in urban ethics, xxxv
species diversity, limited by Industrial Lawn, 16

Spiral Jetty (Smithson), xl, 120
Spirn, Ann, 139
Stapleton Waterfront (Staten Island, NY), *xxi*, xxii–xxiv, *xxvii*
St. Louis Waterfront, *xxii*, xxviii, *xxxi*, 166, 176–182, *184–189*
Steam (Morris), xl
Stern, Robert A. M., 94, 166
stimmung, xviii
stormwater management, 37, 66, 228n3
stormwater parks, 28, 79–86, 144
streets, horizontal and vertical dimensions of, 210
suburban lawn, xii–xiv
Summerson, John, 145
Suna, Alan, 54
Suna, Stuart, 54
sunken gardens, 12, 22
superrealism, 146
sustainability, xvii, 11, 144, 206, 212, 226n4
systematics, 76

tectonics, applying aesthetics to, 145
temporary landscapes, 117: *Robert Smithson's Floating Island to Travel Around Manhattan Island,* 117, 120, *121–127;* Skid Rows, 128–129, *130–131;* Urban Meadow (Brooklyn), 132, *134–135*
Thick Edge, 145–46, 166–67, 190, 222–223; introducing new experience of nature, 182; in Public Administrative Town (Sejong, South Korea), 210; St. Louis Waterfront, 166, 176–182, *184–189*. *See also* interfacing
Thin Edge, 145, 146, 158; Abandoibarra Master Plan and Plaza Euskadi (Bilbao), 166, 167–175; Nippon Telegraph and Telephone Headquarters (Tokyo), 158–160, *161–165*
time: as fourth dimension in landscape, 117, 129; new experiences of, xxxv
Tolle, Brian, 128, 129, 226n25
topographical art work, x
Toronto Central Waterfront, xxviii, *xxxi*
Transitory Gardens, Uprooted Lives (Balmori), xii
Trenton (NJ), xxii
Trust for Public Land, 30, 42
Turner, J. M. W., 146, 158
240 Central Park South (New York), *72–73*

universal art, xxxviii
University College Dublin Gateway, xxviii, *xxx*
urban dwellers, offered experience of community, xxxii
urban forms, inscribing, in larger geographical context, 88–103
Urban Garden (Andersson), *xliii*
urban linear-park movement, xv
Urban Meadow (Brooklyn), 132, *134–135,* 229n8
Urban Revisions: Current Projects for the Urban Realm, 34

Valkenbergh, Michael Van, xv, 229n4
Vaux, Calvert, 14
Vuillard, Edouard, 146, 158

Walker, Peter, xxxvii–xli, xlii, 227n6, 229n1
Walpole, Horace, 91
wasteless city, 206, 212
water levels, affecting public spaces, 112
water pollution, from lawn maintenance, 16

Water Purification Park (Seoul), 28
water supplies, used for maintaining lawns, 16
weaving, importance of, in Balmori's topographical art work, xxvii–xxviii
wet soils, 88, 90
Whitman, Walt, 17
Whitney Museum of American Art, 120
wildlife sanctuary, sign for, *xvi*
Williams, Raymond, 8
Woltz, Nelson Byrd, xv
Wood, William, 12
World Mammoth and Permafrost Museum (Yakutsk, Russian Federation), *xxxvi*

XS Space, 132

yard waste, 16

Illustration Credits

Illustrations courtesy Balmori Associates, with the following exceptions: Diana Balmori, figs. 1, 122, 154; © Bilbao Ria 2000, figs. 16, 19, 38, 181, 182, 183, 184, 185, 186, 187, 188, 189, 190, 191, 192, 216, 217, 218, 219, 220, 221, 222, 223; Bordner Aerials, figs. 107, 108; Michel Conan, figs. 17, 18; Michel Conan © SLA, fig. 40; J. Thomas Dunnó Gateway Arch Riverboats, fig. 193; Mark J. Dye, figs. 81, 82, 93, 96, 97; © Forward Stroke, Inc., figs. 177, 179; Timothy Hursley © Balmori Associates; Joseph Maida, figs. 83, 84, 85; Mitsuo Matsuoka, figs. 174, 176; Reproduced with the kind permission of His Grace the Duke of Malborough, Blenheim Palace Image Library, fig. 159; Mary Beth Meehan, figs. 43, 44, 45, 46; © Margaret Morton, figs. 8, 9, 234; Richard Mosse, fig. 31, 51; National Archives, UK, fig. 158; © Shokokusya Photographers, fig. 178; © SLA, fig. 41; Art © Estate of Robert Smithson/Licensed by VAGA, New York, NY, figs. 137, 141, 142; The State of New Jersey, Division of Fish, Game, and Wildlife Endangered and Nongame Species Program, fig. 13; Courtesy of Brian Tolle Studio, fig. 144; © V&A Images/Victoria and Albert Museum, London, figs. 160, 161; Ro Wilson, fig. 10.